Channeling Knowledges

Channeling Knowledges

WATER AND AFRO-DIASPORIC SPIRITS IN LATINX AND CARIBBEAN WORLDS

Rebeca L. Hey-Colón

University of Texas Press   *Austin*

Requests for permission to reproduce material from this work should be sent to:
Permissions
University of Texas Press
P.O. Box 7819
Austin, TX 78713-7819
utpress.utexas.edu/rp-form

♾ The paper used in this book meets the minimum requirements of
ANSI/NISO Z39.48-1992 (R1997) (Permanence of Paper).

Library of Congress Cataloging-in-Publication Data

Names: Hey-Colón, Rebeca L., author.
Title: Channeling knowledges : water and Afro-diasporic spirits in Latinx and
    Caribbean worlds / Rebeca L. Hey-Colón.
Description: First edition. | Austin : University of Texas Press, 2023. |
    Series: Latinx: the future is now | Includes bibliographical references and index.
Identifiers: LCCN 2022042481
ISBN 978-1-4773-2724-1 (cloth)
ISBN 978-1-4773-2725-8 (paperback)
ISBN 978-1-4773-2726-5 (pdf)
ISBN 978-1-4773-2727-2 (epub)
Subjects: LCSH: Latin American literature—Women authors—History and
    criticism. | Caribbean literature—Women authors—History and criticism. |
    Art, Latin American—Themes, motives. | Art, Caribbean—Themes, motives. |
    Water in literature. | African diaspora in literature. | Borderlands in literature. |
    Water—Latin America—Religious aspects. | Water—Caribbean Area—
    Religious aspects.
Classification: LCC PQ7081.5 H49 2023 | DDC 324.1196—dc23/eng/20221024
LC record available at https://lccn.loc.gov/2022042481

doi:10.7560/327241

Se repartió el saber por el mundo . . .

Contents

Acknowledgements

It is hard to know where to begin to write acknowledgements when every step and misstep I have taken has brought me to this moment. But perhaps a good place to start is where my educational journey begins: in Puerto Rico. I want to thank all of the teachers I had throughout the first 18 years of my life for modeling the possible for me. I would not have considered becoming an educator without you. Siempre estarán en mi corazón.

My move from Puerto Rico to the United States to go to college was jolting, but the Spanish Department at Haverford College made the transition easier by nurturing my love of the written word. In graduate school, the Department of Romance Languages and Literatures at Harvard University helped me develop critical tools I would need to continue on this journey. Thank you to all who walked with me during these formative years.

My move to Maine, another big change, was made easier by the warmth and enthusiasm with which my colleagues at Colby College ushered me into faculty life. Their generosity and support were invaluable. Colby's library and Special Collections staff deserve special mention for always encouraging my projects and helping me bring the Anzaldúa traveling exhibit to Maine. Thank you!

Temple University has been a place of extraordinary growth. Thank you to all the colleagues who have shared their time and insight with me as this book came to fruition. I am especially grateful to Temple's library staff, who, in the midst of a global pandemic, worked hard to make research materials virtually accessible to our community. I could not have written this book without your assistance. I also want to thank Josué Hurtado from Temple's Special Collections Research Center, without whom I would not have found an amazing image of Anzaldúa for this book. ¡Mil gracias!

Access to the Gloria Evangelina Anzaldúa Papers transformed this book. During my time at the archive, the Nettie Lee Benson Latin American Collection staff, and particularly those in the Rare Books and Manuscripts Reading Room, were always willing and able to help with all manner of research questions. Carla O. Alvarez and Daniel Arbino are especially memorable. Thank you so much for everything!

I am indebted to all of the creators and custodians who granted me permissions to include their work in this book: Stuart Bernstein and the Gloria E. Anzaldúa Literary Trust, Eloisa Aquino, Firelei Báez and James Cohan, New York, Professor Henry John Drewal, and Mayra Santos-Febres. The *Chicana/Latina Studies* journal and Lexington Books supported early versions of this project and allowed me to reprint portions of my writing here. I am heartened by your continued support.

I have been fortunate to receive funding for this project at various stages of its development. The Young Scholars Symposium organized by the Institute for Latino Studies at the University of Notre Dame, a Carlos E. Castañeda Postdoctoral Fellowship from the Center for Mexican American Studies at the University of Texas at Austin, a Career Enhancement Fellowship from the Institute for Citizens and Scholars, a Summer Research Award from Temple University, a Center for the Humanities at Temple (CHAT) Faculty Fellowship, the CLARA and LAURA Programs in the College of Liberal Arts at Temple, and Wellesley College's Newhouse Center Faculty Fellowship have all supported my research and writing. Without their invaluable assistance this book would not be what it is.

I would also like to thank everyone at the University of Texas Press for believing in this project. Kerry E. Webb, my acquisitions editor, allowed the book to evolve and become what it was meant to be, and the series editors, Lorgia García-Peña and Nicole M. Guidotti-Hernández, were unwavering in their support. The anonymous readers were critical in helping me take my ideas in new and fruitful directions. On the production side, Lynne M. Ferguson and her editorial team attentively guided me through the project's final stages. Thank you all for engaging with my work.

It would be impossible to name all individuals who have left their mark on my writing and research throughout the years. Still, the following people deserve special mention: Hiram Aldarondo, C. J. Alvarez, Mariola Alvarez, Suzanne Bost, Christian Campbell, Norma Elia Cantú, Arnaldo Cruz Malavé, Richard Deeg, María DeGuzmán, Alicia E. Ellis, Nadia R. El-Shaarawi, Sophie Esch, Alexander Fernández, Carolyn Fornoff, Christina Garcia Lopez, Lorgia García-Peña, Nicole M. Guidotti-Hernández, Laura G. Gutierrez, Monica A. Hahn, Carissa M. Harris, Emily Hind, Rebecca Janzen, Irene Mata, April J. Mayes, Julie Avril Minich, John Morán González, Marisel C. Moreno, Srimati Mukherjee, Kartik Nair, Emily Neumeier, Jess Marie Newman, Ajima Olaghere, Jorge Olivares, Bill Orchard, Vanessa Pérez-Rosario, Sarah Quesada, Terry Rey, Mónica Ricketts, Carmen Serrano, Jay C. Sibara, Sandra L. Suárez, Martin A. Tsang, Hanétha

Vété-Congolo, Ariana E. Vigil, John Waldron, and Kimberly D. Williams. You've all been an integral part of my journey y les estaré agradecida siempre.

I cannot forget to mention all of the students with whom I've discussed many of the ideas and texts included in this book. The classroom is a space of dialogue and exchange, and you have all been invaluable interlocutors. One student in particular, Chloe Huh Prudente, was instrumental in ushering this project through its final stages. Gracias, Chloe, por todo.

My family continues to sustain me in ways I could never articulate and for which I am profoundly grateful. Though I have lost many loved ones along the way, I know they continue to walk with me. This book is a testament to their ongoing guidance. Seguimos.

I give thanks and recognition to every single voice included in these pages; without the wisdom and creativity of so many this conversation would not be possible. Finally, my deepest gratitude to everything the many faces of water have taught me. This book exists because water always finds a way.

Channeling Knowledges

Infusing the Sacred

THE LIQUID KNOWLEDGES OF THE AFRO-DIASPORIC WORLD

In the book *We Are Here: Visionaries of Color Transforming the Art World,* Jasmin Hernandez describes Firelei Báez as a "Dominican-born artist of Dominican and Haitian descent" (115).[1] Movement is intrinsic to Báez's story; she and her family arrived in Miami from the Dominican Republic when she was eight years old, and her studio is currently based in New York. In a 2021 video interview, Báez describes her creative approach in the following way: "I don't want to create narratives of victimhood. I want to flip it" ("Firelei Báez: An Open Horizon"). Báez goes on to discuss the importance of women's bodies in her work and how spotlighting and reinterpreting what society has deemed abject allows her to decenter and repurpose the flows of power. As the artist shares these potent words, the camera offers an indelible image: Báez is wearing a yellow *eleke,* a sacred necklace of Santería/Regla de Ocha, indicating she is in communion with the energies of Ochún, the *orisha* of rivers and sweetwaters.[2]

Just as would happen with a current of water or a flash of light, this moment in the interview comes and goes in a matter of seconds, yet it provides a critical entry point for the conversations I generate in this book. Life-giving, life-sustaining, and latently coursing through our veins, water is omnipresent in our lives. In the worlds of Afro-diasporic religions, water is also a palimpsestic, powerful, nonhuman actor that facilitates the circulation of geographically unbounded Latinx and Caribbean realities. Bringing together the works of Firelei Báez, Mayra Santos-Febres, Rita Indiana, Gloria Evangelina Anzaldúa, and the Border of Lights collective, this book surfaces a discussion of water's sacred infusions. In doing so, I highlight the multiple messages water communicates, the roles it performs, and how it erodes chronological, epistemological, and geopolitical borders to (re)connect us to pasts, presents, and not-yet-imagined futures.

Channeling Knowledges: Water and Afro-Diasporic Spirits in Latinx and

1

Caribbean Worlds opens and closes not with the expected introduction/conclusion dyad, but with a free-flowing prologue and an open-ended epilogue. This stylistic choice mirrors the unruly yet cyclical paths of water that shape these pages. In the prologue, I offer readers a discussion of key terms and the frictions that surround them, first in relation to Firelei Báez's 2014 painting *Ode to la Sirène*.[3] Like much of Báez's art, this painting complicates notions of place, kinship, and belonging. Because Lasirèn is a *lwa* (deity) of Haitian Vodou, Báez's painting sets the tone for my writing's engagement with the liquid knowledges of Haitian Vodou, La 21 División, and Santería/Regla de Ocha.[4] This context is critical since Afro-diasporic religions provide the methodological frameworks of this book. Some of the richest moments for beholding the power of water in Afro-diasporic spiritual traditions take place in initiation rituals. As such, this prologue provides a water-centered discussion of these ceremonies, a process for which Báez's work serves as an invaluable primer.

Readers will find that Santería/Regla de Ocha is the most legible Afro-diasporic system in these pages. Rather than indicate any kind of hierarchy, my primary sources transformed this tradition into the spiritual node of the book. While some of the authors I include evoke Haitian Vodou and La 21 División, Santería/Regla de Ocha is referenced by all: Mayra Santos-Febres's poetry collection *boat people*, Rita Indiana's novel *La mucama de Omicunlé*, Gloria Evangelina Anzaldúa's archive, and Anzaldúa's book *Borderlands/La Frontera: The New Mestiza*. Hence, a latent undercurrent in my analysis is that of *aché*, the life-giving force that connects all beings, human and nonhuman, in Santería/Regla de Ocha's worldview. *Aché* is an indelible component of the Black creative aesthetic (Moreno Vega, "The Ancestral" 46). Water, like all natural elements, is brimming with it.[5]

Before proceeding, I would like to note that while Santos-Febres, Indiana, and Anzaldúa invoke the energies of Afro-diasporic initiations in their written work, they do not go as far as presenting "official" renditions of these rituals.[6] While some might critique their decision, I interpret their creative license as a way of respecting the veil that shrouds these ceremonies.[7] In Santería/Regla de Ocha, only the initiated may witness and participate in *kari ocha* (initiation) (Cabrera, *Yemayá y Ochún* 146). Similarly, in *kanzo*, Haitian Vodou's initiation ceremony, Alfred Métraux observes that "only people who have themselves passed through the *kanzo* rites may enter the room" (202). In response to this reality, I posit that Santos-Febres, Indiana, and Anzaldúa incorporate publicly circulating aspects of these spirited processes to create *literary* renditions of initiation in their texts. This approach allows them to infuse their writing with sacred meaning while respecting the limits of the knowable.

The literary initiations I address in this book dialogue with Margarite Fernández Olmos's concepts of "spirited identities" and "initiated readerships."

Bridging literary analysis and spiritual realities, these terms identify the nonsecular knowledges that can provide access to a plethora of meanings in a work of art or a piece of literature (Fernández Olmos 65). I support Fernández Olmos's theoretical contribution and extend its development by focusing on water. My work posits that the multivalent ways in which water is both a "spirited" and an "initiatory" element in the Afro-diasporic religious world can inform the creation and reception of Latinx and Caribbean expressive culture, whether in art, literature, or civic life.

My research also invites readers to consider the very making of scholarship as a spiritually inflected process. Citations have become a powerful praxis for uplifting the work of multiply marginalized individuals and communities, a practice I fervently uphold. Yet, what is the production of scholarship, especially when it references archives and materials of those no longer living, but another way of speaking and communing with the dead?[8] Inspired by Solimar Otero's concept of the "archival ancestor" (*Archives* 41), I approach writing as a way of honoring the knowledge workers who came before me, and of creating intellectual kinship ties that transcend the limits imposed by academic disciplines. Moreover, the research of many of the scholars I cite overflows with the voices of informants channeled through divination, dreams, possession, and other sacred pathways. My book is committed to honoring those voices. While their names cannot be documented through traditional citational practices, their presence can be acknowledged by expanding our understanding of writing itself. Such an approach evinces that ancestors do not have to be perfect to be remembered because reverence is not inherently blind.[9]

RECALCITRANT TERMS AND FLUID DOMAINS: A NOTE TO THE READER

Identity is a contested terrain; claiming a socially and politically palatable label can entail the dismissal of seemingly incongruent parts of our personhood. Inspired by how water not only sustains but encourages contradiction, I staunchly use "diaspora" *and* "Latinx" alongside each other in my book. These terms inform one another by alluding to something illegible, missing, and/or unplaceable, even as they create friction. As Stuart Hall notes in "Subjects in History":

If you open yourself to the politics of cultural difference, there is no safety in terminology. Words can always be transcoded against you, identity can turn against you, race can turn against you, difference can turn against you, diaspora can turn against you because that is the nature of the discursive. (338)

Hall is well known in diaspora studies, yet his reasoning sharply resonates with the term "Latinx" and the contentious debates surrounding its use.[10] This confluence is also evident in how "the attention to diaspora, its proliferation, explosion, and tropic figuration [results] in serious challenges in defining the term" (Clitandre 14). As in Hall's case, Nadège T. Clitandre's evocation of "diaspora" is an apt description of the current state of "Latinx."[11]

Regardless of one's position, what is undoubtedly true is that the "x" in Latinx is unstable. For Claudia Milian, it describes "one that is falling through the Latin cracks—the spaces between the o's and the a's, the conventional understandings of what it means to be Latino or Latina" (*LatinX* 2). Beyond its critical role in challenging heteronormativity, Nicole M. Guidotti-Hernández articulates that the volatility of "Latinx" is key to its value because it "bears the load of recognition and diversity while representing the power of inclusion without speaking for everyone" ("Affective Communities" 142). The generative possibilities of "Latinx" explain its fervent rejection by many. While the term performs the erosion of binaries, its fluidity makes it an epistemic weapon in the hands of those for whom the "x" is a threat to the established order, be it ethnic, historical, linguistic, racial, sexual, or other.

The inherent instability of the "x" is what drives me to use "Latinx" and "diaspora" together. Their uneasy convergence on the page exposes the constructed disciplinary boundaries I actively push against, an ethos apparent in Frances R. Aparicio's assertion that "Latinx Studies proposes alternative and multiple methodologies that challenge traditional disciplinary approaches" ("Latinx Studies"). My dual use of these terms also posits that ontology often opens the way to epistemology. This reality, evident in the Afro-diasporic religious world, has accompanied me throughout my life. As an Afro-diasporic Latinx woman, I know that while "diaspora" and "Latinx" have distinct academic histories, they intersect in my body in unexpected and oftentimes violent ways.

While the term "diaspora" circulates freely in Caribbean studies, it is less visible in Latinx studies. At times, "diaspora" is subsumed into the "x." At others, it is discarded in an urge to lay claim to alternate spaces and geographies. Dissolving these occlusions is a critical way of "disturb[ing] what appear to be cemented historical narratives steeped in patriarchal nationalisms" (Guidotti-Hernández, *Archiving* 5), allowing us to craft new epistemic paths. Yet, the tensions between "diaspora" and "Latinx" go both ways. Yomaira C. Figueroa-Vásquez asserts that "the long-established sociocultural ties between Latinx Caribbean and Black peoples in the United States requires a rearticulation of Black studies and Latinx studies" (7). By engaging with Equatorial Guinea, Figueroa-Vásquez's research proposes an expansion of Latinx and Caribbean imaginaries, challenging the imposition of (neo)colonial fractures onto Black epistemologies. Hence, as "Latinx" continues to become untethered to US-specific contexts, its cohabitation alongside terms such as "diaspora" will proliferate, revealing newfound continuities. Here, "diaspora" again provides critical context because it indexes a condition that must be historically contextualized even as it is enmeshed in an ongoing process of making and unmaking (Patterson and Kelley 20). As a result of these intimate connections, Afro-diasporic religious waters seep into Latinx and Caribbean worlds, revealing that "diaspora" and "Latinx" index realities that cannot be fully expressed through normative disciplinary thinking.

The uneasy crossroads between the expansive spiritual cartographies of my book and those of diasporic and Latinx worlds are on full display when Afro-diasporic religions are not routinely affirmed as critical sites for the construction of (Afro)Latinx identities.[12] This current state of affairs begets a questioning regarding the place of Haiti in Latinx and Latin American studies. Scholars of Afro-diasporic religions regularly place Haiti in conversation with Brazil, Cuba, and the United States, an inclusive dialogue that resonates with the corpus of this book. Yet, their approach is the exception rather than the rule. Jennifer A. Jones notes that Latinidad "both excludes Blackness and is constructed as proximate to whiteness" ("Blackness" 425).[13] In response to these compromising qualities, Agustín Laó-Montes claims that the field of Afro-Latinidad "reveal[s] and recognize[s] hidden histories and subalternized knowledges" (118). Its ideations of inclusion, however, are tempered by its ties to Latin America, a location implicitly tethered to "Latinidad," a term born out of colonial and hegemonic desire.[14] Hence, although Silvio Torres-Saillant finds that Afro-Latinidad is invested in "expos[ing] the Eurocentric bias at the core of latinidad" (278), its geographic primacy can limit its reach.[15] These constraints are starkly evident when it comes to Haiti.[16]

In 2010 Miriam Jiménez Román and Juan Flores published the edited volume *The Afro-Latin@ Reader: History and Culture in the United States*, a landmark text in the field of Afro-Latinidad. Yet, in their introduction, Jiménez Román and Flores declare that the collection excludes Haiti because "in the context of the United States Haitians have consistently been distinguished—and have often distinguished themselves—from Latin@s. Unlike the case of Afro-Latin@s, Haitians are generally understood to be unambiguously Black" (3). The use of the word "unambiguously" is particularly troubling due to the fluid constructions of race and the diversity of experiences Afro-Latinidad purports to embrace. Brazil is also nonexistent in *The Afro-Latin@ Reader*, an omission remedied by Petra R. Rivera-Rideau and colleagues' 2016 collection, *Afro-Latin@s in Movement: Critical Approaches to Blackness and Transnationalism in the Americas*.[17] Haiti, however, remains absent in this later collection save for one detail: the book's copyright page declares that the logo for the "Afro-Latin@ Diasporas" series, in which *Afro-Latin@s in Movement* is included, is inspired by the Haitian sculptor Albert Mangonès.[18]

Beyond stunting the possibilities of Afro-Latinidad, Haiti's illegibility in Latinx and Latin American studies limits engagement with the term "diaspora." In her introduction to the anthology *The Butterfly's Way: Voices from the Haitian Dyaspora in the United States,* the renowned Haitian American writer Edwidge Danticat explains that "Haiti has nine geographic departments and the tenth was the floating homeland, the ideological one, which joined all Haitians living in the *dyaspora*" (xiv). More than a symbol, for Danticat, the word *dyaspora* describes one's physical and emotional location vis-à-vis the island of Haiti. It is also a weapon wielded by individuals rooted in the island to exclude and marginalize those living beyond its physical borders.[19] Echoing Hall's assertion of the dangers of terminology, Ricardo Ortiz contends that "for a writer like Danticat, the conventional substitution of 'Latin' or 'Latino' for 'Hispanic' must provoke a certain kind of bewilderment" (155). Danticat's comments on *dyaspora* demonstrate that the imposition of geographic borders is part and parcel of the creation and perpetuation of diaspora as an endemic condition.[20]

Given their uses, "diaspora" and "Latinx" are embroiled in the process of "bordering," a term posited by Lorgia García-Peña in her path-opening study *The Borders of Dominicanidad: Race, Nation, and Archives of Contradiction.* For García-Peña, "bordering" is "a continuum of actions that affect human beings" (6), and it can take place in a myriad of situations. Everyday speech can enact bordering, stringently upholding the perimeters of (neo)colonial cartographies despite being enounced thousands of miles away from their physical location. This nefarious quality is on display when Danticat recounts how she is often silenced in conversations about Haiti with the dictum "What do you know? You're a *Dyaspora*" (Introduction xiv). Bordering also sustains academic disciplines, creating an environment in which Patrick Bellegarde-Smith's affirmation that Haiti is "tethered to larger Caribbean, African, and Latin American worlds" (3) is denied. Through this neglect, the borders of Hispanophone Caribbean, Latin American, and Latinx studies conceal Haiti's multiple contributions to knowledge making.[21]

Cognizant of these elisions, in my book I employ a critical language that prioritizes the use of "diaspora" (which includes Haiti) and "Latinx" (which often silently implies a diaspora through current or past migration) and brings them together through the term "Afro-diasporic." This terminology builds upon the fact that "'afro' serves to link struggles and declare a community of experiences and interests" (Jiménez Román and Flores 3). My use also follows Clitandre's proposition of "the diasporic imaginary" as "the creative domain of the displaced subject's imagination and his or her ability to perceive, interpret, and reimagine the world from a diasporic lens" (2). In *Channeling Knowledges,* the term "Afro-diasporic" affirms the multiple ways in which Afro-diasporic identities in Latinx and Caribbean worlds are continually generated and refashioned through their engagement with the spirited waters of Haitian Vodou, La 21 División, and Santería/Regla de Ocha.

It is also important to address my use of the terms "religion" and "spirituality" in relation to Haitian Vodou, La 21 División, and Santería/Regla de Ocha. Here, I am in conversation with Christina Garcia Lopez's *Calling the Soul Back: Embodied Spirituality in Chicanx Narrative*, in which she sustains the following:

> For the purposes of this book, I approach *spirituality* as an active mode of being that consciously centers an epistemology of interconnectivity between elements of existence; I reserve the term *religion* to refer to organized, institutional practices often associated with spirituality. (3, emphasis in the original)

When I began writing this book, I was in complete alignment with Garcia Lopez, going as far as refusing to use the term "religion" when referring to Haitian Vodou, La 21 División, and Santería/Regla de Ocha because one of the distinctive characteristics of these systems is that none revolves around a formalized, state-legible, institutional center. Instead, as conveyed in the title of Nahayeilli Beatriz Juárez Huet's study on Santería/Regla de Ocha in Mexico City, Afro-diasporic religious practitioners have "un pedacito de Dios en casa" (a little piece of God at home).[22]

Still, given their nonhegemonic and rhizomatic roots, practitioners of these frequently maligned traditions have had to seek legal recourse to protect the right to practice their beliefs. Though these tensions have taken place throughout the centuries, a contemporary instance is the 1993 US Supreme Court ruling in favor of the Church of Lukumí Babalú Ayé against the city of Hialeah, Florida (Beliso-De Jesús, *Electric Santería* 66).[23] Beyond granting religious protection, this case established Santería/Regla de Ocha as a legible entity within the US legal system (Palmié, *The Cooking* 17). In the Caribbean, a climactic moment came in 2003 when Vodou was officially recognized as a religion in Haiti, a ruling that Kate Ramsey views as "the vindication of a long and ongoing struggle for religious rights" (13).[24] In addition to these legal instances, I am cognizant of García-Peña's call to pay attention to the terms people and communities use to define themselves. This awareness ensures that we as academics refer to others on their terms rather than impose our own. In this regard, Santería/Regla de Ocha was definitive in encouraging my use of "religion" because it is also often referred to by practitioners as "la religión" (the religion) (Murphy, "Chango" 76).[25] This attentive listening also drives my decision to use the term "La 21 División" to refer to what several scholars deem "Dominican Vodú." I do so because practitioners themselves "nombran 21 divisiones" (name 21 divisions) when speaking of their tradition (Deive 180),[26] and because of how Rita Indiana refers to this Afro-diasporic system in her novel *La mucama de Omicunlé* (59).

But terms are rarely uncontested. Just as my research surfaced frictions between "diaspora" and "Latinx," I learned that the way these traditions are referred to ("Haitian Vodou," "La 21 División," and "Santería/Regla de Ocha") is disputed between practitioners *and* academics, with incongruences within their respective communities and outside of them.[27] Placed alongside the (il)legible strategies of vindication used by practitioners, this realization further blurred the borders between "religion" and "spirituality" in my writing. On the one hand, I began to see the use of "religion" as a way of avowing the legal legibility of traditions that have survived centuries-long campaigns of criminalization. On the other, "spirituality" offered a more decentered way of referring to the complex ontological and epistemological practices of these systems. Hence, I employ the term "Afro-diasporic religion" to refer to the coherent yet fluid corpus that comprises the belief systems of Haitian Vodou, La 21 División, and Santería/Regla de Ocha. I also use "Afro-diasporic spirituality" because this term addresses how the tenets of these religions manifest in the literary and artistic worlds I discuss in this book. Rather than oppose each other, "religion" and "spirituality" function in tandem in my writing, evincing the negation of binaries inherent in the liquid knowledges of the Afro-diasporic world.

INHERITED KNOWLEDGES IN *FIRELEI BÁEZ: BLOODLINES*

Firelei Báez: Bloodlines was published to accompany the opening of Báez's first solo show, *Bloodlines (past forces of oppression become frail and fallible)*. The show was on display at the Pérez Art Museum Miami (PAMM) in 2015, a site bordered by the Biscayne Bay. It was curated by María Elena Ortiz, whom Arlene Dávila describes as a "Black Puerto Rican woman straddling contemporary art circles . . . as well as . . . growingly diverse Latinx communities in Miami whom she seeks to attract to the museum" (25). *Bloodlines* navigates similar complexities. Although Franklin Sirmans, PAMM's director, touted the exhibit as a "celebratory homecoming for the artist" ("Preface" 7), for diasporic artists such as Báez homecomings are never straightforward because "home" is a slippery term. Sirmans's statement is further complicated by Fredo Rivera's claim that Miami functions as "an oceanic borderlands" whose history is intertwined with that of Erzulie Freda, a *lwa* of Haitian Vodou (64), and other Afro-diasporic spirits. While the city's official languages are English, Kreyòl, and Spanish (F. Rivera 64), the political charge of Cuba in the US imaginary has obfuscated Miami's Haitian currents. For example, beyond Little Havana, Miami is home to Little Haiti, a site Terry Rey and Alex Stepick depict as "teem[ing] with Haitian life" (*Crossing* 2).[28] Despite these realities, the book *Firelei Báez: Bloodlines* is only available bilingually (Spanish and English), leaving the artist's ties to Haiti unacknowledged.[29]

My approach to Báez's work troubles how the artist is recurrently described as "Dominican-born" but not bicultural, even though she is of Dominican and Haitian descent. This glossing over reflects the insidiousness of "national privilege" in the art world, an identifying tool that leaves diasporic Latinx artists largely adrift as it focuses on marketing those with direct ties to Latin America (Dávila 9). Furthermore, "Dominican-born" obscures that Báez was born not in the capital city of Santo Domingo but near the border between the Dominican Republic and Haiti.[30] More than an example of Dominican art, then, Báez's work is a manifestation of what García-Peña calls "*rayano* consciousness."

As a polyvalent way of knowing that both precedes and exceeds the nation, "*rayano* consciousness" affirms that the physical bodies of the borderlands peoples of Hispaniola (*rayanos*) are powerful epistemological nodes (García-Peña 137). "*Rayano* consciousness" challenges the hegemony of "national privilege," allowing Báez's work to speak from multiple locations at once. Such a view of artists hailing from Hispaniola, the landmass shared by the Dominican Republic and Haiti, is critical to dislodging what John D. Ribó calls "the geographic, linguistic, and ethno-racial boundaries of Latinidad" (470), an enterprise my work is fully invested in. It is also in line with contesting the "discursive impenetrability" Ramón Antonio Victoriano-Martínez observes in nationalistic discourses (16). Finally, my approach to Báez's art builds on Agustín Laó-Montes's and Mirangela Buggs's affirmation that "border/diasporic decolonial imaginar[ies]" are critical in generating coalitions between Black and Latinx communities in the United States (389). By including Haiti in the conversation, scholars can acknowledge the role island-based and diasporic Haitians have played and continue to play in the production of global Black epistemologies.

Though the publication of *Firelei Báez: Bloodlines* was driven by the 2015 *Bloodlines* exhibit, the book includes earlier works by the artist. In this way, the publication becomes a genealogical artifact, a kind of family album that traces a rich though incomplete intergenerational and transoceanic conversation among Báez's creations. By emphasizing "bloodlines" (with an emphasis on the "s"), the exhibit's title confronts the illusory neatness of borders, bodies, and the truncated taxonomies they engender. The focus on blood also addresses the inextricable bonds between blood, race, and power. Although these ties certainly qualify as "*past forces of oppression*," Báez's art denies them currency by inviting viewers to read blood differently. Here, the Afro-diasporic religious world becomes an essential guide. The bloodlines of Haitian Vodou, La 21 División, and Santería/Regla de Ocha flow into realms that lie beyond the secular and provide access to the previously unimaginable. Rather than create an equivalency between humanness and whiteness, as in the one-drop rule of the

United States or the insidious desire to *mejorar la raza* (better the race) in Latin America, the use of blood in the Afro-diasporic spiritual world allows for energetic transfusions to take place.

Like water, blood is a life-giving and life-sustaining element that circulates all around us. Because there is no blood without water, both liquids are central to the ontological and epistemological frameworks of Afro-diasporic religions.[31] The title of Báez's exhibit, then, can be read as a critique of the establishment of lineages by means intent on stripping peoples of their histories. As María Elena Ortiz asserts:

> *Bloodlines* weaves together Caribbean pigmentocracy and folktales with African American narratives as a vehicle that creates an alternative sense of self, for those whose cultural identities straddle nonlinear, related histories that remain absent from dominant culture. (18)[32]

Positing that other modes of kinship are required to understand Afro-diasporic inheritances, Báez's bloodlines traverse continents and epistemes, making evident that "Báez's interest in the diasporic histories of Africa and Latina America has spurred her to invest in histories that are as of yet often untold" (Báez and Sirmans 78). There are no limits to the times and places viewers can be transported to when gazing at Báez's work, a fact evidenced by the exhibit's utter disregard for chronology (Scalissi 99).

One of the pieces reproduced in the *Bloodlines* book is a 2014 painting titled *Ode to la Sirène (and to muses beyond Jean Luc Nancy's Canon)*. Báez's painting stands at an imposing 108 x 88 inches. Yet the size and scale of the creation are purposeful. The image is inspired by the *lwa* of Haitian Vodou Lasirèn, an anthropomorphic deity who dwells in the sea. Lasirèn is a vital aspect of the visuality of Haitian Vodou. As Elizabeth McAlister notes, she is "particularly popular in paintings and textile arts, which are collected widely by museums and galleries throughout the world" ("Sacred Waters" 261). Hence, while Lasirèn's popularity has accustomed her to dwelling in secular spaces, her presence is always imbued with deeper meaning.

Although Báez's focus on Lasirèn is conjoined with an invocation of the sea, the painting is devoid of the color blue. Instead, the canvas is awash in rust-colored tones, proposing a play between light and dark that creates a subtle allusion to a shimmering and rippling sea. Also absent, at least at first, are the long hair, mermaid tail, and mirror that regularly accompany Lasirèn's visual representations. What the audience readily sees of the *lwa* is one of her eyes, which appears submerged toward what could be taken as the center of the canvas. Taking this eye as a point of departure, viewers can begin to trace what seems to be billowing hair made of vegetation and cowrie shells around the *lwa*'s partially

FIGURE 0.1. Firelei Báez, *Ode to la Sirène (and to muses beyond Jean Luc Nancy's Canon)*, 2014. Gouache, acrylic, and ink on paper and canvas. 108 x 88 in (274.3 x 223.5 cm). Photo © Ian Reeves. Courtesy of the artist and James Cohan, New York.

visible face. By not giving the audience a clear entry point into the painting, Báez evokes the ceaseless movement and circulation of water.

When I gaze at *Ode to la Sirène* I see an evocation of blood in the rust-colored tones chosen by the artist, a reading reinforced by the inclusion of human bodies in the painting. Dramatically smaller in scale compared to the image of the *lwa*, these bodies float below Lasirèn's face, toward the bottom edges of the canvas.

To the left is the silhouette of a woman in a lounging posture. To the right, various figures appear in an array of standing and moving positions; others seem to have fallen along the way. Given that the presence of Lasirèn invokes the sea, Báez's painting continues a critical Afro-diasporic tradition of acknowledging the lives lost in the Middle Passage.

Upon closer examination, the viewer will note that the "sea" in this painting consists of a rich tapestry of symbols that are at once scattered, connected, and layered upon each other. This visual strategy evokes the movements of both "diaspora" and "Latinx," as these terms are the epitome of being both scattered and connected. Notably, many symbols that flow throughout *Ode to la Sirène* are leitmotifs of Báez's art: a raised fist, a comb, and chains. While these emblems have powerful connections to Blackness writ large, each symbol also has profound spiritual meaning. The raised Black fist, evocative of the Black Power Movement, doubles as an *azabache*, an amulet used in Caribbean, Latin American, and Latinx cultures to protect the vulnerable, especially children, from harmful energies. The comb, connected to the natural hair movement, dually indexes Lasirèn and other water deities such as Ochún because long hair is one of their distinctive qualities.[33] Finally, beyond evoking slavery, the broken chains that swirl in the image proclaim the birth of Afro-diasporic religions, revolutionary systems that helped break the physical, mental, and spiritual bondage imposed upon the enslaved.[34] Multiple bloodlines of knowledge thus swirl through and around the liquid body of Lasirèn, summoned by Báez's brushstrokes.

The evocation of water in Báez's painting points to the liquid's spiritual expansiveness. For, while Lasirèn is the most visible *lwa* in the piece, water has several numinous inhabitants. In Haitian Vodou "ancestral spirits (called *lwa*) of the water include the ancient serpent Danbala Wèdo and his rainbow wife Ayida Wèdo, as well as the lady with the fish tail, Lasirèn, a spirit called Simbi Dlo (Simbi of the water), and others, named and unnamed" (McAlister, "Sacred Waters" 259–260). Guided by these words, the audience notes that the top of the painting includes a shape reminiscent of a serpent, hinting at the energies of Danbala and Ayida Wèdo alongside Lasirèn.[35] McAlister's observation regarding the "named and unnamed" spirits in the water provides valuable context in light of the full title of Báez's piece: *Ode to la Sirène (and to muses beyond Jean Luc Nancy's Canon)*.

The unwritten histories of Afro-diasporic waters and all they contain are intrinsic to the painting's titular mention (and dismissal) of the secular Western canon.[36] In 1994 the French philosopher Jean-Luc Nancy published *Les Muses*, a widely circulating collection of essays on European art and aesthetics. Báez's avowal of the *lwa* as muses is a sharp repudiation of the invisibility of Afro-diasporic art in the European canon and an affirmation of the importance of considering Afro-diasporic thought as integral to Western culture.[37] Not surprisingly, Báez notes the importance of making *lwa* such as Lasirèn visible and legible to wider audiences, countering Greek and Roman mythology's hegemonic hold on the popular imagination ("Studio Visit").

Beyond the immense value of Báez's work, my decision to include this artist in the prologue of this book honors how art has often been a place where Afro-diasporic religions have found visibility and credence. This trait is evident in another "bloodline" of these systems, the term "Black Atlantic." Water has always been present, though not necessarily emphasized, in scholarship on Afro-diasporic religions.[38] In fact, one of the first books published on the connection between art and Afro-diasporic spirituality, Robert Farris Thompson's *Flash of the Spirit: African & Afro-American Art & Philosophy*, put forth the term "Black Atlantic" (Patterson and Kelley 12).[39] Thompson's book was published in 1983, ten years before Paul Gilroy's influential *The Black Atlantic: Modernity and Double Consciousness*. As a literature scholar I was often exposed to Gilroy's work, a testament to the many disciplinary boundaries his historical study has crossed. Thompson's *Flash of the Spirit*, however, was a text I had to seek out, though his book has eroded other boundaries. *Flash of the Spirit* is sold in many *botánicas* (Shufro), spiritual stores that supply herbs, books, and other ritual materials necessary to sustain the practices of a variety of spiritual traditions including Haitian Vodou, La 21 División, and Santería/Regla de Ocha.[40] *Botánicas* exist throughout the world, a testament to how Afro-diasporic traditions follow the multiple paths traveled by their practitioners.[41] When I visited Brownsville, Texas, on the US/Mexico border in 2017, I noted how much local spiritual stores (*yerberias/hierberias*) resembled *botánicas*.

My intent in surfacing the genealogy of the term "Black Atlantic" is not in any way invested in discrediting Gilroy's invaluable research or the work numerous scholars have penned to advance the capaciousness of the term. Rather, by underscoring the inception of its use, I affirm the importance of the Afro-diasporic religious world in the generation of Black epistemologies, even within presumably secular disciplinary realms. It is critical to underscore that the gestation of the Black Atlantic was always already spiritual, not in a metaphorical sense but in a very concrete way. For undoubtedly, Afro-diasporic religions are as ethereal as they are tangible, as evidenced by Thompson's discussion of sacred technologies such as Haitian Vodou's *vèvè*, the ritual symbols traced on the ground to invoke the energies of the *lwa*.[42] An awareness of the spiritual currents that fuel the term suggests the importance of acknowledging the epistemological richness of Afro-diasporic religious traditions, a central tenet of my research.

It is also significant that Thompson hails from El Paso, Texas. His background suggests the surreptitious influence of a US-Mexico infusion of Latinidad into the conception of the Black Atlantic, a relationship that merits further study and that my engagement with Gloria Evangelina Anzaldúa's published and unpublished work in this book contributes to. Thompson himself declares, "I loved to cross the Rio Bravo, what we call the Rio Grande, *e inmediatamente la diferencia se ve* [and immediately you see the difference], everything changes" (quoted in Shufro, italics in the original). Though undoubtedly aided by privilege, Thompson's experiences in a majority-minority city fostered a sensibility for living in a world open to cultural contact, one that was facilitated by water, the Rio Grande/Río Bravo, to be exact. An awareness of this genealogy of the Black Atlantic surfaces water's "unapologetic mutability" (Otero, *Archives* 24), a fluid trait that challenges the epistemological hold of rupture.

The construction of the Black Atlantic has been a pivotal framework for the study of Afro-diasporic religions. One example is J. Lorand Matory's influential study on Brazilian Candomblé, another important Afro-diasporic tradition, which bears the title *Black Atlantic Religion: Tradition, Transnationalism, and Matriarchy in the Afro-Brazilian Candomblé*. In his introduction, Matory describes Candomblé as "both the product and one of the greatest producers of a transoceanic culture and political economy known as the 'black Atlantic'" (1). The same can be said of Haitian Vodou, La 21 División, and Santería/Regla de Ocha. Still, I refer to these traditions as "Afro-diasporic" religions rather than "Black Atlantic" religions to purposefully unsettle the sediments of the latter. I accomplish this by extending the bodies of water typically envisioned when evoking the Black Atlantic. In my book, oceans and rivers flow alongside each other. This confluence produces an analysis that engages the saltwaters of the Caribbean Sea, the Atlantic Ocean, and the Pacific Ocean, as well as the sweetwaters of the Rio Grande/Río Bravo on the US/Mexico border, and the Massacre River/Dajabón River and Artibonite River in Hispaniola's border zones. This assemblage is inspired by Édouard Glissant's provocative assertion that "the Caribbean Sea is not an American lake. It is the estuary of the Americas" (*Caribbean Discourse* 139). As a meeting place for saltwaters, sweetwaters, and various Afro-diasporic traditions, *Channeling Knowledges* embodies the estuary, drawing inspiration from the shoal.

In *The Black Shoals: Offshore Formations of Black and Native Studies*, Tiffany Lethabo King proposes thinking of the shoal, an amphibian place that is neither solely land nor solely water, as a productive "space of liminality, indeterminacy, and location of suture between two hermeneutical frames [water and land] that have conventionally been understood as sealed off from each other" (4). I am inspired by how King's shoal-driven methodology centers the intellectual vibrancy of nature. Her approach also resonates with the disciplinary boundaries traversed by my work. Yet, I am also intent on surfacing how traditional academic scholarship constructs and constrains water. Disciplinary fields cordon off the bodies of water I discuss in this book: the Atlantic Ocean is primarily associated with transatlantic studies, the Rio Grande/Río Bravo with Latin American and Latinx studies, and the Caribbean Sea, the Massacre River/Dajabón River, and the Artibonite River with Caribbean studies. Eschewing convention and placing these aquatic bodies in conversation with each other, I emphasize water's capacity to overflow (*desbordar*), unbordering and challenging national, (neo-) colonial, and disciplinary boundaries.

WATER IN AFRO-DIASPORIC RELIGIONS

Afro-diasporic religions are rich and complex systems. This prologue does not put forth a thorough discussion of these traditions because the scholars I continually cite in my analysis have produced this valuable research.[43] What I do offer is a conversation in which Haitian Vodou, La 21 División, and Santería/Regla de Ocha dialogue with each other by focusing on how they each engage with and are sustained by water. Because water is neither stable nor one-directional, readers may struggle to comprehend exactly what water *is* in these spiritual systems. The very act of attempting to grasp water reveals its futility; the liquid will simply slip through our fingers, evading containment. For this reason, my writing does not attempt to impose discursive control through the application of a rigid theoretical framework. Rather, I document the many things water *does* by offering a discussion of its multiple roles in Afro-diasporic religions.

Water is a hardworking element in the Afro-diasporic spiritual world because work is inherent to the ritual practices of Haitian Vodou, La 21 División, and Santería/Regla de Ocha. Water is one of many *herramientas* (tools) an individual can use to perform *trabajos* (ritual work) or *servicios* (ritual offerings) to help maintain balance or mitigate threats to their well-being. Water is also essential to the transference and development of *konesans* (spiritual knowledge or awareness), which lies at the heart of Haitian Vodou. Karen McCarthy Brown offers this description:

> Priestly power is said to reside in *konesans*. This knowledge could be called psychic power, the gift of eyes, empathy, or intuition. It is any and all of these things. Above all, it is knowledge about people. Vodou provides a vast and complex symbol system for thinking about people. *Konesans* is the ability to read people, with or without cards; to diagnose and name their suffering, suffering that Haitians know comes not from God and usually not from chance but from others—the living, the dead, and the spirits. Finally, *konesans* is the ability to heal. (356)

Haitian Vodou's *konesans* exemplifies how water becomes both matter and vehicle, a channel and a mode of channeling that is active and activating. These qualities help explain the liquid's central role in the tradition.

Afro-diasporic waters are physically vital because they are the dwelling places of many *lwa, misterios,*[44] and *orishas.* By harboring the numinous, they connect the living and the dead, the secular and the sacred, and the known and the unknown. For this reason, I often refer to water as an archive. Like water, the word "archive" performs multiple functions; it is a noun and a verb, and it refers to the contents and knowledges that reside inside it and to the willful act of preservation. Yet, perhaps the primary function of water in my book is to sustain contradiction. In the Afro-diasporic world, life and death cyclically collide in the water, transforming this liquid into an element that is as associated with nourishment as it is with destruction. Once we accept this fluid dissonance, we begin to understand that the existence of one reality does not preclude that of another. In this way, a focus on water forces a reckoning with our own epistemological limitations.

Another critical characteristic is water's capacity to challenge the boundedness of geography. To be sure, Haitian Vodou flows from Haiti, La 21 División from the Dominican Republic, and Santería/Regla de Ocha from Cuba. But emanating from a particular place does not mean these systems do not extend elsewhere. Even in seemingly contained spaces such as the island of Hispaniola and Cuba the borders between traditions become blurred, a reality reflected in how Afro-diasporic religions complicate the concept of *nación* (nation).[45] Practitioners of Haitian Vodou, La 21 División, Santería/Regla de Ocha, and other Afro-diasporic religions have broadly "understood themselves as the simultaneous inhabitants of *multiple* nations, some territorial and some transoceanic" (Matory, "The Many" 233).[46] Although this position is not an inherent rejection of the nation-state's ideological and territorial borders, it displays the intrinsic expansiveness of these religious systems, a quality sustained by water's central role in their epistemological and ontological conceptions.

The highly permeable concept of "nation" in Afro-diasporic religion is evident in scholarly texts where these traditions seep into each other.[47] As Carlos Esteban Deive declares in the introduction to his study of La 21 División:

> Como el vodú dominicano aparece tan intrínsecamente ligado al haitiano, he juzgado oportuno estudiar a continuación ambos cultos y establecer sus relaciones y posibles diferencias e influencias. . . . También se indican, a modo de comparación, las correspondencias con otros sincretismos afroamericanos, como la santería y los cultos afrobrasileños, al igual que las simbiosis operadas entre el vodú y el catolicismo.[48] (18)

Deive's statement establishes that to discuss La 21 División it is necessary to draw upon the knowledges and histories of Haitian Vodou, Santería, and Afro-Brazilian religions in addition to Catholicism. Amanda D. Concha-Holmes observes a similar pattern when describing Santería/Regla de Ocha as a system "practiced in Cuba by integrating Yoruba beliefs with Catholic icons, tenets of Kardecian spiritism, along with other African-based religions like Palo and Abakua" (244–245).[49] What these approaches illustrate is that Afro-diasporic religions are constellations. Combining this reality with the multiple and ongoing migrations undertaken by devotees of Haitian Vodou, La 21 División, and Santería/Regla de Ocha, enforcing territorial and epistemological limits onto these systems is a futile but violent act of disciplining, academically and otherwise. As I demonstrate in this book, Haitian Vodou, La 21 División, and Santería/Regla de Ocha are traditions that, while they do not have "edges," represent "distinct" knowledges (King x).

The three Afro-diasporic systems that inform my writing share a belief in a distant yet benevolent supreme deity: Haitian Vodou's Bondye, La 21 División's Gran Dios, and Santería/Regla de Ocha's Olodumare. As a result, these religions are examples of "diffused monotheism," a term proposed by E. Bọlaji Idowu in 1962. The remoteness of the supreme being in all three traditions means that believers quotidianly interact with their emissaries (the *lwa*, the *misterios*, and the *orishas*), transforming these intermediaries into what Mercedes Cros Sandoval calls "symbolic power brokers" ("Santería" 357). The closeness of Haitian Vodou and La 21 División means that many *lwa* have a clear equivalence with a particular *misterio*, while the *orishas* of Santería/Regla de Ocha exhibit a more fluid connection with both *lwa* and *misterios*. The position of the *lwa*, the *misterios*, and the *orishas* vis-à-vis their respective supreme beings explains why relationships between these Afro-diasporic entities and Catholic saints exist.

In their introduction to *Òrìṣà Devotion as World Religion: The Globalization of Yorùbá Religious Culture*, Jacob K. Olupona and Terry Rey bring together various Afro-diasporic traditions by emphasizing a shared devotional center, Yoruba religion, which "often in combination with elements of Native American, European, and/or other African religious cultures, is a taproot of African diasporic life" (4). The *lwa* of Haitian Vodou, the *misterios* of La 21 División, and the *orishas* of Santería/Regla de Ocha are intertwined with Yoruba religion to varying degrees. These connections can be traced to the fact that the Yoruba people of West Africa were among the largest groups forcefully taken from their homelands during the transatlantic slave trade. Undoubtedly, the Middle Passage is the catastrophic womb from which Afro-diasporic religions emerge, an assertion that, like water, is more than a metaphor. For example, David H. Brown notes the circulation of stories about priests who swallowed sacralized stones (*otanes*) infused with the energies of their *orishas* before making the life-altering journey (144).

The *lwa*, *misterios*, and *orishas* are imbued with the horrors of the Middle Passage, slavery, and the dehumanizing afterlives of slavery due to their active witnessing of and participation in the lives of their devotees. But rather than lead to obliteration, these harrowing experiences transformed the deities into mutable forces that allowed practitioners to draw strength and wisdom from worlds beyond bondage, violation, and death. As Michel-Rolph Trouillot observes, "The slaves outsmarted the slave owners. They took the colonists' language, folded it into a bunch of African languages, and produced Creole. They took the colonists' religion, folded it into their own religion, and produced Vodou" (*Stirring* 16). Through numerous acts of invocation and initiation, these transcendent forces have been continually etched on the bodies, souls, and worlds of Afro-diasporic peoples and their descendants. Sacred ceremonies preserved bonds where it would have been secularly impossible to do so. And due to water's ubiquitous use in Afro-diasporic religious rituals (McAlister, "Sacred Waters" 260), it played an inordinate role in both generating and facilitating these processes.

Water is also essential to ancestor worship or reverence toward the dead, a key component of Haitian Vodou, La 21 División, and Santería/Regla de Ocha.[50] Ancestor worship and water are intertwined because watery sites allowed rituals to continue despite the repeated severing of family and community ties initiated by the slave trade and perpetuated through (ongoing) forced migration. Water's connective power informs Otero's contention that "by being and becoming through water, spirits and practitioners create social and cultural change on the earth" (*Archives* 22). Through their radical inclusivity, Afro-diasporic waters carry the dead, the *lwa*, the *misterios*, and the *orishas*. This multimodal channeling is critical for understanding why water is a central element in the initiation rituals of Haitian Vodou, La 21 División, and Santería/Regla de Ocha.

THE RITUAL WATERS OF THE AFRO-DIASPORIC WORLD

In Haitian Vodou, La 21 División, and Santería/Regla de Ocha, initiation is a complex process of transformation that dissolves the borders between life and death. On a technical level, initiation determines access to and depth of knowledge. As C. Lynn Carr expresses, one's status as initiated or not establishes "the practices one is obligated and privileged to perform and the religious knowledge one is permitted to receive" (16). My analyses of Mayra Santos-Febres's poetry collection *boat people*, Rita Indiana's novel *La mucama de Omicunlé*, and Gloria Anzaldúa's archive and published work document the various ways these creators generate literary renditions of initiation. For this reason, an understanding of these Afro-diasporic ceremonies and the roles water plays in them forms a basis for understanding this book.

In her study on Santería/Regla de Ocha in the United States, Elizabeth Pérez describes the decision to undergo *kari ocha* (initiation) as one taking place between "willful spirits and weakened flesh" ("Willful Spirits" 151). Pérez finds that to become initiated is akin to "surrender[ing] to the orishas because [individuals] faced incapacitating infirmity or adversity, and *ocha* stood the only chance of saving them" (153).[51] Attention to the importance of will underscores how, in Afro-diasporic religions, it is the *lwa, misterios,* and *orishas* who determine whether one is destined to become initiated. Kristina Wirtz notes that "most santeros were firm that initiation into Santería is not something a person chooses. Rather, the orichas do the choosing, and they inform their chosen ones of their selection by causing trouble for them" (83). Métraux observes a similar pattern in Haitian Vodou: "In many cases it is the *loa* himself who insists that his servant should be initiated" (193). While a person's awareness of and receptiveness to the knowledges of the Afro-diasporic world may help them recognize and understand the energies of divine entities in their midst, it is ultimately the spirits themselves who determine one's sacred path.

Ritual loss is an integral part of Afro-diasporic religious initiations:

> In order to be born as a priest, a practitioner's identity must be sacrificed, as literally as possible without physically injuring the body soon to become a vessel for the vital energy and primordial substance of the spirits, termed *aché*. For the ill and otherwise suffering, healing is thought to begin with this death, and with the demise of old ways of feeling, behaving, and understanding, to be remade radically through the rigors of the first year of initiation. (E. Pérez, "Willful Spirits" 156)

The way death begets life in *kari ocha* is directly connected to the generative aspects displayed in its language of initiation, which include "metaphors of pregnancy, parturition, and motherhood; both new priests and spirits are said to be 'born' through *ocha*" (E. Pérez, "Willful Spirits" 155). Haitian Vodou's *kanzo* (initiation) echoes much of the energies channeled in *kari ocha*. For McCarthy Brown, *kanzo* is a "rite of fire designed to transform suffering into power" (351). Devotees who undergo this stage of initiation experience both "death and resurrection" (Deren 220; Métraux 193). In his discussion of *kanzo*, Métraux notes how mourning is embedded into the ritual; all who attend the ceremony are aware that something will be lost to facilitate the rebirth of the initiates:

> The initiates will soon return—everyone knows that. But the point is, they will not be the same. They will have become different people and it is for

their symbolical 'death' that spectators are now mourning, no less symbolically. (199)

Understanding the transformative depths of these rituals makes evident that Afro-diasporic religious initiation is "an especially intense form of healing" (McCarthy Brown 352) that should not be undertaken without awareness of its life-altering ramifications.

In contrast, formal initiation has not been historically undertaken by devotees of La 21 División. Many practitioners are simply born with a "'don' o 'luz'" (gift or light) or are initiated in dreams (Davis, *La otra ciencia* 268).[52] Scholarship on the testimonies of those directly initiated by the *seres* (beings) of La 21 División reveals that several of these spiritual activations took place at the age of seven or were inherited through kinship systems (Deive 196).[53] Martha Ellen Davis notes that the expansion of La 21 División into urban centers spurred the formalization of initiation through the ritual of *bautizo* (baptism) (*La otra ciencia* 277).[54] While La 21 División's *bautizo* does not emphasize death and rebirth in the same way *kanzo* and *kari ocha* do, its purpose is to grant protection and strength to the initiate, an objective that unifies the three rituals. By spiritually harmonizing the *corrientes* (spiritual currents or energies) of the initiate, a *bautizo* fortifies the spiritual and secular aspects of their life, particularly when they are in a state of diminished health (Davis, *La otra ciencia* 278). The beginnings and endings of the initiation practices of Afro-diasporic religions thus reveal their sensibility for the constant cycles of creation and destruction that give shape to the natural world.

Rest is an essential element of Afro-diasporic initiations, structurally countering the dehumanization and compulsory able-bodiedness imposed upon many who are sustained by these traditions.[55] In Santería/Regla de Ocha, *kari ocha* takes approximately seven days. During this time, the *iyawo* (initiate) is considered to be a newborn whose bathing, clothing, and nutritional needs must be tended to by their spiritual community.[56] Similarly, for a *bautizo* in La 21 División, initiates are given "una serie de siete baños de colores, aplicados uno por uno, durante el transcurso de una semana" (a series of seven baths of different colors, given one by one, throughout the course of a week) (Davis, *La otra ciencia* 279). Dagoberto Tejeda Ortiz notes that *bautizos* may take place in nature, oftentimes near bodies of water, such as "un río, arroyo, laguna, bosque, montaña o en la orilla del mar" (a river, stream, lagoon, forest, mountain or at the seashore) (151). A notable difference between the *bautizo* and *kari ocha* is that while community engagement and support are critical in both, the seclusion demanded of the *iyawo* is not expected of the newly birthed *servidores* (those who serve the *misterios*). However, initiates of La 21 División may be advised against partaking in certain activities (Davis, *La otra ciencia*

279), conveying a sense of the restriction that distinguishes the Santería/Regla de Ocha ceremony.

Haitian Vodou's *kanzo* is a more intense ritual. Like *kari ocha*, *kanzo* takes approximately seven days and, as Karen E. Richman finds, "novices are dressed in white cloth and are treated as though they were delicate, vulnerable newborns" (130).[57] In addition to being attended to and served by the spiritual community, *ounsi* (initiates) must stay lying down during *kanzo*, a process that begins with the ritual "'putting-to-bed' ceremony (*le coucher*)" (Métraux 195). *Kouche* emphasizes the stillness of *kanzo*: "to lie down, sleep, make love, give birth, and, less frequently, to die—is the verbal form used for all levels of initiation" (McCarthy Brown 351). Infusing the understanding of ritual with the history of Afro-diasporic religions, the *kouche* aspect of *kanzo* evokes the Middle Passage when "the entire cohort of novices lies together in spoon fashion on their left sides, their ankles bound together with vines" (Matory, "Free to Be" 415). The symbolic presence of historical death is integral to Haitian Vodou's initiation process. It underscores the resurgence of the initiates and their ability to face otherwise insurmountable challenges due to the spiritual assistance they now carry within. The fortifying qualities of the ceremony explain why *kanzo* entails ritual contact with fire, ultimately making initiates impervious to it (Hurston 175). Blending intense rest with extreme power, *kanzo* and *kari ocha* promote the integration of new spiritual energies by creating a protective barrier between newly birthed (and thus spiritually vulnerable) community members and the outside world, emphasizing each tradition's engagement with and understanding of (permeable) borders.

In Santería/Regla de Ocha, *kari ocha* begins at the river. Here, the initiate is presented to the *orisha* of sweetwaters, Ochún, before performing a cleansing river bath, the first of several depurative acts that involve water. Lydia Cabrera, whom Martin A. Tsang identifies as the "textual *madrina* (godmother) to many aspiring students of Afro-Cuban religions and Spanish-language readers" ("On Becoming" 63), paid close attention to this ceremony. Cabrera notes that contact with the "agua viva" (living water) of the river is the gateway to initiation, and "sin 'saludar,' rendirle homenaje a la dueña del río [Ochún], sin purificarse en sus aguas, no se efectúa ningún asiento" (without paying respects to the owner of the river [Ochún], without purifying oneself in her waters, no initiation can take place) (*Yemayá y Ochún* 139). Once respects are paid to Ochún, water continues to play a crucial role; during the seven-day ritual period, a series of sacred herbal baths is given to the initiate and their newly birthed *orishas*. This depurative water, the *omiero*, is defined by Cabrera as:

"agua sagrada" que purifica, regenera y cura, pues en ella se concentra el poder mágico y medicinal de las plantas y las influencias de los Orichas que les infunden sus energías ["sacred water" that purifies, regenerates, and cures, as it is infused with the magical and medicinal power of plants and with the energies bestowed upon it by the Orichas]. (*Yemayá y Ochún* 156)[58]

The *omiero* cleanses and regenerates the body, tempering the fusion between the physical and spiritual energies taking place within the recently sacralized flesh.[59] It enhances the channeling of water in *kari ocha* that began at the river with the presentation to Ochún.

Kanzo also relies on the use of water and herbs. Although full-body baths are essential to the purification aspects of this ritual, a vital aspect of *kanzo* is the *laver-tête* (washing of the head), an act in which the *ounsi's* head is washed with water infused with medicinal herbs and nourished with a mixture of sacred elements (Métraux 200). This mixture is left on the *ounsi's* head until the end of *kanzo*, at which point it is removed and the head is once again washed with the sacred waters prepared at the start of the ceremony. Métraux notes:

> The main effect of the *laver-tête* is to establish a permanent link between the neophyte and a *loa*. In ritual language this ceremony corresponds with the placing of the *loa maît'-tête* (the *loa* master of the head). (200)

In this manner, water again serves as a channel and infuser of sacred energy. It cleanses and regenerates the initiate's body, particularly their head, which in the corporeal realm of Afro-diasporic religions is the human body's most sacred part.

Vodou's *laver-tête* is integral to understanding the preparation for the *bautizo* of La 21 División, a process also called the *refresco de cabeza* (refreshing of the head) (Davis, *La otra ciencia* 285), evidencing its close ties with the Haitian ritual.[60] According to Davis:

> En Santo Domingo, la preparación para poder trabajar como servidor de misterio consiste en echar aguas en la cabeza que hayan sido santiguadas por los diferentes misterios [In Santo Domingo, the preparation to become a devotee of the *misterios* consists of pouring water blessed by the different *misterios* upon the head]. (*La otra ciencia* 283)

The sacred baths, described by Davis as "baños divisionales" (divisional baths), are often bestowed upon the devotee by another *servidora* (initiate/devotee) in a state of possession (*La otra ciencia* 283). These baths culminate in the *bautizo*, which, much like the *laver-tête* and the *omiero*, seeks to create unity and harmony for the newly birthed initiate:

El propósito del baño usado en el bautizo es "para luz, paz y perfecto enten-
dimiento y claridad para los caballos de misterios, para los cinco sentidos, en
el nombre de las Veintiuna Divisiones" [The purpose of the bath used in the
bautizo is to generate "light, peace and perfect understanding and clarity for
the horses (initiates who can become possessed) of the *misterios*, for the five
senses, in the name of the 21 Divisions"]. (Davis, *La otra ciencia* 288)

Like the waters of the *omiero* and of the *laver-tête*, the fluid blessed by the *misterios* is infused with an array of sacred materials (Davis, *La otra ciencia* 283). The
resonance between the *laver-tête*, the *omiero*, and the *refresco de cabeza* evidences
how in the Afro-diasporic religious world water facilitates the spiritualization
of the body while also generating a path toward transformation and rebirth.[61]
Deive observes that water is "garantía de un nuevo nacimiento y símbolo de
curación" (the guarantee of rebirth and a symbol of healing) (199). In this context, an understanding of water's ability to transmit energies and knowledges in
the Afro-diasporic world surfaces its potential for serving as a methodological
tool able to generate conversations across disciplinary and geographical divides.

THE ORGANIZATION OF *CHANNELING KNOWLEDGES*

The structure of this book emanates from the bodies of water that traverse it. Chapter 1 straddles the Caribbean Sea and the Atlantic Ocean; chapter
2 centers the Caribbean Sea; chapter 3 focuses on the Pacific Ocean with influences from the Atlantic; chapter 4 brings together the Rio Grande/Río Bravo
and the Pacific Ocean; the epilogue centers the Massacre River/Dajabón River
and ends with the Artibonite River flowing into the Caribbean Sea and Atlantic
Ocean. This sequence follows neither the delineations of geography nor chronological time because Afro-diasporic waters eschew linear standards of measure-
ment. By centering water, the book's structure offers an opportunity to consider
the potential of circuitous ceremonial time as a site for knowledge transference.
Chapter 1, "Channeling the Undocumented in Mayra Santos-Febres's
boat people," presents a spiritually driven reading of this 2005 poetry collection. Although Santos-Febres is one of the foremost Afro–Puerto Rican and
Afro-Latinx writers of our time, her collection's emphasis on water frees it
from static geographic coordinates. My reading addresses how *boat people*'s sea
becomes a multifaceted narrator infused with the energies of Afro-diasporic
deities such as Yemayá, Olokun, Lasirèn, and Mami Wata. I contend that the
spiritual charge of *boat people*'s living waters enables the collection to channel
the souls of the innumerable undocumented migrants who have succumbed

to the ocean throughout the centuries. Cognizant of how initiation in the Afro-diasporic religious world is necessarily constructed as a process in which death begets life, I argue that in *boat people,* the sea offers spiritual asylum to the drowned migrants, unleashing the potential for recovery and communion imbued into Afro-diasporic waters.

In chapter 2, "The Techno-Resonances of Rita Indiana's *La mucama de Omicunlé,*" I delve into the convergence between cyber and religious technologies in Indiana's apocalyptic 2015 novel. Written approximately a decade after *boat people,* Indiana's book makes the presence of Afro-diasporic spirituality hypervisible but not necessarily legible. While the novel is primarily read as science fiction, knowledge of Afro-diasporic religions furthers the reach of *La mucama de Omicunlé* by enabling readers to consider the limits of the secularly and spiritually knowable. The *orisha* of Santería/Regla de Ocha who embodies the limits of knowledge is Olokun, the androgynous ruler of the depths of the ocean. Olokun is of critical importance in the novel because Acilde, the text's transgender protagonist, is infused with Olokun's power in an attempt to save the ocean from cataclysmic demise. In this chapter, I propose the concept of "techno-resonance" to critically mine the collapsing of secular and spiritual worlds in the text. I argue that *La mucama de Omicunlé* deftly uses technology to present a reality in which spiritual updates and downloads take place alongside secular ones, leading readers to reflect on how these processes give shape to and perhaps might even help save the world.

In chapter 3, "Afro-Diasporic Currents in the Gloria Evangelina Anzaldúa Papers," I honor Anzaldúa's commitment to "bridging" disparate spaces, ideas, and even worlds by connecting Caribbean and Latinx communities through the circulation of Afro-diasporic waters and the knowledges they carry.[62] This chapter relies heavily on the Gloria Evangelina Anzaldúa Papers (GEA Papers) as I identify select documents from the archive to address pivotal moments of Anzaldúa's life regarding her lifelong relationship to water. I begin by discussing her near-drowning at South Padre Island, an experience that caused a spiritual awakening. I then pay attention to the migrations Anzaldúa underwent when going from Texas to the West and East Coasts, movements that left their mark on the development of her lifelong connection to Yemayá, the *orisha* of saltwaters in the Americas. I also propose new insights into moments of Anzaldúa's life referenced in her published works, such as her hysterectomy in the 1980s. Ultimately, I offer a genealogy of the watery presences in Anzaldúa's life and of her evolving understanding of Yemayá's sacred energies, priming readers for my reading of the Afro-diasporic waters of Anzaldúa's best-known work, *Borderlands/La Frontera: The New Mestiza.*

In chapter 4, "*Orishas* in the Borderlands," I offer the first in-depth analysis of how the Afro-diasporic spiritual world manifests in *Borderlands/La*

Frontera. A reading of Anzaldúa's borderwaters evinces the value of using a Caribbean-infused epistemological framework when considering the work of this Rio Grande Valley Chicana. Though rarely spoken of in this way, *Borderlands* is a text that opens and closes with water. The first body of water it presents is the Pacific Ocean, and the last one it references is the Rio Grande/Río Bravo. Through close readings of key moments in *Borderlands,* particularly its opening poem, I posit that water functions as an energetic portal through which Anzaldúa channels Afro-diasporic knowledges. To be sure, Yemayá is a fundamental part of this process, but *orishas* such as Eshu/Elegguá (the path opener) and Oyá (the *orisha* of winds and transformation) are also vital. Adding nuance to current readings of Anzaldúa's foundational work, my engagement with *Borderlands* showcases the reach and adaptability of Afro-diasporic spiritual traditions.

The epilogue, "Water and Light: The *Bóveda* as Counter-Archive," flows from the borderwaters of Hispaniola's Massacre River/Dajabón River, where I revisit the intersections of memory, trauma, and water through a discussion of the candlelight vigil organized by the Border of Lights (BOL) at the river's edge. A motley crew of activists, artists, and scholars from Hispaniola and its diaspora, BOL organizes a yearly act of remembrance for the 1937 Massacre, a violent act of border control perpetrated by the Dominican state against Haitians and Dominicans of Haitian descent. I propose that reading BOL's candlelight vigil as the enactment of a binational spiritual *bóveda* (altar) gives visibility to this moment of historical trauma and appeases the souls of the victims of the Massacre and their descendants. Finally, I address the current state of border affairs in Hispaniola by discussing *TC/0168.13 (Anthropophagist wading in the Artibonite River),* a painting by Firelei Báez that avows the healing powers of salty and sweet Afro-diasporic waters in the face of ongoing state violence.

My research has shown me that water is a physical and metaphysical site of submerged importance in Latinx and Caribbean studies. When spiritually accessed, water offers alternatives for healing, transformation, and sustenance that challenge the excesses of violence and trauma etched on the bodies, souls, and worlds of Afro-diasporic peoples. Combining my awareness of water's energies with how the body becomes a vessel of spiritual knowledge and power in Afro-diasporic religions, my book argues that texts and cultural practices can become empowered through their engagement with water. Read through the lens of Afro-diasporic sacrality, the ocean and the river have the capacity to channel the energies and knowledges swirling in their currents, and these liquid knowledges, which have survived inordinate cycles of violence, continue to provide strength and possibilities beyond the secularly knowable.

Channeling the Undocumented in Mayra Santos-Febres's *boat people*

In October 2012, Mayra Santos-Febres, a leading Afro–Puerto Rican author, signed my copy of her 2005 poetry collection *boat people*.[1] Her inscription, "Por el mar que nos une. Aché" (For the sea that unites us. Aché), was revelatory. Undeniably connecting the collection's portrayal of water with the transformative power of Afro-diasporic religions, Santos-Febres's inscription became the portal through which I became aware of the text's spiritual valence. The word *aché*, which in the epistemological framework of Santería/Regla de Ocha is the divine life force that flows throughout the physical and spiritual world, is paradoxically not found in *boat people*'s poems. Hence, only when I allowed Santos-Febres's inscription to guide my reading did the underlying spirituality of her work surface. Doing so disclosed that the power of all that is unnamed in the collection is boundless.

Consisting of only twenty poems, some no longer than a page, *boat people*'s brevity belies its depths. In this chapter, I probe the crevices of Santos-Febres's collection to fathom its veiled engagements with Afro-diasporic religions. I argue that *boat people*'s narrator is the sea itself, a complex entity that responds to the names of Yemayá, Olokun, Lasirèn, Mami Wata, and countless Indigenous forces. In addition to embodying these deities, *boat people*'s lyrical maritime voice channels the energies of the thousands of human bodies and spirits it has engulfed throughout the centuries. When the sea proclaims, "ah mi morenita cae" (ah, my little Black one falls), the possessive pronoun "mi" evinces the water's omnipotent agency as witness and guide (Santos-Febres 11). By attending to the multiple undocumented maritime migrations that continue to occur in the Caribbean Sea and Atlantic Ocean, *boat people* invokes the present as much as the past, evincing the generative possibilities of challenging the violent imposition of linear time and rigid taxonomies.

I begin by addressing the complexity of the collection's title, which incites a conversation about how water challenges legally prescribed notions of belonging. I then analyze the first three poems to create a compass that allows readers to access the spiritual sanctuary the sea offers to the souls of the drowned migrants. The last poem in the collection, "20. aquí al fondo danzan concejales—" (here at the bottom, council members dance), reveals that the culmination of the boat people's journey comes when the sea claims them. When the souls of the drowned descend to the bottom of the ocean they undergo a radical act of spiritual initiation that creates a submerged repository of Afro-diasporic knowledges and coalitions. Such an understanding transforms *boat people* into an elegy proclaimed by the only one who can attest to the final resting place of the undocumented migrants submerged in the waters: the ocean itself.[2]

THE FLOWING BORDERLESSNESS OF *BOAT PEOPLE*

Due to Santos-Febres's positionality as a Black Puerto Rican woman, critics have read *boat people* as primarily acknowledging undocumented Dominican migration to Puerto Rico through the perilous Mona Passage (Moreno; J. P. Rivera).[3] Although this is an essential part of the conversation, the title of Santos-Febres's collection makes legible the plurality of migrations that take place in the Caribbean and beyond. It also showcases how water can collapse time and geography. In "7. en el vientre de los nuevos animales" (in the belly of the new beasts), Santos-Febres suffuses recent experiences of undocumented migration with those of the Middle Passage, a critical origin point for the histories of the African diaspora in the Americas as well as for understanding the impact of undocumented migration in the hemisphere. For, although logs of slave ships exist as documentary evidence, the enslaved were recorded only as cargo, unwillingly transformed into the region's first undocumented migrants. Sounding the echoes of this foundational undocumented migration and connecting them with current iterations, this poem's appearance in the middle of *boat people* rather than at the beginning illustrates how all sense of time on these journeys emanates from the swirling water. The narrative voice declares that the unnamed boat person "aún da fe de que está vivo" (still proclaims he is alive) (21). Offering evidence of resistant life that transcends the hold of chronological time, the voice simultaneously evokes the Middle Passage, the twenty-first century, and the borders placed upon bodies of water by empires and governments.

To grasp the radical possibilities of Santos-Febres's collection, one must grapple with the nuances of its title. The term "boat people" conveys invisibility and hypervisibility by concurrently highlighting and obscuring the presence of the sea; it zeroes in on the body while stripping it of nationality, leaving it adrift. Critics have commented that the moniker is distinctly associated with Haiti due to the existence of the Kreyòl term *botpipèl*. Sarah Banet-Weiser adds that the term "functioned to not only strip away agency from the Haitians but also to conjure a specific image of race" (164). In Santos-Febres's collection, however, "boat people" is historically and racially laden. Though the poems are centered on the Afro-diasporic experience, the title also gestures toward those who fled the violence in Vietnam between 1975 and 1980 (De Maeseneer and De Beule 99). Such an assertion forces an acknowledgement of the multiple Asian migrations that took place on Atlantic and Caribbean waters, stories that are slowly being recovered but about which much remains to be said.[4]

As a collection, *boat people* elucidates how the shared experience of violent migration challenges divisions erected by national boundaries. In this manner, Santos-Febres's poetry responds to the call of oceanic studies, which Hester Blum understands as an opportunity to "derive new forms of relatedness from the necessarily unbounded examples provided in the maritime world" (671). The term "boat people" is employed precisely because of its borderlessness. To be at sea is to be nowhere and everywhere at the same time. Therefore, beginning with her chosen title, Santos-Febres's collection defies epistemological and geographical boundaries because, as poem 5 states, "es tanto el mar" (the sea is so vast) (18).[5] The breadth of water in the collection pushes past archipelagoes, heralding its ability to provide connection in the face of trauma and truncation.

The organizational structure of *boat people* reveals fissures in current constructions of citizenship and belonging. Neither the poems nor the migrants are easily discernible because Santos-Febres only uses numbers to identify the printed poems and the physical bodies they index. While the use of numbering is common in poetry, Santos-Febres's deployment of this technique underscores the violence of reducing undocumented lives to mere statistics (De Maeseneer and De Beule 95). Taken alongside the author's decision not to capitalize the book's title and to largely eschew capitalization throughout her poems, *boat people*'s format reflects its indictment of documentation by resisting conventions.[6] This position helps explain how and why the various nationalities of the collection's boat people (Cuban, Dominican, and Haitian) are referenced not by naming their countries of origin but through the author's deliberate use of culturally specific vernacular and orthography. For example, poem 5 recounts the plight of "indocumentado 4" (undocumented 4), whom the reader identifies as Cuban given Santos-Febres's use of the words "balsa" (raft) and "jaba" (bag) (17). This linguistic tactic showcases how *boat people* fosters the creation of another kind of community, one that emanates not from state-sanctioned modes of documentation but through an engagement with the lived experiences that take place in and through the water.

Questions of language surround the book's English title, an authorial decision that suggests the neocolonial presence of the United States in Caribbean-Atlantic waters as well as the haunting shadow of the so-called American Dream. In this way, *boat people* dialogues with Ana Lydia Vega's 1982 "Encancaranublado" ("Cloud Cover Caribbean").[7] Vega's story narrates the experiences of three Black Caribbean men (a Haitian, a Dominican, and a Cuban) who are "rescued" at sea by a US ship manned by a crew that includes a Black Puerto Rican man. Myriam J. A. Chancy finds that the masculinist tone of Vega's story "testif[ies] powerfully to the absence of women's voices and presence in the formation and formulation of national identities in all three nation-states" ("A Solidarity" 28), a reality *boat people*'s inclusion of women openly disrupts. And although both texts are committed to centering Blackness, "Encancaranublado" reinscribes the power of ships and islands while Santos-Febres's poems are irrevocably anchored at sea.[8] For, while *boat people*'s title may gesture toward the primacy of the ship evident in Gilroy's conception of the Black Atlantic (4), the collection's discussion of undocumented maritime migration nuances this approach by harnessing the power of Afro-diasporic religions to reinterpret and reimagine history and belonging.

The centering of water in *boat people* allows Santos-Febres to identify the echoes of undocumented migrations beyond the Caribbean Basin. For Chicanx and Latinx scholars, this becomes particularly salient when, in the collection's eighteenth poem, Santos-Febres directly entwines the boat people's plight with that of migrants who are "vadeando algún río / trepando alguna verja / cruzando algún desierto" (wading through some river / climbing some fence / crossing some desert) (43). Given the importance of the river, the fence, and the desert in the discourse of undocumented migration on the US/Mexico border, Santos-Febres's verses create a powerful opening through which to explore the humanitarian crisis birthed by the hegemonic establishment and policing of borders in the Global South.[9] Surpassing geopolitics, Santos-Febres's affirmation of the migratory resonances between the Caribbean and the US/Mexico border illustrates how an Afro-diasporically infused understanding of water can instill life into fossilized identitarian constructs.[10]

The title of Santos-Febres's collection reflects her engagement with the radical revisionary ethos of Afro-Latinx feminisms. By emphasizing the body in the collection's title and in the poems, Santos-Febres affirms that the corporeal is epistemological. This assertion lies at the heart of "theory in the flesh," a mode of theorizing that departs from one's lived experiences and that was initially proposed in the ground-breaking anthology *This Bridge Called My Back: Writings by Radical Women of Color*.[11] It is also sustained by the tenets of African spirituality, as exemplified by Yolanda Covington-Ward's contention that "the body is not just a means of learning or expressing social norms or conventions; it is also a means of doing, creating, and transforming the world around oneself" (9). Santería/Regla de Ocha espouses a similar view in which, as Vanessa K. Valdés indicates, "there is no difference between the sacred and the secular" (*Oshun's Daughters* 2). These complementary interpretations reflect how *boat people* capitalizes on the conception of the Afro-diasporic body as a sacred site, a reading that seeps into Santos-Febres's construction of the sea itself. In the collection, the living waters recover the souls of the migrants discarded by their countries of origin not because of legal obligation but in recognition of subsumed historical and spiritual alliances.

While Covington-Ward addresses how quotidian bodily gestures produce social and political realities, Marta Moreno Vega emphasizes that in Afro-diasporic religions "the colors, symbols, altars, and the body of practitioners serve as sacred receptacles for the sacred energy force, àshe, of the orisás" (Moreno Vega, "The Candomblé" 158). These views explain why the Afro-diasporic body is a place from which numinous knowledge emanates, in life and in death, given the foundational role of ancestor worship in Afro-diasporic religious systems. Furthermore, intergenerational and ancestral relationships catapult the Afro-Latinx body into what Omaris Z. Zamora deems "(trance) formation," a multifaceted process intersected by the movements of migration, the experiences of trauma, and the charge of memory (2). The spiritual energies channeled by the Afro-diasporic body empower the drowned migrants in *boat people* to become part of an extraordinary underwater archive capable of countering incomplete historical narratives. The existence of this archive is compelling because historical omissions largely silence women, especially Black women (García-Peña 84). In this way, *boat people* exemplifies how water and the Afro-diasporic body become nodes of epistemological power that manifest unorthodox and multifaceted ways of knowing. By channeling ancestral reservoirs of knowledge, these nodes can create new narratives and ontological practices that assert our humanity.

"1. BOAT PEOPLE"

The painful connection between drowning and initiation in *boat people* is evident from the first poem, "1. boat people," which begins at the open sea with a graphic portrayal of physical death. The narrative voice presents the boat people as "carnes trituradas" (shredded flesh) surrounded by sharks and pelicans (9). The presence of these creatures in the sea's ecosystem is suggestive of the deepest waters of the ocean and the sky above it, attesting to the totality of water's domain in the collection. The only witnesses to the boat people's demise are the ocean and its nonhuman inhabitants. Such a description in the collection's opening scene may conjure what Jenny Sharpe calls "the totalizing effect of the vastness of the Atlantic Ocean as a graveyard" (59). Nonetheless, despite the sobriety of the initial image, the subsequent verses reveal a subtle sense of communion emanating from the spiritual charge of water in the Afro-diasporic religious world:

cuerpos hinchados como moluscos	bodies bloated like mollusks
buscando en el fondo del mar	searching the bottom of the sea
el cielo	for the roof
de la boca	of the mouth
que es su vientre.	that is their womb.
(9)	

In these lines, water functions as an infusion that reconfigures the shredded flesh of the migrants. As their skin and organs expand through the intake of fluid, water fills every crevice and rupture. The sea endows the bodies of the migrants with a new sense of wholeness, ultimately transforming them into mollusks. This visceral transmutation is facilitated by the permeability of the human body, which is largely made up of water, and is driven by the inherent receptivity of the sea toward the migrants. The water's embrace is particularly stark given that even before the boat people board their vessels and set out to sea, neoliberalism and capitalism have already reduced them to human debris.

As a presumed end gives way to an ongoing underwater journey, the collection's opening poem makes clear that the impetus to search for a better life is so entrenched within the migrants that it transcends death, akin to generational trauma. The desperate yearning that saturates *boat people* is apparent from the collection's title; the migrants cast themselves onto the waters due to the unbearable hope that opportunity awaits somewhere across the ocean. In her discussion of undocumented Dominican migration to Puerto Rico, Milagros Ricourt relays that people risk their lives at sea because "'there is no life here' (*aquí no hay vida*)" ("Reaching" 226, italics in the original). Karen E. Richman describes an eerily similar response provided by Haitian migrants who believe that "to live in Haiti, . . . you have to pursue life Outside" (69). In both instances, migrants envision life as residing elsewhere. Affectively challenging geopolitical borders, their words display a violent process of self-abjection that illustrates the power of capitalist structures to determine what life is and where it can be found. Santos-Febres's collection exposes and subverts the overwhelming power of this life-negating process by engaging with the spiritual energies of Afro-diasporic waters.

Given that *boat people* centers migrants who never reach another shore, the collection agonizingly underscores that even when faced with death, the boat people's longing for a better life does not end, nor is it deferred. Yearning filters through the membranes of time and currents as their bodies descend to the bottom of the sea, becoming a beacon that leads the migrants through the deepest folds of the water. Santos-Febres's use of "buscando" (searching) to describe the ongoing nature of their quest underscores the timelessness of their actions. Yet, in transforming their search from one driven by capitalism to one directed by the sea's spiritual agency, *boat people* defies the trope of victimhood that dominates narratives of undocumented maritime migration. This approach is evident in poem "5. indocumentado 4" (undocumented 4) where "todo tiempo se detiene / en medio del mar" (all time stops / in the middle of the sea) (17). The explicit cessation of linear time in the water speaks to the chronological alterity of Afro-diasporic ceremonial time (Desmangles 77). Reiterating the importance of using a spiritual lens when navigating the poems, the absence of linear time forces the reader to consider that a ritual or ceremony may be taking place in Santos-Febres's collection. On a more literal level, this powerful verse is further evidence of how the boat people's seeking is always happening *right now*, in a space that is only accessible by contemplating the mythical dimensions of the maritime.

Going back to *boat people*'s initial poem, the combination of the unrelenting nature of the search undertaken by the migrants with their transformation into sea creatures (mollusks) brings attention to two key visual and corporeal elements: the mouth ("la boca") and the womb ("el vientre"). The importance of the body in Santos-Febres's poetry is inextricably linked to the religious undercurrents of the text. The physicality of the spiritual energies ascribed to water stresses how it serves as a channel and a dwelling space for the sacred in Afro-diasporic religions. Specifically, the mouth and the womb connect to the act of speaking or being silenced and to generating life, becoming Santos-Febres's first direct allusion to religious initiation.

The intertwining of mouth and womb is intrinsic to the initiation ceremonies of Santería/Regla de Ocha, as specific prayers and songs are recited to invoke the ancestors and the *orishas* and garner their blessings (Cabrera, *Yemayá y Ochún* 149–155). The mouth and the womb are also evident in the shape and function of the cowrie shells of the *diloggún*, one of the divination systems of Santería/Regla de Ocha. While the feminine form of the shells connects them with the womb and with female genitalia, the grooves on the cowrie shells resemble the teeth in the human mouth (Fernández 44–45). These qualities enhance the *diloggún*'s connection to the human body and its channeling power. The fact that cowrie shells come from mollusks encourages a reading of the boat people's drowning and ensuing transformation as one linked to spiritual initiation, deepening the collection's collapsing of life and death in the waters.

That Santos-Febres combines the mouth and the womb through the word "cielo" is also telling. While in Spanish "el cielo de la boca" refers to the roof of one's mouth, the term "cielo" is compatible not only with "sky" but also with the celestial construct of "heaven." Despite being shrouded in death, the multiple meanings of this verse illustrate that *boat people*'s poems drip with *aché*. The *patakís* (mythical stories) of Santería/Regla de Ocha provide further evidence of the collection's spiritual wavelengths, as they posit that the world's origins lie in the water.[12] Nonetheless, water is also essential to the generation of knowledge since the *diloggún* initially belonged to Yemayá and Ochún, the two *orishas* most associated with water, salty and sweet (Fernández 45–47). The channeling qualities of water are thus on display whenever the *diloggún* is consulted. That all of these signifiers appear in *boat people*'s first poem underscores the role of the Afro-diasporic religious world in the collection, a presence not evident to those not looking for the signs in the book's living waters. Additionally, these verses indicate that Santería/Regla de Ocha is one of the central spiritual systems from which Santos-Febres's ritualized sea draws. By seeking to understand this tradition's knowledges and practices, readers can begin to apprehend the spiritual charge of *boat people*'s sea and how its currents embrace contradiction without seeking to neutralize it.

Whether salty or sweet, water is an intrinsic part of Santería/Regla de Ocha's cosmology. It is a portal and a spiritual entity in and of itself, an understanding shared by other Afro-diasporic traditions.[13] In Santería/Regla de Ocha, the first *orisha* that comes to mind in relation to the sea is Yemayá, who is believed to have birthed the *orishas* and the world (Fernández Olmos and Paravisini-Gebert 52). A visit to the river to pay respects to Ochún, Yemayá's sister, is the first step in Santería/Regla de Ocha's *kari ocha* (initiation), furthering the connection between birthing and water (Cabrera, *Yemayá y Ochún* 139). These religious tenets add nuance to how in the collection's first poem water is infused with the presence of the mouth and the womb, avowing its spiritual agency.

In her ground-breaking work on Afro-Cuban religiosity, the self-taught ethnographer Lydia Cabrera recurrently acknowledges the importance of the aquatic in the life cycles of Santería/Regla de Ocha. While Cabrera was not formally initiated, she knew she was a daughter of Yemayá, and her attention to this *orisha* is evident in her writing.[14] The Afro-diasporic sacrality of water located in the ocean (Yemayá) and the river (Ochún) propels her text *Yemayá y Ochún: Kariocha, Iyalorichas y Olorichas*. Here, Cabrera and her informants describe water as follows:

> "La bebemos al nacer, la bebemos al morir y ella nos refresca el camino cuando nos llevan a enterrar." Porque de Yemayá es la frescura que apacigua el espíritu de los muertos y de los vivos ["We drink it when we are born, we drink it when we die and she (water and Yemayá) refreshes our path when we are to be buried." Because the freshness that soothes the spirits of the dead and of the living belongs to Yemayá]. (24)

The totality of water's presence in Santería/Regla de Ocha's life cycles is unquestionable. Cabrera's linking of Yemayá to the realms of the living and the dead also suggests the depths of the traumas submerged in the water, a narrative *boat people* extends. Like the rest of the *orishas*, Yemayá arrived alongside her children in the so-called New World because of the transatlantic slave trade. This experience forever altered her presence in the Americas. While in Nigeria Yemayá's worshippers associate her with sweet waters and the River Ogun, across the Atlantic she is venerated at the ocean (Sellers 132). In this manner, Yemayá too is a boat person, pushed into the sea by forces beyond her control.

For Kimberly Juanita Brown, Yemayá is "the necessary repository for all earthly slave traumas" (143). The poems in *boat people* acknowledge this legacy by presenting a sea that recognizes the largely invisible plight of contemporary maritime migrants and in response claims and archives their undocumented lives. Furthermore, as Santos-Febres endows her living waters with the ability to shelter those who have perished at sea, she engages a Caribbean, Latin American, and Latinx tradition because, as Susan C. Méndez contends, "Santería empowers Latinas, Afro-Cuban, and Cuban women to survive tragedies" (127). This stance is affirmed by how Afro-Latinx and Chicanx spirituality enable recovery and healing through writing (Irizarry 2; Garcia Lopez 9). These scholarly antecedents make evident that Afro-diasporic spirituality is pivotal to *boat people*'s movements and to the conversations it can generate, conversations that resonate far beyond the Caribbean Basin. In this manner, Santos-Febres's emphasis on the complex femininity and spirituality that reside in the water distinguishes her approach from that of well-known Caribbean critics and the predominantly male vision of contemporary maritime migration.[15]

The Cuban *balsero* crisis that took place during the Special Period of the 1990s is one example of the masculinist tone surrounding undocumented maritime migration.[16] Of the thousands of people who set out to sea on perilous rafts trying to reach Miami, none is better known than Elián González.[17] Problematically, the story of this Cuban odyssey emphasizes masculinity. It focuses on Elián, the little boy miraculously saved by dolphins and found floating alone on an inner tube; his father, Juan Miguel González, who, from Cuba, was desperately trying to lay claim to his son; and the "monster," Fidel Castro, who, according to Miami Cubans, saw Elián as a pawn in a much larger and dangerous political game.[18] In his editorial for the *LA Times*, Latinx writer Francisco Goldman describes the Elián story as a "biblical, mythical, magic realist, national epic: A story, essentially, about a miraculous boy savior sent by God to destroy the Monster." In the exile community in Miami, the story took on spiritual dimensions when Santería/Regla de Ocha practitioners attributed Elián's survival to the divine intervention of Yemayá and/or Ochún (Acosta 55).[19] Yet, a key figure missing in all these narratives is the boy's mother.

The omission of Elián's mother, Elisabet, triggers a reengagement with one of the literary Caribbean's foundational mother-son dynamics, that of Caliban and Sycorax in Shakespeare's *The Tempest*.[20] Elián became a *balsero* only because his mother, Elisabet Brotons, decided to take her chances at sea. Still, like Sycorax, Elisabet was forgotten and Elián became a symbol for the future of Cubans and Cuban Americans, a fact cemented by how the home he resided in while in Miami was turned into a shrine (De La Torre 118–119). In this manner, Elián's story parallels that of Caliban, whom Roberto Fernández Retamar transformed into a metaphor for the future of the Caribbean in *Calibán: Apuntes sobre la cultura en nuestra América*. Elisabet's narrative elision is reinforced in that her body was never recovered and her voice was never recorded, mirroring the plight of the migrants that populate *boat people*'s pages, especially the female ones.[21] Silenced forever, Elisabet was discarded by the male actors who would soon take over her son's life.[22] This cycle of devaluation of the feminine connects to the muted and utilitarian presence of an often-feminized sea (Tinsley 196).

In stark contrast to Elián, who mobilized two countries and incited an international conversation, the bodies in *boat people* are those no one seems to care for and for whom no political saga has been written. They are bodies like Elisabet's. In response, the collection buoys the lives of the drowned undocumented female migrants through the spiritualization of the water. Bringing attention to these women is a subversive act on Santos-Febres's part since dangerous maritime migration is normatively coded as male. Although Frank Graziano notes that "the great majority of yola migrants—about 70 percent, . . . —are Dominican males between eighteen and forty years of age" (55), studies such as Ricourt's 2007 "Reaching the Promised Land" document the particular dangers experienced by women who undertake this journey. Santos-Febres's collection acknowledges these high stakes and makes them legible, radically contesting their erasure by the media (J. P. Rivera 181). Even the plight of the *balseros* did not receive much coverage in the United States until the Elián González story broke, and arguably, when that happened, the political stakes extended far beyond the *balseros*.

But Santos-Febres's poems do not only address the *balseros*. Although Silvia Pedraza finds that "from 1985 to 1993, close to 6,000 *balseros* managed to reach the United States safely [and] more than 34,000 left just in the summer of 1994" (8), they were not the only ones setting sail. From 1991 to 1994, more than 90,000 Haitian *botpipèl* took to the sea in an attempt to seek political asylum in the United States (Rey, "Vodou" 205).[23] Hence, while the Haitian *botpipèl* traversed the water alongside the Cuban *balseros*, their plight was much less visible due to each island's distinct political relationship with the United States. By titling her collection *boat people* Santos-Febres addresses the *botpipèl's* experiences, denouncing their pervasive erasure.

In Santería/Regla de Ocha, initiation is a complex act that necessitates the symbolic death of the initiate to fathom their ritual birthing (E. Pérez, "Willful Spirits" 156). In *boat people*, however, death is not a metaphor. The allusions to life and death implicit in *kari ocha* are explicit in Santos-Febres's poems. While the depiction of drowning is central to underscoring the dangers faced by the boat people as they traverse the ocean on makeshift rafts, it also alludes to the transformative power of initiation in Afro-diasporic religions. This multilayered understanding of death and drowning provides vital context for the collection's second poem, "2. ah mi morenita cae" (ah, my little Black one fall[s]), which presents Santos-Febres's first female protagonist. By centering the unnamed woman's drowning, this act becomes thematically and aesthetically linked to the pulsating spirituality of Santos-Febres's water. Though it is a real threat faced by the boat people (and the author does not take this lightly), drowning proves essential to the collection's message of transformation and its offering of spiritual sanctuary.

Reminiscent of the opening poem, in which the boat people's bodies become mollusks, the act of drowning in the second poem marks a change in the female migrant's trajectory, establishing a crucial link between these undocumented bodies, the region's past, and the churning currents of history. The way Santos-Febres's second poem is printed on the page literally emulates the woman's body succumbing to the waters:

cae   fall(s)

    cae   fall(s)

        cae   fall(s)

y dale de comer a todo pez.   and feed each and every fish.
(11)

By performing the act of drowning on the page, the poem reinforces the inextricable connection between the human body and the sea in *boat people*. Yet, in contrast to how the first poem gives the boat people a sense of agency through the ongoing search that continues even after they become mollusks, here the water is in complete control. The indefatigable currents triumph when the woman's body is submerged. Her demise suggests the relentless power play between humans and nature, with nature invariably having the upper hand. This view is supported by the way "cae" can be read as a description and an active command, demonstrating water's dual role as witness and agent in relation to the drowning woman. The initial sense of connection between the boat people and the sea extends through the feminine body's response to the call of the water, a process M. Jacqui Alexander voices when she contends that Ocean "will call you by your ancient name, and you will answer because you will not have forgotten. Water always remembers" (285). Still, Santos-Febres problematizes the act of communion by gesturing toward consumption. When the woman fully merges with the sea, it is clear that the fish that dwell in its waters will ingest her. That this theme surfaces in a poem anchored on a female subject can be read as an acknowledgment of how Black bodies, particularly those of Black women, are consumed by contemporary society, an idea Santos-Febres's continual use of the word "carne" (flesh) throughout the collection emphasizes.[24] This reality, however, does not preclude additional readings of *boat people*'s living waters, emphasizing the liquid's ability to sustain variable meanings at once.

As in the first poem's connection to the mouth and the womb, in "2. ah mi morenita cae," the sea is imbued with a human attribute, a voice. The water actively witnesses and narrates the woman's drowning, demonstrating its archival agency as it emerges as the collection's omniscient narrator. This lyrical moment epitomizes Solimar Otero's contention that "the sea gives but also takes away voice, reaffirming her awesome and mysterious power over sound and divination" (*Archives* 164).[25] The second poem also offers the first tangible connection to the *orisha* Yemayá, whose sacred number is seven. As the woman falls into the depths, "siete manos" (seven hands) receive her (11). Yet, the allusion to Yemayá here also serves as a portal, given her role as the universal mother of the *orishas* and the fact that she is the only female *orisha* in "the unique position of and [with the] ability to speak for other male *orishas*" (Tsang, "A Different Kind" 118). For these reasons, the number 7 that synecdochically represents Yemayá can simultaneously allude to las Siete Potencias Africanas (the Seven African Powers), which represent the core *orishas* of Santería/Regla de Ocha: Elegguá, Ogún, Obatalá, Orula, Changó, Yemayá, and Ochún. The activation of the water that manifests in this poem elucidates how and why the sea claims the woman's body even before she drowns. The sea's agency is evident in the narrative voice's use of the possessive pronoun "mi" (my), the use of the diminutive *morenita*, which implies not only familiarity with the woman but also power over her, and the command "cae" (fall). Death, then, is understood as a return to one's spiritual home, a place where the *orishas*, the ancestors, and other spiritualities await.

The collection's second poem is integral to developing the transculturated spirituality of Santos-Febres's ocean.[26] While Santería/Regla de Ocha is one of the spiritual systems accessed by *boat people*, it is not the only one. In "2. ah mi morenita cae," the use of orthography allows for a deeper reading. The poem describes the woman's body as thin, given the hunger that pushed her to undertake this dangerous migration. Her thinness, however, reflects that she often went "sin harina / sin más sal quel salitre" (without flour / without any salt but sea salt) (11). Here, Santos-Febres gestures toward Haitian Kreyòl by using "quel" when Spanish grammar rules would dictate the use of "que el." This acknowledgment of the cultural diversity that permeates *boat people*'s aquatic domain goes back to Santos-Febres's initial assertion of the sea's *aché* while simultaneously moving past it, ushering in additional spiritual undercurrents.

The allusion to Kreyòl in the second poem is a moment of spiritual and historical kinship in *boat people*, two threads often intertwined in Afro-diasporic religions. Terry Rey contends that much pain was infused into Vodou's water when the Haitian *botpipèl* "seeking refuge *across the water* in America . . . tragically w[ound] up as ancestors *under the water* instead" ("Vodou" 198, emphasis in the original). Rey's assertion collapses time and space to give visibility to the Haitian migrants who took to the sea in the hopes of receiving political asylum in the United States.[27] Furthermore, Rey's comments regarding movement across and under the water echo the work of various scholars of Haitian Vodou who discuss the watery realm in which the *lwa* live. In "Vodoun, or the Voice of the Gods," Colin (Joan) Dayan describes this spiritual reservoir:

> The loa [*lwa*] live *en bas de l'eau*, under the waters, in an unlocatable place called "Guinée." Though clearly distinguished from *les morts*, the spirits of the dead, they share their home with the ancestors. When loa come to visit their "children," whether in a formal, public ceremony or in private times of dream or individual communion, they come by way of the *chemin de l'eau*, or water road [which they share with the dead]. (17)

Rey and Dayan profess that Vodou's spirituality is water-laden. Rey goes as far as asserting, "In Vodou, water is essential to cosmology, healing, pilgrimage, baptism, and purification, and along with blood, leaves, and stones, water is the religion's material lifeblood" ("Vodou" 199). This statement, which leaves no doubt about water's powerful role in Haitian Vodou, is capaciously applicable to Santería/Regla de Ocha, La 21 División, and other Afro-diasporic spiritual traditions. In this way, water becomes an essential channel through which the distinct yet interconnected lineages of these traditions intersect and resonate with each other.

Dayan's and Rey's research attests to water's capacity to create communal sites of spiritual power.[28] Housing the *lwa* and the ancestors, the sea enables transmission and connection, as it is through the "water road" that communion between the sacred and the secular occurs. This view is supported by Vodou's construction of water as a mirror, a tool often used for divination: "Gazing into the water, a woman sees her own reflection, and through it, simultaneously, she sees the *lwa*. Superimposed on the faces of the *lwa*, she sees the faces of her ancestors" (McCarthy Brown 284).[29] At the same time, in Vodou water becomes a portal for connection, underscoring the reality that the word "diaspora" carries both destructive and edifying energies (Pressley-Sanon 14). During the Middle Passage, slavery's merciless uprooting of millions of people severed ancestral ties. As a result, rites that would typically take place at burial sites were transposed onto the water (Rey, "Vodou" 204). Water's central role in Vodou, then, while always tinged with pain, also carries the possibility for regeneration and transformation. A similar coexistence occurs in Santería/Regla de Ocha, given that Yemayá and other *orishas* reside in the sea, but the dead can also be found there (Alexander 305).

In their exploration of *boat people*, Rita De Maeseneer and Jordi De Beule include the above quote from Dayan to discuss the presence of a particular *lwa*, Carfour (one of the names of Legba, the path opener) in the poem "12. tinta para este poema sobre dejar una isla" (ink for this poem about leaving an island) (100). While fleeting, the attention to Carfour is key for understanding *boat people*'s Vodou-infused sea, a fact furthered by Dayan's observation that "Legba opens the way to memory, not fantasy" (25). As Benjamin Hebblethwaite contends, Legba is also "the barrier between the living and the dead and between the natural and the supernatural" (*Vodou Songs* 255). Legba/Carfour's invocation in *boat people* is thus an invitation to consider the permeable barrier between worlds, one that can inform a reading of the multiple functions of water in the text.

Although Carfour is the only Afro-diasporic deity invoked by name in *boat people*, even his name lacks capitalization.[30] His presence in the collection is connected to the role of the water road described by Dayan, evidenced by how the Kreyòl word for crossroads is *kalfou* (Smartt Bell 16). The spiritual water road imbues additional meaning to the undocumented migration taking place on the ocean. As Edwidge Danticat notes, "In Haitian Creole when someone is said to be 'lòt bò dlo,' on the other side of the water, it can either mean that they've traveled abroad or that they have died" ("All Geography" 60). Carfour's inclusion in the collection is potent because Legba is routinely invoked at the start of ceremonies. As the gatekeeper, his blessing is always needed to proceed (McCarthy Brown 54). In *boat people*, Carfour appears when the poetic voice mentions the existence of "un carfour hecho de agua" (a watery crossroads) (Santos-Febres 31). In this verse, the *lwa* is suggestively linked to Puerto Rico due to the island's role as a geopolitical crossroads between Caribbean and Latinx worlds.[31] In this way, the collection presents an opaque and textured Caribbean Sea that contains the *lwa*, the *orishas*, the ancestors, and as the poems themselves give testimony to, the undocumented migrants who never reach another shore. By fusing the heart-wrenching pain of loss with the effervescence of spirit, Santos-Febres shows that despite centuries of land-centered nationalistic discourse proposing otherwise, the potential for strength and unity for the Caribbean and its diasporic communities is undoubtedly "submarine."[32]

Dayan's description of the spiritual realm of Guinée as an "unlocatable place" in the waters inspires a deeper dive into Santos-Febres's next poem, "3. el aire falta" (air is lacking) (13). This poem is the first in the collection to speak of "la ciudad ilegal al fondo de los mares" (the illegal city at the bottom of the seas) (13), and it centers on lack, the driver of the desperate searching described in the first two poems. The description of the city as illegal suggests an experience of migration that, bureaucratically, is reduced to a matter of either having or lacking documentation. The collection's initial poems thus revolve around each other; the first one begins with the death of the boat people, the second describes the process of one of them dying, and the third plumbs the depths of why they have perished.

The lack of air and documentation that characterizes the third poem metonymically embodies the denial of life that occurs when one is deprived of basic human rights. Scarcity and lack are why the boat people set out to sea in the first place. Devastatingly, the poem states that, yes, air is lacking underwater, but "cuál la diferencia con arriba / si arriba falta todo lo demás" (what is the difference with above / when above everything else is lacking?) (13). While these lines certainly express hopelessness, it is important to remember that although the boat people do not reach the places they believed would be their final destinations, the migrants are not left adrift. Once underwater, their journey veers toward "la ciudad ilegal al fondo de los mares" (13). Santos-Febres's inclusion of this place is perhaps the most compelling reason a reading of the collection must be infused with a spiritual understanding of water and its unbridled initiatory power.

Following Dayan's description of the spiritual realm of the ancestors and the *lwa*, *boat people*'s underwater city can be connected to the existence of Guinée, a vision Danticat echoes in her essay "We Are Ugly but We Are Here." In this personal narrative Danticat, a renowned Haitian American writer who also centers women in her stories, attests to the spirituality of the ocean in Haitian culture and to the call of this submarine realm. As she concludes her discussion of the overall invisibility of the violence inflicted upon Haitian women, some of whom are also boat people, Danticat states:

> The past is full of examples of our foremothers showing such deep trust in the sea that they would jump off slave ships and let the waves embrace them. They believed that the sea was the beginning and the end of all things, the road to freedom and their entrance to Ginen. (25)

Although Danticat does not explicitly name the *lwa*, by mentioning the freedom found in Ginen (another spelling for Guinée), she implicitly acknowledges the currents of the spirits and the water road depicted by Dayan. Capitalizing on the multiple wavelengths of water, *boat people* dialogues with both texts. The poem's illegal submarine city is unlocatable on any map, but it is a place where the migrants hope to find freedom from the lack that has haunted them above the water. In this manner, the underwater city echoes the spiritual and physical resistance imbued into "the Quilombos of Brazil, the Palenques of Colombia and the remnants of maroon communities in Puerto Rico, Cuba and other locations [that] are spaces of African affirmation" (Moreno Vega, "Afro-Boricua" 78). These sites of Afro-diasporic religious practice and preservation are also undocumented, as secrecy was integral to their survival. Hence, when the narrative voice indicates that "entre las algas brillan unas lucecitas" (in between the algae, little lights glimmer) (13), readers are offered literal glimmers of hope through the possibility that a place of respite for these undocumented bodies exists somewhere in the depths of the sea.

Yet, the resistance Santos-Febres infuses into her illegal underwater city is laced with violence. The most readily accessible allusion refers to the migrants themselves, who are often described as "illegal" (im)migrants in news outlets and political discourse to strip them of their humanity. In terms of spirituality and memory, however, the transgressive nature of the submarine city places it in dialogue with the violence directed toward Vodou and other Afro-diasporic spiritual traditions. Hegemonic and heteronormative ideologies have repeatedly targeted these systems due to their presumed primitiveness and supposedly threatening nature.[33] One example of this persecution is the 1941–1942 anti-Vodou *campagne anti-superstitieuse* (anti-superstition campaign) led by the Catholic Church in Haiti.

Agents of the *campagne anti-superstitieuse* raided sacred spaces to seize and burn ritual artifacts, a tactic Laurent Dubois explains as aimed at "pressur[ing] Haitians to renounce Vodou" (307). The ritualized violence of this campaign echoed what had taken place in Haiti during the 1915–1934 US occupation of the island, making evident the longevity and cyclical nature of these spiritual assaults (Ramsey 200).[34] The desecration of Vodou continued in 1957 when François "Papa Doc" Duvalier came to power. Beyond presenting himself as the spiritual father of the nation, Kate Ramsey notes that Duvalier "constructed his persona through visual motifs of [spirits known as] the Gede *lwa*, associated, in part, with cemeteries and the dead, and theatricalized such associations by donning the characteristic dark vestments and hat of these spirits and their leader, Bawon Samdi" (250).[35] This sinister use of sacred imagery transformed Vodou, a spiritual worldview meant to provide resilience and hope, into another tool for terror and violence (Dayan 27–28).[36]

Duvalier's use of Vodou as a tool of repression was particularly harrowing since the Gede *lwa* are homegrown spirits; according to Zora Neale Hurston, the Gede are "entirely Haitian. There is neither European nor African background for it" (219). The Duvaliers controlled Haiti for almost three decades; after his father's death, Jean-Claude "Baby Doc" assumed the presidency. Altogether, the violence of the regime claimed between 20,000 and 50,000 lives (Bellegarde-Smith 129). Upon the ousting of Baby Doc, the process of *Déchoukaj* began. Described by Jana Evans Braziel as "a literal uprooting of all cultural and historical elements affiliated with the Duvaliers," *Déchoukaj* generated "a backlash against Vodou, because *oungans*, or priests, were believed to have supported Duvalier" (6). An awareness of the interweaving of violence, repression, and spirituality during the Duvalier years explains Santos-Febres's mention of the regime in the last poem of her collection. This historical inclusion recognizes the physical and psychic violence the dictatorship inflicted on the Haitian people, leading to more bodies seeking refuge in the water.

"11. CAMBIAR DE NOMBRE"

After the first three poems, *boat people* recounts the stories of a series of individual though still unnamed migrants. The sea speaks of the travails, the exploitation, and the fear the migrants experience before, during, and after their journeys. Santos-Febres continues to develop the cultural breadth of the waters by incorporating island-specific vernacular such as "balsa" and "jaba" to evoke Cuban *balseros*. The terms "yolas" (vessels) and "tiguere" (hustler) refer to a Dominican *yolero* who perishes when he is thrown overboard (23). Finally, the poems explicitly address the need to leave behind the old and new "tontonmacoutes," making a direct allusion to the Haitian *botpipèl* fleeing violence and oppression on their island (31). By using language as the sole identifier of these unnamed bodies, *boat people* emphasizes how the documentation crisis is another example of hegemonic violence's desire to erase and diminish Black bodies. This idea reaches a critical point of inflection in "11. cambiar de nombre."

The poem "11. cambiar de nombre" (to change names) speaks of the dehumanizing need for documentation faced by those rendered stateless.[37] The poem declares, "cambiar de nombre / de células de identidad / cédulas de igualita celda / dos por dos" (to change names / from identity cells / identification cards of the same cells / two by two) (29). Here the narrative voice describes the experience of creating a fictitious identity through falsified paperwork with the hopes of cobbling together a path toward legitimacy and legibility. The futility of this attempt is evident in the disturbing conflation of "células" (biological cells), "cédulas" (identification cards), and "celdas" (jail cells). The uneasy flow between these terms attests to the ravages of documentation narrated in the poem and throughout the collection, beginning with its title. Though only a page long, "11. cambiar de nombre" fuses the desperation of accessing documentation with the dangerous act of undertaking maritime migration, marking them both as extreme measures of survival. The migrants' desire for a new identity clashes with the undercurrents of death and drowning that permeate the collection. This dissonance is expressed through the use of recursive nautical imagery such as "y otra vez al mar" (and once again to the sea) and "y de nuevo al mar" (and again to the sea) (29).

Still, the poem's emphasis on naming allows it to be read through the frameworks of Afro-diasporic religions, particularly the naming practices embedded into Santería/Regla de Ocha's processes of initiation. Once the body of the newly consecrated initiate, the *iyawo*, has been infused with their tutelary *orisha's* energies, they are provided with a series of epistemological and ontological tools to help them navigate secular and spiritual life. Many of these tools are given to the *iyawo* in a ceremony called *itá*, which takes place on the third day of the seven-day initiation process. The *itá* is a complex divination ritual that provides the *iyawo* with information and insight regarding their past, present, and future (Cabrera, *Yemayá y Ochún* 179–180).[38] The final piece of information the *iyawo* receives in the *itá* is their new religious name, their "*orukó*—the priestly name the iyawó is given at initiation process and by which he or she will be known by during ritual functions from that day forward" (Tsang, "Write" 241). The way information circulates in the *itá* reinforces Santos-Febres's language regarding mouth and womb. It is through the conferral and confirmation of the *iyawo's* religious name (mouth) that their new life (womb) comes fully into being in the divine realm of the *orishas* and the earthly community of practitioners.[39]

Although Afro-diasporic religions rely heavily on oral traditions, recent scholarship has underscored their incorporation of the written word. For example, writing is an integral part of Santería/Regla de Ocha initiations. While the divination process of the *itá* is an oral one, a written log of the counsel provided to the *iyawo* is recorded in what will become their personal *libreta* (notebook). Described by Tsang as "sacred initiatory pedagogy" ("Write" 230), the *libreta* is created by one of the attendees of the *itá*, the *ofeicitá*.[40] The role of *ofeicitá* is habitually performed by women and is akin to that of a court reporter (Fernández 57). The existence of the *ofeicitá* reflects Santería/Regla de Ocha's historical incorporation of what Alexander Fernández describes as the "secret and forbidden privilege" of learning to read and write during slavery (57).[41] In contrast to government documentation, the *libreta* is a source of subversive and empowering knowledge that provides evidence of female resistance to enslavement. As an unregulated mode of documentation, the *libreta* is a critical tool in ensuring the transmission and longevity of religious knowledge.[42]

In *Yemayá y Ochún*, Cabrera explains that choosing an *iyawo*'s religious name is a collaborative process between the attending practitioners and the *orishas* because the deities give final approval of the selection (224). Cabrera observes:

> Ese nombre religioso no se divulgará para evitar que lo "amarren", embrujen o le 'roben el Angel' a quien lo lleva, pues en el nombre se encierra la esencia del ser de la persona." [The religious name will not be divulged to protect the initiate from being "worked on," bewitched, or suffering the loss of their "Guardian Angel" (titular *orisha*), since the name contains the essence of the individual.] (*Yemayá y Ochún* 224)[43]

This explanation confirms that access to the religious name of an initiated practitioner increases their susceptibility to harm by others with spiritual knowledge. As a preemptive measure, many practitioners use a different name in public, keeping their religious name private to protect themselves (Cabrera, *Yemayá y Ochún* 224).[44] The care taken with naming in Santería/Regla de Ocha illustrates that the *iyawo*'s religious name is the seal that puts forth their new identity, just as documentation has the power to transform the status of the undocumented. Contrary to identification documents, keeping one's name private and secure in the Afro-diasporic religious world is of utmost importance as a mode of spiritual protection. An understanding of these spiritual processes shows that creating a new identity is a critical element for migration and initiation, and "11. cambiar de nombre" forcefully collapses them in the circularity of the water.

The polyvalent meaning of names and identification invoked in "11. cambiar de nombre" highlights the violent cacophony of documentation in contemporary life. Awareness of the spiritual subtext of this poem does not diminish the dehumanization of legal documentation. On the contrary, by acknowledging this undercurrent, the exclusionary practices that predetermine who can acquire these official documents become more salient. Santos-Febres's employment of the Afro-diasporic religious world shines a light on the callousness of bureaucracy, taxonomy, and classification by showing that this is not the only way in which documentation can work. In "11. cambiar de nombre," once the undocumented migrant enters the world of falsified documents, they fall prey to a system that refuses to recognize their humanity, even before they begin their dangerous maritime journey. Rather than opening a path toward legitimacy, the false paperwork they carry gives way to the "selva de agua / con su ciudad enorme de muertos / hinchados en sal" (water jungle / with its enormous city of the dead / whose bodies are swollen with salt) (29). When the migrants disappear underwater, no traces of them will be left because the documents they have with them will fail to reveal their true identities. The boat people will be irrevocably lost to the water unless the spiritual agency of the currents is asserted. This, precisely, is what the final poem of the collection enacts.

"20. AQUÍ AL FONDO DANZAN CONCEJALES—"

The "selva de agua" that houses the city of the dead is ultimately found to be filled with vitality and resistance in *boat people*'s closing poem, "20. aquí al fondo danzan concejales—" (here at the bottom, council members dance).[45] This poem, the longest of the collection, reveals that the deaths of the maritime migrants are a "rito necesario" (a necessary rite) (28) embedded into the continual making and remaking of the Caribbean-Atlantic seascape and its memory. The depiction of death as a "rito necesario" resonates with the concept of "residence time" in Christina Sharpe's *In the Wake: On Blackness and Being*. Sharpe's "residence time" refers to "the amount of time it takes for a substance to enter the ocean and then leave the ocean" (41). Since "human blood is salty, and sodium . . . has a residence time of 260 million years" (C. Sharpe 41), the constant mention of salt in *boat people* goes beyond the materiality of the sea and into how the very lifeblood of the migrants circulates in the water. The term "residence time" also speaks to the place one inhabits, alluding to how these mysterious council members "manage" the underwater city toward which the perished boat people flow. The connection between life underwater and drowning extends the reach of Afro-diasporic spirituality in the collection. This powerful undertow is also reflected in how the image of the "concejales" dancing points to the importance of bodily movements in the rituals of Afro-diasporic religions, enhancing *boat people*'s portrayal of the sea as an active site of recurring ceremony, particularly initiation.

"20. aquí al fondo danzan concejales—" is *boat people*'s most direct engagement with the transformative power of Afro-diasporic religious initiation. That it comes at the end of the collection is an invitation to reread the entire work with this climax in mind, to understand that the ending is merely the beginning or continuation of yet another cycle. In the context of the unceasing migrations that push people to undertake such dangerous journeys, repetition is akin to condemnation, but an emphasis on the reiterative nature of Afro-diasporic initiation rituals dislodges the power of any definitive reading. Hence, the placement of this poem evidences the importance of preservation in *boat people*. While any one individual only undergoes initiation once within a respective tradition, the repeated undertaking of this ritual is critical to the transmission and endurance of the knowledges of Afro-diasporic religions. These initiations also continue to transform people and communities while mitigating repeated experiences of rupture and subjection.

In the second stanza of this final poem, the poetic voice confirms that the inhabitants of this underwater dwelling are "ahogados todos del Caribe" (all Caribbean drowned) (47), a term that includes those who experienced the Middle Passage, Indigenous peoples of the region, and migrants fleeing the dictatorships of Trujillo in the Dominican Republic, Batista in Cuba, and the Duvaliers in Haiti. By placing drowning at its center, the poem makes the vastness of *boat people*'s waters indisputable; the experiences the ocean chronicles in this collection surpass geographical and temporal boundaries. Such an opening also makes necessary the consideration of another vital water deity in Afro-diasporic spiritual practices: Mami Wata.[46]

Akin to how being at sea is a way of being nowhere and everywhere at the same time, Mami Wata challenges notions of belonging and place. As part of not one spiritual tradition but many, Henry John Drewal describes Mami Wata as "a water spirit widely known across Africa and the African diaspora, [whose] origins are said to lie 'overseas,' although she has been thoroughly incorporated into local beliefs and practices" ("Sources and Currents" 23). Mami Wata is intrinsic to the migration of goods and of spirituality. Her history is traversed by the multiple paths of secular economic systems because Mami Wata's presence across the waters is tied to the advent of maritime trade. In this way, Mami Wata also experienced the onslaught of (neo)capitalism lived by the boat people.[47] Often described as half human and half fish or as a mermaid, Mami Wata embodies water's power to sustain contradiction and multiplicity. She signals the possibility of connection despite all odds, evident in how her energies have transmuted into those of various Afro-diasporic water entities. Her enormous power also instills fear (Drewal, "Charting the Voyage" 2).[48]

Perhaps one of the most relevant connections facilitated by Mami Wata in relation to *boat people* comes through her resonances with the figure of Santa Marta la Dominadora, a *misterio* (deity) of La 21 División.[49] The image created by Nadine Fortilus depicts a common representation of this enigmatic *misterio*. While Santa Marta is not directly connected to water, her affiliation with Mami Wata is evident through the presence of the snake that often appears in both of their portrayals.[50] Firelei Báez's more abstract rendition of Mami Wata's energies focuses on the power of her snake. Emphasizing how Mami Wata "bridges cultural and natural realms" (Drewal, "Charting the Voyage" 2), the snake is an attribute that links Mami Wata to various water-based Afro-diasporic deities.

Mami Wata's undercurrents in *boat people* are significant because they open the door to a discussion of La 21 División, a system that appears to be largely absent in *boat people*. Such an absence might seem incongruent in a collection that is often read as centering undocumented Dominican maritime

FIGURE 1.1. Nadine Fortilus, *Santa Marta Ora*, 2007. Satin, beads. 104.1 x 91.4 cm. Private collection. Courtesy of Henry John Drewal from his book *Mami Wata: Arts for Water Spirits in Africa and Its Diasporas*, edited by Henry John Drewal, Fowler Museum at UCLA, 2008.

migration. Yet, this elision is another way of harkening to the violence of documentation, this time in academic scholarship. In comparison to Haitian Vodou and Santería/Regla de Ocha, La 21 División is understudied and sometimes even subsumed to the structures of Haitian Vodou because of the intimate connections between these two traditions. Going back to the importance of naming practices, the very concept of "21 Divisions" is asserted as being distinctly Dominican (Ricourt, *The Dominican* 116). Once again, however, it is in *boat people's* waters that a submerged connection to La 21 División appears, one that elicits a reckoning with the points of contact between Blackness and Indigeneity.

FIGURE 1.2. Firelei Báez, *Becoming New (a tignon for Mami Wata)*, 2016. Acrylic on canvas. 48 x 34 in (121.9 x 86.4 cm). Courtesy of the artist and James Cohan, New York.

Indigeneity is intrinsic to the Afro-diasporic belief systems of Haitian Vodou, Santería/Regla de Ocha, and the broader spiritual world of the Americas due to the intimate contact between Indigenous and Afro communities as a result of colonization and slavery.[51] Although Paul Christopher Johnson and Stephan Palmié note that these relationships often lie "beyond documentary reconstruction"

(451), Indigeneity is particularly legible in La 21 División due to it having a particular division inhabited by Indigenous spirits, la División de los Indios (the Indian Division). Also referred to as la Corte Indígena (the Indigenous Court), this division is strongly associated with water.[52] This spiritual background adds weight to the moment in *boat people*'s final poem where some of the council members are described as "ciboneyes todavía suicidándose en rituales de mar" (*ciboneyes* still committing suicide in sea rituals) (47).[53] By invoking one of the Taíno cultures of the region, the presence of the *ciboneyes* purports the sacredness of water in the autochthonous spiritual cultures of the Americas, one that is preserved in the associations between water and Indigeneity in La 21 División.[54] This verse also marks the ocean as a sacred place that carries remnants of colonial violence and subjugation and that remembers a predocumentary time devoid of geopolitical borders. By using the word "todavía" (still) when referring to the death rites of the *ciboneyes*, the poem continues to underscore that ceremonial time reigns at sea. Past, present, and future converge in the water, increasing the coalitional power asserted by the end of the collection.

The mention of the *ciboneyes* in the depiction of *boat people*'s submarine dwelling speaks to Ana-Maurine Lara's contention that "There is no [Latinx] or [Afro] without [indigenous], just as there is no [Latinx] without [queer]" ("I Wanted").[55] Lara's inclusive worldview is contrary to what nation-states, hegemonic cultures, and canonical texts have often claimed in that it reinforces that Afro/Black, Indigenous, Latinx, and Queer identities are not mutually exclusive. Such a declaration speaks to the oft-repeated claim Sherina Feliciano-Santos's research seeks to upend: that because "Taíno survival is not documented, Taíno identity is not possible" (12). This fluid position has always already existed in the spiritual realm, illustrated here by the resonances between Mami Wata and La 21 División's Santa Marta (connected to Blackness), and the Corte Indígena (connected to Indigeneity). That the coming together of these seemingly disparate identities takes place underwater compounds *boat people*'s scripting of the sea as a culturally inclusive space of submersion/subversion, transforming it into a pulsating node for the continuous emergence of Afro-Latinx thought. By putting into motion the "contested epistemologies of possibility," *boat people*'s ocean calls attention to the multiple ways relating to ancestral pasts can be informed by Black and Chicana feminist theory (Feliciano-Santos 12).

In an epistemological sense, then, *boat people* transforms the water into what Maria Paula Chaves Daza's work on coalitional Latina practices describes as a "horizontal contact zone." Informed by the work of Mary Louise Pratt and Gloria Anzaldúa, Chaves Daza defines horizontal contact zones as "social spaces where *marginalized* communities come into contact with *each other* in everyday interactions that informally set the stage for more formal coalitional networks" (83, emphasis in the original). This framework elucidates how Santos-Febres creates an alignment between the resistance of the *ciboneyes* with that of dissidents from the Trujillo, Batista, and Duvalier regimes, all twentieth-century Caribbean dictatorships in the Dominican Republic, Cuba, and Haiti, respectively, as well as with maroon communities ("cimarrones") (47). Santos-Febres's decision to bring all of these peoples together toward the end of the collection is a direct subversion of how in the Spanish-speaking Caribbean, notably in Puerto Rico, the Indigenous ancestry of the nation is often exalted through the recollection of a nostalgic past while its Black heritage is relegated to the margins or erased (Duany 70; Herrera 42–43).[56] In contrast, *boat people*'s portrayal of Blackness recognizes its profound entanglements with Indigeneity, rendering them visible through the water.

The collection's closing lines leave no doubt as to the spiritual power of initiation Santos-Febres ascribes to the ocean:

esta es tu casa morenito	this is your house morenito
ven deja que te abrace	come let me embrace you
al fin estás conmigo	at last you are with me
al fin puedo dejarte de embrujar.	at last I can stop bewitching you.
(50)	

By the end of the collection, the reader has witnessed the boat people's transformations and that of the water. While the sea appeared as an omnipresent but silent protagonist in the opening poem, in "20. aquí al fondo danzan concejales—" the water is fully activated. In these verses, the ocean reveals that it has been calling for the boat people to come home. Its living waters are infused with the lineage of various Afro-diasporic and Indigenous traditions, and laden with the literal blood and bones of countless slave ships, shipwrecks, rafts, *yolas*, and more. The waters hold within their profundity more than they will ever disclose.

The spiritually powered ending of *boat people* encourages a reading of the sea's voice as one that includes Lasirèn, a deity of Haitian Vodou and one of Mami Wata's numerous progeny.[57] Often depicted as a blend of a mermaid or a whale, this mysterious *lwa* is described as having a magnetic pull: "When people catch a glimpse of Lasyrenn beneath the water, they feel her beckoning them to come with her back to Ginen, to Africa, to the ancestral home and the dwelling place of the *lwa*, *anba dlo* (beneath the water)" (McCarthy Brown 223). This nurturing aspect of Lasirèn is the focus of Evelyn Alcide's rendition of the *lwa* and her children. Still, as Deborah O'Neil and Terry Rey indicate, Lasirèn may also "snatch" women and "bring them under the sea to impart sacred knowledge" (180), an unorthodox initiation by the divine in which spiritual forces unilaterally decide that one should undergo the life-changing rituals.

FIGURE 1.3. Evelyn Alcide, *Lasirène matennelle* (Maternal Lasirèn), 2005. Satin, beads. 82.6 x 120 cm. Private collection. Courtesy of Henry John Drewal from his book *Mami Wata: Arts for Water Spirits in Africa and Its Diasporas*, edited by Henry John Drewal, Fowler Museum at UCLA, 2008.

The energies attributed to Lasirèn are in alignment with the various spiritual forces that manifest in *boat people*. Although Santos-Febres never loses sight of the tragedy experienced by the undocumented migrants, her poems seek to provide them with spiritual asylum. This strategy is especially poignant in light of Lasirèn as this *lwa* "may have roots that connect, like nerves, to the deepest and most painful parts of the loss of homeland and the trauma of slavery" (McCarthy Brown 224). For this reason, Lisa Ze Winters contends that Lasirèn's "pull upon her subjects into the sea and back to Africa invokes a reversal, an undoing of the Middle Passage" (103). Affirming Santos-Febres's contention that the undocumented migrants can finally find the sustenance *anba dlo* (beneath the waters) that was denied to them in the world above, Lasirèn's currents reinforce the spiritual power of *boat people*'s waters.

Due to the ocean's boundless reach in *boat people*, other Afro-diasporic entities can be generatively summoned in the last poem, particularly Olokun, a Santería/Regla de Ocha deity closely related to Yemayá.[58] Miguel Barnet describes Olokun as "a deity who lives at the bottom of the sea tied to a chain, the sight of whom can bring sudden death" (92). A powerful and feared *orisha*, Olokun inhabits the depths of the ocean and represents the limits of the knowable. Possessor of great riches, Olokun is connected to the origins of life and is believed to be both male and female (Cabrera, *Yemayá y Ochún* 28; Beliso-De Jesús, *Electric Santería* 133). The life-giving and life-preserving qualities of the ocean are asserted through the evocation of Olokun at the end of *boat people*, a presence that adds nuance to Yemayá's initial invocation in the text. The way sea-dwelling *orishas* open and close the collection mirrors the boat people's journey; they start at the water's surface, Yemayá's realm, and make their way to the ocean's depths, Olokun's domain. That Yemayá and Olokun bookend the journey reflects John Mason's view that these two *orishas* "represent the means of salvation and rebirth for those that have been abandoned, exiled and given up for dead" (*Olóòkun* 17). This labor of healing and recovery is precisely what Santos-Febres offers through her text's engagement with the living waters of Afro-diasporic spirituality.

In *boat people*, the sea has knowledge that transcends the knowable and that humans are unable to resist. The attraction between the migrants and Santos-Febres's waters is akin to how practitioners understand the pull toward initiation as a battle between "willful spirits and weakened flesh" (E. Pérez, "Willful Spirits" 151). The water claiming the boat people is a heart-wrenching balm for the plight faced by these migrants, whose bodies enter the sea and seemingly disappear without a trace. What "20. aquí al fondo danzan concejales—" makes clear is that this reality is linked to many moments of violence and colonization in the Caribbean, the Atlantic, and beyond. It emphasizes that while lives have unquestionably been lost, enduring traces of those who succumbed to the waters are archived in the depths of the ocean.

In Santería/Regla de Ocha there is a saying: "Nadie sabe lo que hay en el fondo del mar" (No one knows what lies at the bottom of the sea). Mayra Santos-Febres's *boat people* acknowledges this chasm as well as the mystery of the boundless and unbridled nature of water. In response, the collection enables the only entity able to testify to its history, the sea itself, to speak. By recognizing the injustices, the scarcity, and the violence that lead the boat people into the water as well as through her envisioning of a numinous yet illicit underwater city, Santos-Febres's poems assert that water is paramount to spiritual life and resistance. This powerful depiction of water draws inspiration from Afro-diasporic rituals of initiation, ceremonies that open the gateway toward spiritual development and action in the human realm. As a collection, *boat people* recurrently underscores water's potential for generating new collaborations within and between Afro-Caribbean and Afro-Latinx studies. Not bound by the constraints of governments or nationalities, engaging the living waters of the ocean can radically alter our understandings of community, grief, and survival, ushering in possibilities of connections with other sacred reservoirs of healing and creation throughout the world.

CHAPTER TWO

The Techno-Resonances of Rita Indiana's
La mucama de Omicunlé

R ita Indiana's 2015 novel *La mucama de Omicunlé* begins by depict-
ing Acilde Figueroa, the novel's transgender protagonist, indif-
ferently watching the execution of an unidentified Haitian man.[1] Described as
"uno de los muchos haitianos que cruzan la frontera para huir de la cuarentena
declarada en la otra mitad de la isla" (11), the man repeatedly presses the doorbell to the apartment where Acilde works as a *mucama*, a maid, in an attempt to
seek refuge.[2] Upon hearing the sound of the doorbell, rather than interact with
the man, Acilde activates the connection between their eye and the apartment's
security cameras by bringing their thumb and index finger together. After completing this gesture, Acilde, whose body is fully embedded into the intricate
technological webs of 2027 Santo Domingo, gains access to the scene taking
place outside.

As the camera's feed streams into their mind, Acilde watches the apartment's
security system scan the Haitian man's body. When the machine detects that
the man is infected with the mysterious virus that plagues the Western side
of the island of Hispaniola, it swiftly emits a poisonous gas to exterminate the
perceived threat. Acilde waits until the man's body stops moving before discon-
necting from the feed and returning to their cleaning duties. Soon, the Haitian's
lifeless body is collected like trash by Chinese scavenger robots gifted to the
Dominican Republic to "aliviar en algo las terribles pruebas por las que pasan
las islas del Caribe tras el desastre del 19 de marzo" (12).[3] This chilling start to
La mucama illustrates why the text has primarily been read through the lens of
science fiction or ecological disaster (De Ferrari; Duchesne-Winter; Rogers).
However, when I read Indiana's opening scene, I also see evidence of the currents of Afro-diasporic spirituality that run throughout the book.

From the start, *La mucama* scripts Acilde's body as a site viscerally inhabited by multiple channels of consciousness, Acilde's own and those streamed

by the apartment's surveillance cameras. Though this depiction could solely be read as evidence of the technological advances that lie in humanity's near future, Acilde's expanded consciousness runs parallel to the experience of spiritual mediumship, a practice that often functions alongside Santería/Regla de Ocha and other Afro-diasporic religious traditions. Intimately connected to Espiritismo, spiritual mediumship is essential to the development of Afro-Latinx religious subjectivities.[4] Espiritismo is also compatible with the language of secular technology because, as Kristina Wirtz notes, "unlike the technologies of divination, mediumship uses the human mind as . . . a radio transmitter of spirit messages" (101). Beyond emphasizing the innovative undercurrents of Afro-diasporic divination, Wirtz's decision to refer to spiritual processes as technologies is an explicit way of rejecting the stigma of backwardness often attributed to Afro-diasporic religions. It also makes clear that the transference of knowledge that takes place through mediumship is part and parcel of technology's function in the digital sphere. As Rachel Afi Quinn observes, "digital technologies . . . facilitate the rapid flow of beliefs, images, meanings, and emotions" (2). In this way, the novel's introduction to Acilde invites readers to ponder how the overt presence of technology in Indiana's text is never devoid of Afro-diasporic religious resonances.

La mucama de Omicunlé recurrently collapses religious and secular technologies to spotlight the inherent adaptability of Afro-diasporic religions. This literary strategy generates what I call "techno-resonances" between cyber and spiritual worlds and between distinct Afro-diasporic spiritual traditions. My proposition of this term stems from the premise that Afro-diasporic religions function in sync with technology and regularly update in response to technological advances. Scholars have demonstrated as much by noting the convergence between the oral (traditional) and virtual (contemporary) transmission of sacred knowledge (Brandon, "From Oral to Digital"; Murphy, "Òrìṣà Traditions"; Tsang, "¿Tienes memoria?"). More recently, terms such as "ochascape" or "ochasphere" address how the circulation of knowledge about the *orishas* online has commodified teachings and ritual practices as spiritual downloads (Beliso-De Jesús, *Electric Santería* 236n9).[5] Paul Christopher Johnson and Stephan Palmié find that the digital circulations of these religions, particularly in the diaspora, "allow and even require that previously distinct and separate groups begin to engage each other, forge cross-referential identifications, and collectively build an African diaspora meta-religion" (474). The notion of a virtually mediated Afro-diasporic "meta-religion" is an apt framework from which to consider how techno-resonance is produced in *La mucama* through religious and technological confluence.

A critical concept that informs my reading of techno-resonances in Indiana's novel is Aisha M. Beliso-De Jesús's theorization of copresences in Santería/Regla de Ocha:

> Copresences are Santería ontologies—they are the sensing of a multiplicity of being (and beings joined together) that are felt on the body, engaged with spiritually, experienced through television screens and divination, and expressed in diasporic assemblages. The various oricha, dead spirits (egun), energies of good (*iré*) or bad (*osogbo*) that influence practitioners' lives are copresences that haunt transnational Santería interactions. (*Electric Santería* 9)

Copresences are essential to techno-resonance because they underscore the quotidian nature of multiplicity in the Afro-diasporic religious world. Rather than a fantastical experience, the embodiment of multiplicity is a daily occurrence in Santería/Regla de Ocha. As a touchstone of a sacred reality, copresences emphasize the dissolution of a chronologically defined time-space continuum, mirroring the novel's eschewing of secular order. The time travel that critics have primarily attributed to *La mucama*'s engagement with science fiction can also be read as a techno-resonance that hinges on the convergence between the secular imagination and Afro-diasporic religious consciousness. This observation is especially potent considering that Indiana herself has extensively researched Santería/Regla de Ocha ("A Conversation").[6]

La mucama's opening scene presents the first display of techno-resonance by intertwining spiritual mediumship and virtual streaming in Acilde's body. Mediumship and streaming both interrupt the flow of linear time.[7] This disruptive quality is particularly salient because, as Guillermina De Ferrari articulates, the novel "moves among several time periods in the Dominican Republic—1606, 1991 to 2001, and 2027–2037" (2).[8] The pivotal connector between all epochs is Acilde, who is depicted as spiritually and technologically permeable from the start. Supporting conflicting yet coexisting realities, the techno-resonances that shape Acilde's character steer the relationships between Acilde and their corresponding male avatars in the text, Giorgio and Roque.[9] By underscoring the importance of acknowledging the concentric nature of Afro-diasporic spiritual time, techno-resonances can placate readers of Indiana's difficult text.

Rather than attempt an all-encompassing reading of Indiana's novel (a feat that might well be impossible), in this chapter I identify critical moments of techno-resonance in *La mucama de Omicunlé* and provide the religious background to apprehend them. My analysis challenges the prevailing view that Afro-diasporic religions are primitive traditions that have no place in the contemporary world.[10] It also posits that Indiana's novel exemplifies how several fundamental tenets of these traditions such as channeling, divination, and initiation mirror the processes of virtual and scientific technologies, generating instances of techno-resonance that broaden the reach of the text. As a point of departure, I suggest that the ocean, a critical component of the climate fiction and ecological readings of the novel, is a techno-resonant being in *La mucama*. In the text, this liquid body functions as a sacred reservoir of Afro-diasporic religious knowledge and as a virtual allusion to the incessant circulation of information on the Internet. The ocean is also in grave danger in the novel, and despite the disaffection with which Acilde is introduced, they are the character tasked with saving it. My discussion hinges on Indiana's portrayal of Esther Escudero (Omicunlé), Eric Vitier, and Acilde Figueroa, characters directly tied to the novel's spiritual nexus through their affiliation with the sea. By offering a reading of select moments of techno-resonance in *La mucama*, I contend that the convergence of past, present, and future in the novel shatters the hold of scripted endings and charges readers with the responsibility for imagining alternate paths.

WHO IS OLOKUN?

Though they are often shrouded in the language of cyber technology, water and Afro-diasporic religion are present in *La mucama de Omicunlé* from the start. The novel's first line reads, "El timbre del apartamento de Esther Escudero ha sido programado para sonar como una ola" (11).[11] The sonic reference to water produced by the doorbell reveals that although the liquid marks the space through which readers enter the novel, it is not physically present. Like so much in *La mucama*, what appears is a virtual representation of the sea, achieved here through sound. The doorbell functions as a haunting synecdoche for the current state of the Caribbean's waters, described by Rosana Herrero-Martín as "a dead sea, contaminated beaches teeming with unrecoverable corpses and submerged scrap" (61). On the one hand, that the sea has been reduced to a virtual existence demonstrates the planetary destruction experienced in the Dominican Republic. On the other, the technologically generated sound of the wave marks Esther Escudero's house as the latent repository for the ocean amid disaster. This dual construction of the ocean is cemented by Esther's profession. Also known as Omicunlé, Esther is a Dominican *santera* initiated to Yemayá, the *orisha* of the sea in Santería/Regla de Ocha.

When pondering the depths of the novel's opening line, readers would do well to consider the title of the first chapter: "Olokun." Not as well known as other *orishas*, Olokun is the androgynous ruler of the unfathomable depths of the ocean in Santería/Regla de Ocha. Given Olokun's habitat, they are also intimately linked to Yemayá.[12] Establishing a hierarchical relationship between these entities is ill advised, however, because power among the *orishas* is of a fluid and recurrently shifting nature (D. H. Brown 128). The novel's blurring of the borders between these *orishas* is visible in Esther Escudero's religious name, Omicunlé. In Lukumí, the creolized Yoruba tongue spoken in Cuba, her name means "el manto que cubre el mar" (23).[13] Esther's name reflects the tenets of Santería/Regla de Ocha, in which Olokun is often conceived as being a part of Yemayá herself, one of her *caminos*, paths, since all *orishas* are both one and multiple.[14] Yemayá and Olokun are simultaneously the same but different, heralding the power of Afro-diasporic waters to sustain contradiction and multiplicity. The relationship between them exemplifies religious techno-resonance due to their complementary yet distinct energies.

To fully gauge Olokun's breadth in Indiana's text, an awareness of the origins of this *orisha* in Santería/Regla de Ocha is needed. This history is pivotal to understanding Olokun's ties with knowledge and healing, central themes in *La mucama*. In Santería/Regla de Ocha, it is impossible to think of Olokun without considering the figure of Fermina Gómez, whose religious name was Ocha Bi (Beliso-De Jesús, *Electric Santería* 127).[15] Gómez was a powerful Cuban *santera* initiated to Yemayá who "gave the oricha Olokun to uninitiated black Cubans suffering from spiritual turmoil due to slavery" (Beliso-De Jesús, *Electric Santería* 116). Despite her undeniable influence in updating this spiritual tradition, Gómez was not without her detractors, particularly in terms of gender because some believe that only certain male priests, *babalawos*, can perform Olokun rituals (Ferrer Castro and Acosta Alegre 50). The transgression and controversy that surrounds Olokun's genealogy is central to their role in *La mucama*.

Despite the challenges she faced, Fermina Gómez is credited with growing the cult of Olokun in Cuba and its diaspora. Beliso-De Jesús explains:

> In an effort to calm the instability and racial violence of the time, Gómez decided to give Olokun to nonpriests. "Giving" a santo entails a material manifestation of oricha in which sacred stones and shells housed in a pot or soup tureen are consecrated and then "received" by a practitioner, who must care for and worship the deity. Such responsibility is usually reserved for priests, who commit themselves for life to the religion. By giving Olokun to nonpriests, Gómez allowed for them to bypass costly initiation rites and appease their spiritual turmoil with less initial investment. Olokun, an androgynous oricha of the depths of the sea, is said to calm tragedy and change destiny. As a result of this move, Gómez is credited with bringing Olokun to the Cuban Yoruba diaspora. All Olokuns in Cuban Santería are thus said to have originated from her pot. (*Electric Santería* 132–133)

Olokun's genealogy in Cuba and its diaspora reflects the transnational ideas of migration and redemption found in Santería/Regla de Ocha and in Indiana's novel. In addition, this historical background underscores that this *orisha* is integral for those seeking transformational healing.

Olokun's limitless capacity for healing does not minimize the fear they instill in believers. In *Yemayá y Ochún*, Cabrera observes that *santeros* dreaded making offerings to Olokun at sea because invariably at least one of them perished during the ceremony (27). As the notion of the sublime makes clear in European aesthetics, the unknowable or unfathomable is as fearsome as it is intriguing, and this is precisely what Olokun represents in the Santería/Regla de Ocha pantheon. Olokun reigns in the darkest depths of the ocean. They embody the profundity of knowledge as well as the impossibility of accessing it. In this sense, Olokun is associated more directly with the mysterious creation power of the universe than with direct contact with the human world (D. H. Brown 125). The rawness of Olokun's power attests to how energy can be used as much for healing and creation as for destruction, an apt description of the role of secular and spiritual technologies in the contemporary world.

DIVINING THE PATH:
ESTHER, ACILDE, AND TRANSNATIONAL TRANSACTIONS

La mucama engages Olokun's historical legacy by tasking Esther, a priestess of Yemayá, with initiating "the chosen one" to the cult of Olokun to create an opportunity to save the sea. Esther is a Black queer woman born in the Dominican Republic during the Balaguer years. These twelve years, fruit of the usurpation of the island's possible futures by yet another US occupation in 1965, function as a shadow period in the nation's history. The shadows are evident in Esther's personal life; she lives in denial of the flashes of spiritual insight she receives and of her queerness. When she falls dangerously ill due to a hex placed upon her after falling in love with a married woman, her childhood caretaker, a Black woman named Bélgica, appears at her bedside and takes her to Cuba to become initiated to Yemayá. Esther's *kari ocha* (initiation) takes place in Matanzas, the region of Cuba where Fermina Gómez practiced and where Olokun's legacy in the Americas begins. This literary move expands the territories of the novel and intertwines the energies of Yemayá and Olokun in *La mucama*, emphasizing the techno-resonance between secular and spiritual histories. It also transforms Esther into a transnationally birthed priestess, a Dominican *santera* with Cuban spiritual lineage. Through the religious technologies embedded into *kari ocha* Esther recovers her ancestry, evidencing one of the most powerful truths of Afro-diasporic knowledges: what is not known has not necessarily been forgotten, though it must be accessed differently.

Esther Escudero's religious name, Omicunlé, brings together depth and knowledge. It also addresses the relationship between Olokun, who represents the limits of the knowable, and Yemayá, who is largely associated with the power of prophecy due to her propensity for divination.[16] When it comes to water, Yemayá is associated with the upper realms, most commonly the waves and seafoam. Her connection to the ocean's surface explains why, as Margarite Fernández Olmos and Lizabeth Paravisini-Gebert note, when Yemayá takes possession of her children "she swirls around quickly, swaying like the waves of the sea" (52). This portrayal elucidates why Esther's spiritual name alludes to the covering of the sea, or perhaps more appropriately, given the threats faced by the ocean in Indiana's novel, to shielding the water.[17]

Esther's connections to Yemayá and Olokun point to the significance of water in Santería/Regla de Ocha. For example, one of Cabrera's best-known texts, *Yemayá y Ochún*, was inspired by the sacredness of water as Yemayá and Ochún respectively represent the sea and the river. In the opening discussion of her work, Cabrera writes, "De Yemayá nació la vida. Y del mar nació el Santo, el Caracol, el Ocha verdadero" (Life was born from Yemayá. And from the sea came the Saint [*orishas, santos*], the [cowrie] Shells, and the true Ocha [gods, religion]) (*Yemayá y Ochún* 21). Cabrera returns to this assertion when quoting a practicing priest who declares, "sin *agbó, omí,* y *ewe,* –carnero, agua y yerba– no hay Santo" (without *agbó, omí,* y *ewe,*—ram, water and herbs—there is no Saint) (277). Cabrera's research resonates with the movement of Haitian Vodou's *lwa* across and below the water as well as with Terry Rey's conception of water as "the lifeblood" of Haitian Vodou ("Vodou" 199). Such a description focuses on the centrality of water to life and knowledge in Afro-diasporic traditions. This coalescence of meanings is essential to understanding what is at stake in *La mucama*. Beyond the threat of environmental disaster, whole systems of knowledge are at risk of extinction due to the poisoning of the Caribbean Sea.

The connection between water and knowledge in *La mucama* is palpable in Omicunlé's role as spiritual advisor to Said Bona, the first Dominican president to declare that the official religion of the island is "las 21 Divisiones y su mezcla de deidades africanas y santos católicos" (*La mucama* 59).[18] This moment marks an important techno-resonance between Santería/Regla de Ocha and La 21 División as Afro-diasporic religious traditions born in the Americas. It also challenges the political invisibility of La 21 División on the island, given its historical condemnation by the Dominican state (Ricourt, *The Dominican* 112). And, although Bona is a fictional character in the novel, his last name coincides with that of a priestess of La 21 División who had ties to government officials (Tejeda Ortiz 102). His character thus makes legible the largely undocumented historical complicity between sanctioned and unsanctioned discourses of power.

The existence of Esther's political influence in *La mucama* is undeniable, but its effects are murkier:

> Según las redes, la victoria y permanencia en el poder del presidente Bona son obra de esa señora encanecida que arrastra sus pantuflas de seda azul hacia la cocina y se sirve en una taza profunda el café que Acilde le ha preparado minutos antes. (13)[19]

The word "redes" (webs or networks) capitalizes on the techno-resonances between cyber and spiritual knowledge as it invokes the Internet as well as social networks common in Afro-diasporic religious communities.[20] Yet, despite Esther's advice or perhaps because of it, Bona decides to store biological weapons in the Caribbean Sea, setting the stage for their unexpected detonation in 2024 by a cataclysmic tidal wave. This incident, which creates the need for Acilde's heroic mission, illustrates Eugenio Matibag's contention that "divination may mediate between individual desire and the social context, although its 'misuse' can also work against the interests of the collectivity" ("Ifá" 152). In *La mucama* there are multiple ways of accessing knowledge, but the application of that knowledge falls on the shoulders of the individuals who dispense and receive it.

Like Esther, Acilde Figueroa struggles with the weight of responsibility. The novel emphasizes this compromised position by providing information about Acilde's birth that marks them as the product of an encounter between a Dominican sex worker and an Italian man:

> Su padre había permanecido junto a su madre lo que había tardado en echarle el polvo que la preñó. Jennifer, su madre, una trigueña de pelo bueno que había llegado a Milano con un contrato de modelo, se había enganchado a la heroína y terminó dando el culo en el metro de Roma. Se había sacado seis muchachos cuando decidió parir *el séptimo* y regresar al país para dejárselo a sus padres, dos campesinos mocanos amargados, que se habían mudado a la capital cuando el fenómeno de La Llorona y sus dos años de lluvias acabaron con su conuco para siempre.[21] (*La mucama* 18, my emphasis)

Although this passage appears to transmit solely secular information, there is a significant moment of techno-resonance. That Acilde is Jennifer's seventh pregnancy links them to the sacred waters of Santería/Regla de Ocha. Yemayá's divine number, 7, is also the number of the entities in las Siete Potencias Africanas. Olokun is often associated with the number 9 but can be connected to the number 7 due to their ties to Yemayá. Seven is also intimately linked to the initiation practices of Afro-diasporic religions; it marks the spiritual incubation period for the rituals of *bautizo*, *kanzo*, and *kari ocha*. Thus, this passage scripts

Acilde's body from its very conception in Jennifer's amniotic fluid as a site ripe for techno-resonance between the sacred and the secular and between various Afro-diasporic traditions.

The brief narration of Acilde's conception is one of the few instances in which their racial background is addressed. The narrator describes Jennifer, Acilde's mother, as "trigueña," a term that reflects the pigmentocracy that reigns in the Caribbean. Ginetta E. B. Candelario establishes that "trigueña" means "lit. wheat-skinned; fig., brown-skinned" (*Black* 32).[22] The references to Jennifer's "pelo bueno" (good hair) make evident the relentless waves of anti-Blackness that circulate in the Caribbean and in the United States, where "good" hair is prized due to its relative proximity to straightness and thus whiteness. In light of these physical descriptions of Jennifer, readers can deduce that Acilde's mother is a nonwhite passing albeit "attractive" Dominican woman.

Acilde's birth story identifies them as a product of the diaspora even though they never move beyond Dominican soil, illustrating that "the Dominican Republic has always existed as a transnational space" (Quinn 2). Furthermore, by gesturing toward the expansion of the Dominican diaspora to Europe, a move driven by the forces of capitalism, the novel extends the conversation on Dominican migration far beyond the United States and Puerto Rico, the locations of its initial diasporic communities. Jennifer's presence in Europe also subtly suggests the global spread of La 21 División and other Afro-diasporic spiritual practices.[23] That the sexual encounter that leads to Acilde's procreation takes place between a Dominican woman and an Italian man is one more link in the chain of sexual exploitation and addiction that imprints Acilde's DNA with ancestral trauma.[24] Their historical and genetic predisposition to suffering primes them for their techno-resonance with Olokun's energies, as this *orisha*'s unbounded capacity for healing trauma is linked to the unfathomable depths of their own injuries and sorrows.[25]

In *La mucama*, the narrative of Acilde's birth viscerally connects them to the ocean:

> Durante la transacción de la que Acilde era producto, su papá le había dicho a su madre que deseaba conocer las playas dominicanas. La isla era entonces un destino turístico de costas repletas de corales, peces y anémonas. (26)[26]

To read Acilde as a "product" of the economic transactions that shipped her mother to Italy and led her to become a substance-abusing sex worker painfully invokes the prevalence of sex tourism in the Caribbean, one of the region's primary "exports."[27] Yet, beyond the troubling presence of tourism in this passage, the narrator subtly mentions the sea and the sacred anemone that will change Acilde's life, making clear that the sea has always been a part of Acilde's story. That the text makes all these interactions revolve around the word "transacción" is a prime example of techno-resonance between spiritual and neoliberal economies.[28]

Spiritual transactions are the currency of Afro-diasporic religions. While Christianity and other hegemonic religions emphasize the need humans have for the divine, a need that is understood in strictly hierarchical terms, in Afro-diasporic religions the ancestors, *lwa*, *misterios*, and *orishas* also need humans. The recurrence of transactions, contracts, and agreements among and between humans and the divine is particularly evident in the terminology of Haitian Vodou and La 21 División, whose devotees are often referred to as *serviteurs* or *servidores*, those who serve the deities.[29] In Santería/Regla de Ocha, it is customary to offer the ancestors and the *orishas* "un servicio" (a ritual offering), evidencing the need to be in a process of constant exchange and receptivity with the sacred. Spiritual transactions ensure the circulation of power and *aché*; what flows from the divine toward the human endows practitioners with the ability to better care for and serve their ancestors, *lwa*, *misterios*, and *orishas*. This kind of symbiotic relationship lies at the core of Afro-diasporic religious systems, underscoring the cyclical nature of their temporalities. A transaction, however, also implies that debt can be incurred, and Indiana's novel does not shy away from this aspect.[30]

Water and Afro-diasporic religions also offer a productive framework from which to read Acilde's transgender identity. The seamless flow between binaries and contradictions in Afro-diasporic waters is one of the characteristics that makes this element a critical part of the epistemological and ontological methodologies Indiana deploys in *La mucama*. Gender fluidity is essential to Yemayá, Olokun, and other *orishas*.[31] Although Yemayá is recurrently portrayed as female, she is believed to provide special protection to gay men (Matory, "The Many" 259). Olokun, however, is androgynous (Cabrera, *Yemayá y Ochún* 28; Beliso-De Jesús, *Electric Santería* 133).[32] Some *patakís* (mythical stories) go as far as to make the violence experienced by Olokun when others rejected their body as the reason for this *orisha*'s desire to destroy the world (Ferrer Castro and Acosta Alegre 22–23). In this way, Acilde's role as Olokun's heir is connected to how embodying fluidity can engender violence in a forcefully cisgendered world.

Despite the rich convergences between Acilde and Afro-diasporic religiosity, Acilde has neither knowledge nor interest in these traditions. Acilde arrives at Omicunlé's house not to seek spiritual counsel but because they have been promised easy and lucrative employment. Even though Acilde is not shown as outright rejecting Esther's religious practice, there is a great deal of ambivalence surrounding their relationship to Omicunlé. Regardless, Esther introduces Acilde to the energies of Olokun through an impromptu divination session.[33] Here, she offers Acilde the saying "Nadie sabe lo que hay en el fondo del mar" (*La mucama* 25).[34] This proverb, associated with Olokun given the *orisha*'s connection to the depths of the ocean, signals "the arrival of something hidden or unexpected, the unknown" (Matibag, "Ifá" 154). It evidences water's function as a channel for and a reservoir of knowledge in Santería/Regla de Ocha, calling attention to how water's techno-resonance is critical to secular and spiritual survival. The saying acquires more weight in that this is the only moment in the novel that incorporates the use of the *diloggún*, one of the divination technologies of Santería/Regla de Ocha. The fact that this religious practice relies on the use of cowrie shells transforms this moment into one where the sea speaks to Acilde through Omicunlé, a daughter of Yemayá.

While Omicunlé is only alive during the novel's first chapter, her presence sets the tone for much of Acilde's tenuous relationship to religious knowledge and responsibility. This ambivalence is on display when Omicunlé gifts Acilde a consecrated Olokun necklace:

> De Brasil, Esther le había traído un collar de cuentas azules consagrado a Olokun, una deidad más antigua que el mundo, el mar mismo. "El dueño de lo desconocido", le explicó en el momento de colocárselo. "Llévalo siempre porque aunque no creas te protegerá. Un día vas a heredar mi casa. Esto ahora no lo entiendes, pero con el tiempo lo verás." Omicunlé se ponía muy seria y Acilde se sentía incómoda. No podía evitar sentir cariño por aquella abuela que la cuidaba con la delicadeza que nunca habían tenido con ella sus familiares de sangre. (*La mucama* 28–29)[35]

Beyond referring to the possibility of inheriting Esther's literal apartment, which is where Acilde currently resides and works, in this moment Acilde is unceremoniously declared the protector of the sea and by extension of planetary life and Afro-diasporic religious knowledges. For Alexandra Gonzenbach Perkins the immensity of this transaction "transforms Acilde into a proxy for salvation" (52). Yet, the religious implications of this moment in *La mucama* cannot be overstated. Beaded necklaces called *elekes* are one of the primary technological artifacts of Santería/Regla de Ocha. To receive them is to undergo one of the initial rites of passage of this religious system. *Elekes* do not singularly denote that one will become initiated, but they are a prerequisite for initiation (E. Pérez, "Willful Spirits" 155). *Elekes* are a tangible representation of a sacred commitment between human and divine actors. For this reason, some practitioners view the necklaces as "el anillo de compromiso que el novio le da a la novia" (the engagement ring the fiancé gives the soon-to-be-bride) (Cabrera, *Yemayá y Ochún* 121). The nonchalance of Acilde's reaction foreshadows what is to come throughout the novel, when the fate of the world will, quite literally, rest upon their noncommittal head.

Omicunlé's placement of Olokun's *eleke* on Acilde, which happens without

Acilde's explicit consent, can be read as another moment of techno-resonance between diverse Afro-diasporic spiritual traditions through the inclusion of Candomblé, an influential Afro-diasporic religion born in Brazil. Candomblé has much in common with Santería/Regla de Ocha but is a distinct system with a unique history and particular rituals. Its insertion in *La mucama* reiterates that presenting Yoruba religious culture as a globalized phenomenon disrupts neoliberal circuits by signaling alternative modes of exchange (Olupona and Rey 6–7). Through its reference to Candomblé the text emphasizes how spiritual techno-resonance is neither limited nor obliterated by political or technological divides. Still, this necklace's connection to Olokun and the sea raises the stakes in the novel by expanding the geographical reach of the ocean's plight. Although Acilde's story takes place in the Dominican Republic, just as all waters are connected, the future predicted for Hispaniola implicates the rest of the world's waters.

PUNISHING KNOWLEDGES:
THE COSTS OF IMPROVISATION

While my initial discussion of techno-resonance in *La mucama de Omicunlé* centered on productive convergences, the presence of Eric Vitier in the novel illustrates that connections between systems of knowledge do not always lead to positive outcomes. Eric and Omicunlé are crowned (initiated) by the same Santería/Regla de Ocha priest, described by Esther as "Belarminio Brito, Omidina, un hijo de Yemayá más malo que el gas" (23).[36] They are spiritual kin because they belong to the same religious *ilé* (house).[37] Like Esther, Eric receives valuable information about his spiritual destiny when he is initiated at the age of nine:

> En la profecía que se hace al iniciado, se le reveló que él encontraría al hijo legítimo de Olokun, el de las siete perfecciones, el Señor de las profundidades; y por esto su padrino le puso Omioloyu, los ojos de Yemayá, confiado en que *un día el pequeño pícaro sabría hallar en la carne del mundo* a aquel que sabe lo que hay en el fondo del mar. (*La mucama* 68, my emphasis)[38]

As Esther's right-hand man, Eric fulfills his spiritual destiny literally because it is through contact with the flesh (sex) that he meets Acilde and brings them to Omicunlé's house. Yet, the way Eric behaves upon discovering that Acilde is Olokun's heir warrants close attention. His actions provoke a traumatic moment of techno-resonance that hinges on sexual and divine understandings of the body.

In contrast to Acilde, Eric is a privileged character in *La mucama*:

> Médico, cubano y con rasgos de película, Eric no necesitaba pagar para tener sexo, pero los blanquitos de clase media que se prostituían para comprar tuercas, las pastillas a las que eran adictos, lo volvían loco. (14)[39]

A *santero* and a medical doctor with a fetish for power, Eric is a dangerous possessor of divine and secular knowledge. When he propositions Acilde, who engages in sex work to earn the money they need to pay for a synthetic drug that will give them the male body they covet, the encounter begins like any another. Suddenly, however, Eric is transformed after Acilde performs oral sex on him:

> Acilde se la chupó *dejando que [Eric] le agarrara la cabeza*. . . . Acilde no había terminado de decir "dame mis cuartos, maricón" cuando Eric se le fue encima, la inmovilizó boca abajo y ahogó sus gritos de "soy hembra, coño" con la grama contra su boca. A esas alturas a Eric no le importaba lo que fuese, le metió una pinga seca por el culo y, cuando terminó y Acilde se levantó para subirse los pantalones, sacó un encendedor para acercarse y confirmar que era verdad, que era mujer. "Te voy a pagar extra por los efectos especiales", dijo. Y ella, al ver la cantidad que le pasaba, aceptó su invitación a desayunar. (*La mucama* 14–15, my emphasis)[40]

I read this passage as one that underscores the violent techno-resonance that emerges from the combination of Acilde's physical body and Eric's penchant for subjugation. As a transgender man, Acilde is surrounded by currents of abuse. Eric is not the first man to rape them, which helps explain the almost mechanical way Acilde moves from fury to compliance when shown the right amount of money. Yet, at this moment, Acilde's body is once again inscribed by multiple registers. Afro-diasporic religion transforms Acilde's body into sacredly legible flesh that Eric can read and that honors Acilde's trans identity given Olokun's androgyny. Furthermore, water is surreptitiously present in this scene through the word "ahogar" (to drown), subtly invoking Olokun. Given that Olokun abused their power and almost destroyed the world, this moment exemplifies how even sacred knowledge is sometimes unable to shield the vulnerable from harm.[41]

The decision to rape Acilde clashes with the divine mandate Eric was given at his initiation, setting him up for the multiple transgressions he will commit in the narrative. Eric perpetrates the crime and then desecrates Acilde's head, a part of the body he, as an initiate of Santería/Regla de Ocha, knows to be sacred.[42] Devastatingly, Eric rapes Acilde *as a result* of identifying them as "the chosen one." While the reader is unaware of this detail when the violation occurs, it is revealed in the novel's third chapter as Eric officiates Acilde's initiation to Olokun. Indiana writes:

> La cabeza de Acilde exhibía una corona de lunares, puntos oscuros en círculo alrededor de la coronilla que Eric había distinguido cuando aquella chica . . . se arrodilló para mamárselo una noche en el Mirador. (*La mucama* 69)[43]

As a visual representation of the spiritual crown an *iyawo* receives upon being initiated, the moles on Acilde's head are the techno-resonant bodily markings that lead Eric to realize he is about to fulfill the prophecy of his initiation.[44] Yet, rather than protect the person who represents the climax of his sacred mission, Eric rapes them. After his violent transgression, Eric offers Acilde a job at Esther's house, seemingly fulfilling his spiritual mandate. The distorted way he does so exemplifies how easily spiritual knowledge can be used nefariously. It also explains how and why Eric attempts to avoid Acilde's initiation in the first place, a decision that ultimately costs him his life.

While Acilde's presence in Esther's *ilé* appears to signal that Eric is committed to complying with his sacred destiny, in reality he is plotting his next steps. When Esther travels to Brazil for the conference on African religions where she acquires the Olokun *eleke* she bestows upon Acilde, Eric makes his move:

> Eric se quedó con Acilde en la casa. Esta pensó primero que la bruja no confiaba en ella; luego entendió que la anémona necesitaba de atenciones especiales que Eric le brindaría en su ausencia, teoría que confirmó cuando lo vio pasar horas muertas encerrado en el cuarto de santo. A su regreso, Esther encontró a Eric enfermo, con diarreas, tembloroso y con manchas extrañas en los brazos. Lo mandó para su casa y le dijo a Acilde: "Se lo buscó, buen bujarrón, no le cojas las llamadas". A pesar de las advertencias de Omicunlé, Acilde visitaba al enfermo para llevarle comida y las medicinas que él mismo se recetaba. Eric permanecía en su habitación, en la que reinaba una peste a vómito y alcoholado. Había días en los que deliraba, sudaba fiebres terribles, llamaba a Omicunlé, repetía: "Oló kun fun me lo mo, oló kun fun." Acilde volvía a casa de Esther y le contaba todo para ablandarla: sólo conseguía que la vieja lo maldijera aún más y lo llamara traidor, sucio y pendejo. (*La mucama* 27–28)[45]

Readers soon learn that Eric has attempted to initiate himself as Olokun's heir, unleashing catastrophic consequences due to the wrath of the *orishas*.[46] Knowing she would die as a result of welcoming the savior of the seas into her home, Omicunlé had passed on secret ritualistic knowledge to Eric to ensure he would be able to initiate the *Omo Olokun* (child of Olokun) in her absence. Transforming his body into a locus of cacophonous techno-resonance, Eric attempts to supplant his own crown of Yemayá's energies with those of Olokun, damage from which he never recovers.[47] Eric falls prey to an illness of the soul that does not respond to any of the medical knowledge he possesses. Although Acilde brings Eric all the allopathic medicines he prescribes for himself, what ails him cannot be solved through pharmacological means. Acutely aware of the cause of his disease, Omiculné refuses to help him. Eric's predicament exemplifies how "divine and human sanctions serve to reinforce collective religious aims by policing those who would adapt the religion to their own ends" (Wirtz 138). For Eric, spiritual and medical knowledge converge to condemn rather than save because he has abused both for personal gain.

To complicate matters, Eric presumably abuses the spiritual instruction he received from Omiculné because he is thinking of the "greater good":

> Eric quería a la vieja [Omiculné] como a una madre y, creyendo poder evitar el desenlace fatal de la profecía, improvisó una salida. Si él se coronaba como Omo Olokun podría deshacerse de Acilde, la supuesta elegida, pero sus experimentos con la anémona a espaldas de Esther terminaron por enfermarlo y enojaron a la bruja. (*La mucama* 68)[48]

This passage provides Eric's justifications for his actions: he wants to save Omiculné from premature death. Yet, close attention to Eric's prior behavior shows that he has been repeatedly hostile toward Acilde, from his initial violation to his ultimate desire to "deshacerse de Acilde" (get rid of Acilde). Although the novel does not provide much additional information about Eric, who dies as soon as Acilde's initiation is complete, what is clear is that his designated role as supporting spiritual actor clashes with his ambitious nature.

ACILDE'S AFRO-DIASPORIC REALITIES: INITIATING THE *OMO OLOKUN*

Afro-diasporic religious initiations are moments of border crossings: borders of time, place, life, and self. For this reason, it is not surprising that Acilde's initiation gives shape to the novel's third chapter, aptly titled "Condylactis gigantea."[49] The number 3 is spiritually charged in Santería/Regla de Ocha because it is associated with Eshu/Elegguá. In the Western world, Eshu/Elegguá is often aligned with the role of the devil, a move that fails to acknowledge that the binaries of Christianity cannot contain the expansive dimensions of Afro-diasporic spiritual traditions. Eshu/Elegguá is a complex *orisha* who effortlessly moves between worlds. As the path opener, he must be invoked at the start of any ritual. Eshu/Elegguá's fluidity can be appreciated through his multilingualism: "being privy to the creation of the world he has seen all languages develop and can communicate in any dialect" (Tsang, "Beguiling Eshu" 218). The energies of Eshu/Elegguá manifest in the religious worlds of La 21 División and Haitian Vodou, where the deity goes by the name of Legba. Due to his ubiquity, Eshu/Elegguá/Legba is a formidable deity to consider in regard to techno-resonance in *La mucama*, and perhaps the place where these energetic convergences most richly abound is at Acilde's *kari ocha*, a ceremony known for its capacity to "multiply the spirit space" (Beliso-De Jesús, *Electric Santería* 69).

Even though Acilde had never heard of Olokun before arriving at Omicunlé's apartment, they agreed to take the job at Esther's because they needed money to buy the pharmaceutical Rainbow Bright.[50] This drug, which represents another key moment of techno-resonance in the novel, potently fuses religious and medical knowledge, as indicated in the following description:

> [Era] una inyección que ya circulaba en los círculos de ciencia independiente y que prometía un cambio de sexo total, sin intervención quirúrgica. El proceso había sido comparado al síndrome de abstinencia de los adictos a la heroína, aunque los indigentes transexuales que habían servido de conejillos de Indias decían que era mucho peor. (*La mucama* 20–21)[51]

In the novel, Rainbow Bright is depicted as a life-altering drug that generates a new body, opening the door to a new life. Such a description recalls the death and rebirth cycles of Afro-diasporic initiations. But Rainbow Bright is prohibitively expensive for Acilde; it retails for US $15,000. This exorbitant price deftly comments on the ever-rising costs of initiation in the Afro-diasporic world, a direct result of the commercialization of these rituals.[52] Acilde turns to sex work to procure money to pay for the serum and through this work meets Eric, who ultimately takes them to Omicunlé. Acilde's plot to steal the sacred sea anemone from Omicunlé, which causes Esther's death, is driven by their desire to sell it on the black market and secure the money needed to purchase the life-altering injection. Intertwining science, technology, and spirituality, Rainbow Bright is a critical node of techno-resonance in *La mucama*, a trait clearly on display during Acilde's initiation to Olokun.

The story of Rainbow Bright's creation is directly connected to how the novel addresses the ethics of medical, scientific, and religious knowledge. These ethics are already in crisis due to Eric's actions; he does not comply with his Hippocratic oath, let alone with religious mandates. Nonetheless, it is critical to remember that the spiritual systems of the Afro-diasporic world provide a great deal of medical support for their communities.[53] In her discussion of La 21 División, Martha Ellen Davis states:

Las actividades privadas, o sea las consultas, sirven para sanar y orientar a los 'pacientes'. Y después de sanos, se ofrece una fiesta de acción de gracias, o sea, un evento público [Private activities, or consults, are used to heal and orient the 'patients.' Once healed, a celebration to give thanks is offered, which is a public event]. (*La otra ciencia* 222)

When addressing the medical dimensions of La 21 División, Davis underscores issues of logistical and economic access. In areas not serviced by allopathic medicine, knowledgeable *servidores* become the "curandero-servidor" (healers) of their communities (*La otra ciencia* 223).[54] Ricourt confirms the longevity of the medicinal underpinnings of La 21 División through her discussion of Papo, a *servidor* of Belié Belcán, Saint Michael: "People come to him with tumors, infections, aches, and other *quebrantos* (illnesses) that doctors cannot cure but that, through vision given to him by the mysteries, he can diagnose and heal" (*The Dominican* 122). In this way, La 21 División and other Afro-diasporic spiritual traditions are self- and community-sustaining practices in which healing knowledge is generated from and for the Afro-diasporic body.

In contrast, the development of Rainbow Bright is an indictment of how medical and scientific knowledge has often been extracted through and from marginalized bodies and monetized for the economic gain of others.[55] Consent is impossible to attain when no other choices are available. These realities converge in the use of the words "indigents" and "guinea pigs" when discussing members of the trans community who become test subjects for Rainbow Bright. Furthermore, the novel lays bare the pain induced by the drug, bringing to mind the construction of the Black "superbody" in the nineteenth century. In *Medical Bondage: Race, Gender, and the Origins of American Gynecology*, Deirdre Cooper Owens asserts:

Enslaved women were perfect medical subjects for gynecological experimentation because doctors deemed them biologically inferior to white women based on their research findings, yet black women supposedly had a high tolerance for pain. Also because of the low status of black women, white doctors felt no obligation to give merit to their thoughts on the matter. (23)

The supposed inability to feel pain attributed to the Black female body leads Owens to coin the term "medical superbodies." This construct addresses how medical practitioners assumed that "these women's bodies were somehow

'super' in their abilities to transcend pain," a concept that "shaped early gyne-
cologists' behavior toward them on operating tables and in examination rooms"
(Owens 115). Showcasing an awareness of the echoes of slavery in the United
States and the Caribbean, Indiana's portrayal of Rainbow Bright addresses how
the recognition of pain continues to be a privilege afforded only to certain bodies. Afro-diasporic religions actively counter this narrative as they arise through
and from the pain of the Black body to provide opportunities for healing and
freedom.

Beginning with the obliteration of the virus-ridden Haitian man at the start
of the novel, to the trans community members in the medical trials for Rainbow
Bright, to Acilde and the sexual abuses they recurrently endure, the marginalized
bodies in La mucama are denied access to an acknowledgment of pain. Instead,
they function as superbodies expected to take whatever is thrust upon them.
Owens's documentation of Dr. Marion Sims's use of restraints supports this
view. Considered by many to be the father of modern gynecology, Sims "held
fast to the practice of restraining surgical patients because he knew so many of
them would physically resist being cut by his surgeon's blade, even black women
who were allegedly impervious to surgical pain" (Owens 112). This practice
is reflected in La mucama when, presumably following orders from Rainbow
Bright's creators, Eric physically restrains Acilde to the bed to administer the
drug. Acilde, who initially rejects being tied down, ultimately complies.

The portrayal of Acilde's body as their greatest currency evokes techno-
resonance by conflating secular and divine economies. This is evident in how
Acilde's initial decision to engage in sex work leads Eric to identify them as
Olokun's heir. The techno-resonance of Acilde's body reaches a screeching cre-
scendo after Omicunlé's death, a death that is caused by Acilde's desire to sell
the sea anemone on the black market. In hiding from those hunting for Esther's
killer, Acilde reaches out to Eric to negotiate what they believe is a purely economic exchange: they will give Eric the coveted sea anemone in exchange for the
delivery and administration of Rainbow Bright. Despite his precarious health,
Eric readily agrees to Acilde's terms and travels to Villa Mella, where Acilde has
sought safe haven.

The location Indiana selects for Acilde's refuge and initiation is revelatory.
Within the Dominican Republic's capital city of Santo Domingo, Villa Mella
is a stronghold of Blackness, evidenced by the presence of the cofradía (religious sisterhood/brotherhood) of the Congos of Villa Mella.[56] Like the Cuban
cabildos, the Dominican cofradías were mutual-aid societies structured around
Afro-religious worship. Lorgia García-Peña notes that "these spiritually based
societies also performed a political purpose: they were charged with representing free blacks in front of colonial law" (62). Villa Mella thus functions
in La mucama as a spiritual and historical techno-resonant node that places

Acilde's spiritual birth in the pulsating heart of La 21 División's presence in Santo Domingo, from colonial times until now. That this is the only chapter in *La mucama* that mentions La 21 División by name reinforces the circumscribed visibility of Blackness on the island.[57]

When Eric arrives in Villa Mella he immediately instructs Acilde to "ponerse un enema, darse un baño, afeitarse la vulva y la cabeza" (*La mucama* 64).[58] While these acts might appear to simply be preparation for the medical procedure that will soon take place, a techno-resonant understanding of Rainbow Bright signals the need to also view them as attributable to Afro-diasporic purification rituals. Bathing the body is a vital aspect of initiations and many rituals in Haitian Vodou, La 21 División, and Santería/Regla de Ocha.[59] Shaving the head is also an integral part of *kari ocha* and is one of the acts traditionally performed by the *obá-oriaté*, the Santería/Regla de Ocha priest who officiates at initiations and other important rituals.[60] The novel's description breaks with Santería/Regla de Ocha convention by having Acilde shave their own head as well as having them shave their vulva.[61] Although not often a part of the traditional protocol of Santería/Regla de Ocha, this bodily depilation is experienced by initiates in Haitian Vodou's *kanzo*: "the priest cuts a lock of hair from the tops of their heads, removes the hair from their arm-pits and pubes, and takes nail-parings from their left hands and feet" (Métraux 199). The removal of hair is a common aspect of Afro-diasporic initiations because it implies purification and rebirth. After shedding or offering a part of one's body, its regrowth is evidence of the nascent strength of an initiate's newly birthed spiritual life.

Once Acilde has finished performing the mandated tasks, Eric tells them to lie down on the bed, evoking *kanzo*'s practice of *kouche*, lying down.[62] Eric has placed a white sheet around the bed, creating a kind of chamber to "mantener estéril el espacio alrededor de su cuerpo" (*La mucama* 65).[63] In medical terms, to keep a space sterile is to prevent anything harmful that could cause infection from entering. *Kari ocha* and *kanzo* enact a similar kind of protection by creating an enclosed birthing chamber through Santería/Regla de Ocha's *igbodu* or *cuarto de santo* and Haitian Vodou's *djèvo*. The white sheet Eric uses is tied to the Afro-diasporic world; the color white is ritualistically used in the initiation ceremonies of Santería/Regla de Ocha, Haitian Vodou, and even in the *bautizos* of La 21 División.[64] The techno-resonance of Acilde's initiation in *La mucama de Omicunlé* is also evident in Stephan Palmié's description of Santería/Regla de Ocha initiations as "a series of ritual operations linking the initiate's head with vessels containing the objectified presence of the deity in question" (*Wizards* 166). Hence, what at first glance can appear to be a solely medical procedure for Acilde must be understood as a moment of climactic techno-resonance between the many technologies and copresences that inhabit their body.

Acilde believes they are only preparing for an infusion of Rainbow Bright, the coveted drug Eric is about to administer, but the injection's techno-resonances with the Afro-diasporic religious world are multiple. First, since it is a serum, it is subtly connected to water and to this element's transformative and channeling spiritual qualities. Second, the drug's connection to the rainbow can be read as an affirmation of queerness, a reminder that all members of this Afro-diasporic religious triad—Esther, Eric, and Acilde—are queer-identified. Third, colors are technologies of the *misterios*, *lwa*, and *orishas*. In Santería/Regla de Ocha, the rainbow is a marker of las Siete Potencias Africanas. Each *orisha* is associated with a color, making the representation of las Siete Potencias a multicolored one. The techno-resonance of the rainbow increases in light of Joseph M. Murphy's observation that "the famous chromolithograph of the *òrìṣà* as the 'Seven African Powers' appears to have arisen under the influence of Spiritism" ("Òrìṣà Traditions" 477). In La 21 División, the *jarro divisional* (divisional pitcher) used at the beginning of any ritual to offer a libation of sacred water to the *misterios* is decorated with the colors of all the spiritual divisions (Davis, *La otra ciencia* 314).[65] These overlapping techno-resonances reveal that the setting of Acilde's life-altering medical procedure is ritualistically aligned with elements of Afro-diasporic religious initiation.

Despite this context, Acilde is only interested in the allopathic qualities of Rainbow Bright. They become alarmed when Eric places offerings of raw rice at the four corners of the bed where they will be tied down. Eric explains that these are "ofrendas para que todo salga bien" (*La mucama* 65).[66] Acilde's disregard for Afro-diasporic religious knowledge is showcased when they describe the rice offerings as "folkloric," a view that reflects how nation-states have traditionally depicted Afro-diasporic traditions (Palmié, *The Cooking* 18). Nonetheless, even Acilde recognizes that in addition to his medical supplies, Eric has come equipped with *cascarilla*, a white eggshell chalk powder used in Santería/Regla de Ocha for purification and protection that Acilde had seen Omiculné use in her apartment. In Acilde's initiation, Eric uses *cascarilla* to draw symbols on the floor and the wall to spiritually charge the makeshift initiation chamber he has constructed in Villa Mella.[67] The novel does not reveal much more about the symbols or describe what they look like, but the Afro-diasporic religious world offers an opportunity to identify them as another moment of techno-resonance.

Cascarilla can be used to create sacred designs for protection or invocation, and chalk designs are often used in Benin for Olokun worship (Rosen; Mason, *Olóòkun* 57). Continuing with the scene's engagements with *kanzo*, Haitian Vodou's sacred symbols (*vèvè*) provide the most direct entry point for identifying the techno-resonance of Eric's actions.[68] Notably, La 21 División uses *vèvè*, although the Dominican rendition of these symbols may be called *claves* (keys), and they are less embellished than their Haitian counterparts (Davis, *La otra ciencia* 312–313).[69] Métraux notes that "*vèvè* reveal the presence of the god in a tangible form," and "merely by tracing them out a priest puts pressure on the *loa* and compels them to appear. Their function is to summon *loa*" (165). Bridging the physical world with the spiritual, *vèvè* are one manifestation of Solimar Otero's contention that "in Vodoun metaphysics, sacred spaces are drawn, created, and the potential for communication between the worlds is induced by ritual and ceremony" ("Èṣù" 200). Otero's recent book, *Archives of Conjure: Stories of the Dead in Afrolatinx Cultures*, is in dialogue with my concept of techno-resonance in that she argues that *vèvè* "provoke an efficient and dense construction of a third dimensional space analogous to holographic and virtual experiences of connectivity" (39). Beyond blurring the borders between ritual and secular technologies, *vèvè* dissolve the boundaries between physical and sacred realms, allowing energies and entities to be spiritually downloaded.

While Santería/Regla de Ocha does not use *vèvè* or *claves*, it does employ the *osun*. *La mucama* invokes the *osun* through the crownlike markings on Acilde's head. These birthmarks, through which Eric identifies Acilde as Olokun's heir, become the focal point of the connection between Acilde and the *orisha* during initiation, bringing to mind the role of the *osun*. Used after the first day of *kari ocha* has taken place, the *osun* is the "signature of the governing orisha, a series of painted designs using impermanent pigments emanating from the apex or crown of the head indicating a lifelong bond between the deity and the person" (Tsang, "The Power" 137). Like *vèvè*, the *osun* promotes the energy of a particular entity. It also functions as a spiritual seal as it brands the *iyawo* as the child of their tutelary *orisha* and helps promote the physical integration of the spiritual process of initiation that has already taken place. Innovation surrounds the sacred technology of the *osun* since some of its elements "have no direct Yoruba or diasporic parallels" (D. H. Brown 200). Hence, while in Acilde's initiation the drawing of the *osun* is not performed traditionally, its specter surrounds the ceremony in the tell-tale moles on Acilde's head. The changes Rainbow Bright causes in Acilde's body underscore the importance of their spiritual crown; when the injection enables Acilde's body to transition from female to male, their epidermal *osun* remains intact.

The crown of moles on Acilde's head serves as the physical entry point for the energy that initiates them as Omo Olokun.[70] This ritual operation takes place when Eric, determined to fulfill his spiritual mandate before his imminent death, places the tentacles of the sea anemone in contact with Acilde's head, plugging Acilde into the spiritual force of the ocean, Olokun.[71] Eric is able to proceed with the Santería/Regla de Ocha ritual unchallenged because Acilde is restrained to the bed and is severely debilitated by the scouring effects of the Rainbow Bright injection. Yet, Acilde never consents to initiation; they have not even been informed that this would happen, something that would be unheard of in the initiation processes of La 21 División, Haitian Vodou, and Santería/Regla de Ocha.

Although unable to stop the process, Acilde curses when Eric begins praying to Olokun and simultaneously places the sea anemone's tentacles in direct contact with the moles on Acilde's head. The initiation presented in *La mucama* becomes the final violation of Acilde's body, a disturbing techno-resonant moment that transforms what should be a chosen act of salvation into a perpetual state of exploitation. Now, not even Acilde's body belongs to them.

Upon completing Acilde's initiation to Olokun, the last words Eric Vitier says to Acilde are "Esther sabía todo lo que iba a pasar. Yo ya estoy pago, te dimos el cuerpo que querías y ahora tú nos has dado el cuerpo que necesitábamos" (70).[72] In this crucial moment, the toll of Eric's transgression becomes apparent through the phrase "estar pago" (to no longer be in someone's debt). Upon completion of the initiation ritual, Eric dies, paying the debt incurred by his spiritual transgressions. What this makes clear is that in the religious world of *La mucama*, it is the spirits who are keeping score, and only they can decide who is indeed "pago," debtless. Eric's final words also reveal that although Acilde has received something priceless through initiation, they have also incurred an outstanding debt. As described by Palmié:

> Once established by metonymically installing the deity in the initiate's head . . . such relationships cannot be terminated by either party and must be maintained in what is thought of, ideally, as a chain of reciprocal prestations. (*Wizards* 166)

It will now be up to Acilde to discover what they have been initiated into and how they will settle the score.

Despite being bequeathed the enormous task of saving the sea and by extension the world, Acilde does not receive a formal *itá*. The *itá* is a life-determining divination session that takes place on the third day after initiation and is traditionally performed by the *obá-oriaté*. In *La mucama*, the importance of the *itá* is evident in the lives of Esther and Eric, as through it they are informed of their spiritual destinies. Nonetheless, due to the dire circumstances under which Acilde is initiated, Acilde is left without a religious community. Rather than be cared for by their spiritual family, as would be the case in a traditional *kari ocha*, Acilde is rescued by President Said Bona. Bona, a child of Legba who had been the recipient of Esther's spiritual advice for years, had been warned that the time would come for him to administer his support to "the chosen one." Unbeknownst to Acilde, Bona is prepared to offer whatever is needed to fulfill Acilde's sacred mission.

The problem is that Acilde has no idea what their mission is. All they receive as guidance is a virtual message from Esther recorded before her death, another distinct moment of techno-resonance in the text.[73] Bona projects the recorded hologram for Acilde in the hospital, where they are still recovering from the life-altering physical and spiritual procedures they have undergone. Echoing the digital sound of the wave that opened the novel with the electronically programmed doorbell, this moment furthers the novel's blending of cyber and religious technologies. In this virtual message, a phantasmagoric Omicunlé tells Acilde, "Said cuenta contigo, utiliza los poderes que recién empiezas a descubrir para el bien de la humanidad. Salva el mar, Maferefún Olokun, Maferefún Yemayá" (*La mucama* 114).[74] Esther's techno-resonant transmission makes clear that Olokun and Yemayá are vital energies in Acilde's life and mission through the use of the Lukumí word *maferefún*, which evokes thanks and praise.[75]

The power Acilde slowly discovers they have access to is their ability to exist simultaneously in multiple time periods through male avatars. These alternate existences are facilitated in the 1990s and 2000s through Giorgio and in the seventeenth century through Roque. The moment Acilde wakes up in the hospital after the initiation and the Rainbow Bright transition have taken place, the first thought they have is "*Tengo dos cuerpos o es que mi mente tiene la capacidad de transmitir en dos canales de programación simultánea?*" (*La mucama* 110, italics in the original).[76] This wording appears in a chapter titled "Update," elucidating the novel's investment in capitalizing on the techno-resonances between Afro-diasporic religious currents and secular technology. What could be understood as a complex state of possession, a key trait of many Afro-diasporic religions, is rendered into the cyber language of transmission and programming. Techno-resonance explains why Herrero-Martín argues that the "time-space coordinates of the novel" are woven together through "engram-based streaming," defined as a "narrative thread [that] basically features the chemical-neural weaving of synapses or associations of thoughts, feelings and emotions" (58). *La mucama* presents all of these times as occurring simultaneously for Acilde, whose enhanced level of consciousness is only possible after *both* the scientific and the spiritual operations that have radically altered their being transpire. In other words, to read the multiplicity of Acilde's consciousness as one that bridges secular and religious time, it is essential to consider how the techno-resonances between these systems determine Acilde's life before, during, and after their physical transition/spiritual initiation.

Spiritual possession is often described as a displacement of one's consciousness from one's body while the energy of an ancestor, *lwa*, *misterio*, or *orisha* floods into it. However, other understandings are possible. According to Roberto Strongman:

> Many experienced priests of the religion confess to having developed the ability to retain such full consciousness while the divinity is on their heads that they are able to go about their quotidian life as they easily slip in and out of trance throughout their day. (*Queering* 251)

The same concept is expressed in Haitian Vodou's *nan dòmi*, a state of lucid dreaming (Smartt Bell 29). Precisely, this collapsing of time and space is what Acilde experiences through their avatars, underscoring the importance of looking to moments of techno-resonance in the novel to understand how the epistemologies and ontologies of Afro-diasporic religions help shape *La mucama de Omicunlé*.

Regardless of their professed powers, Acilde is a new initiate, an *iyawo*. What this means is that once their initiation is complete, Acilde is thrust into an exceptional positioning, as described by C. Lynn Carr:

> The *iyawo* is a distilled embodiment of identification on the margins. Not only is the *iyawo* considered to be and treated as inhabiting a liminal status in the Lukumí rite of passage, but the *iyawo*—like the Heinleinian "cat who walks through walls," regularly crossing the borders of religion, gender, ethnicity, minority and majority, mainstream and occult, sacred and profane— epitomizes the multiplicity and fragmentary nature of identification for many in contemporary pluralism. (10)

Santería/Regla de Ocha's process of *iyaworaje*, a transitional phase that lasts a year and a day from the initiate's *kari ocha*, is an experience of simultaneously dismantling and reconstructing the world. Such a perspective allows the reader to see Acilde's connection to Giorgio and Roque not as a fantastical side effect of contact with the sacred sea anemone but as a process of recalibrating one's position in the world after breaking down the barrier between the secular and the sacred.

Like so much in *La mucama*, Acilde's *iyaworaje* is anything but typical. Acilde does not understand the spiritual processes they are undergoing or why they are happening, and they lack the direct guidance of religious elders. Still, the novel preserves the sense of isolation that distinguishes the *iyaworaje*. With Bona's assistance, Acilde agrees to go to jail to appease those demanding justice for Esther's murder. Even as Acilde's prison stay severely limits the physical rhythms of their life, it emulates the spiritual purpose of the *iyaworaje*, which is to allow the initiate to develop a relationship with their *orishas* and spirits, understanding themselves as no longer being one but multiple. In prison Acilde meets Iván de la Barra, a Cuban man who is not formally initiated but who possesses knowledge of Espiritismo and of Santería/Regla de Ocha and provides Acilde with some spiritual instruction.

Acilde's time in prison is eerily pleasant; for the first time in their life all of their needs are met. Their day-to-day routine consists of resting and connecting to their avatars. Acilde is not allowed to have a data plan in prison, but their initiation as Omo Olokun keeps them perpetually plugged into the universe. Acilde's time in jail exemplifies how the techno-resonance between secular and spiritual technologies enables Acilde to develop a new operating system. Despite their seemingly constrained location, Olokun and Acilde are intrinsically uncontainable. As Norma Rosen notes, "Because there is water in the air, Olokun can move freely" (53). In this regard, the unbounded quality of Olokun's energies within Acilde parallels how knowledge, virtual and otherwise, functions in the novel.

Acilde's stay at the prison, ominously named La Victoria (Victory), is so pleasant that it extends far beyond the year and a day of the *iyaworaje*. At Acilde's request, it lasts a decade. During their imprisonment, Acilde, through access to their avatars Giorgio and Roque, has carefully orchestrated a plan to save the sea by buying (privatizing) a pristine section of the beach in Sosúa called Playa Bo. Acilde believes that by using cutting-edge technology in Playa Bo to develop strains of coral that can be replanted into the ocean they can fulfill their sacred mission. This, in turn, would give them the privilege of enjoying life as a white-passing European man, Giorgio Menicucci, in the Dominican Republic of the 1990s and 2000s.[77] But everything comes crashing down when Acilde-Giorgio realizes that all they have devised is not the fulfillment of their mission but rather an intricate buildup to an encounter with a young Said Bona, the very man who, as president, has allowed Acilde to design their life as Giorgio from inside La Victoria prison.

Bona is the one responsible for the maritime disaster that destroys the Caribbean Sea, and it is this crisis Acilde, as Olokun's child, has been birthed to avert. Acilde quickly realizes that in order to save the sea they must sacrifice everything they have painstakingly built through their lives as Giorgio and Roque, a crisis that is compounded by their looming eviction from La Victoria:

> Tras diez años en La Victoria, cómodo, tranquilo, sin más responsabilidad que comer y respirar, saldría ahora al mundo exterior, donde el asfalto se quedaba pegado a las suelas como chicle. Tendría que trabajar, por ejemplo. ¿Cómo iba a atender sus asuntos, sus otras vidas, sus negocios? (*La mucama* 168)[78]

Faced with the destruction of the oasis they have built for themselves, Acilde goes rogue. They pull the plug rather than fulfill their divine mission as Omo Olokun, opting for suicide when faced with life outside La Victoria prison.

Acilde overdoses on sleeping pills, suddenly and terminally severing the connection between themselves, Giorgio, and Roque. The last sentences of *La mucama* read:

> Podía sacrificarlo todo menos esta vida, la vida de Giorgio Menicucci, la compañía de su mujer, la galería, el laboratorio. [...] En poco tiempo se olvidará de Acilde, de Roque, incluso de lo que vive en un hueco allá abajo en el arrecife. (180-181)[79]

Acilde's decision to commit suicide sacrifices their life for Giorgio's, completing a horrific cycle of devaluation that began in their mother's womb, was perpetuated by their family and by Eric Vitier, and ultimately ends by their own hand. Rather than being an egotistical decision, however, Acilde's apparent refusal to complete their sacred mission elucidates the failure of collective support. Without the networks of care and knowledge that would have allowed Acilde to understand the depths of their responsibility, they relinquish the opportunity to save the world and instead opt for individual survival through the guise of Giorgio. This decision shows that although the spiritual and secular technologies to support Acilde's mission were in place, the teachings that would have enabled them to understand their purpose were absent. Hence, the collapse of the Esther-Eric-Acilde religious triad leads to the dissolution of the techno-resonant triad of Acilde-Giorgio-Roque.

The novel's ending reveals that the energies of Olokun and Yemayá cannot create a miracle on their own. While Santería/Regla de Ocha generates the possibility of an alternative script, in order for the narrative to change, those with access to spiritual knowledge and power (Esther-Eric-Acilde) must take proper action, something each one is unable or unwilling to wholly do. Here, Beliso-De Jesús's words become urgent, a prophecy in their own right:

> Santería does not offer a utopia. Rather, it assumes the terrors of violence and negotiations with negativities as part and parcel of the everyday. Copresences are haunting conjurings of seething imperfections, partialities that link injustice and marginality but also produce new problematic relationships. In their analytic capacity, copresences provide visibility and opportunity but also might be complicit with new lines of power. (*Electric Santería* 102)

Beliso-De Jesús's warning of how the copresences of Santería/Regla de Ocha can become "complicit with new lines of power" is precisely what Indiana's novel exposes when Esther's, Eric's, and Acilde's plan to save the sea is aborted.

OTHER ALLIANCES, OTHER FUTURES: TECHNO-RESONANCE AS POSSIBILITY

In *La mucama de Omicunlé* hope is a barely perceptible wavelength found in the (un)expected techno-resonances between Afro-diasporic and Indigenous spiritual knowledges, both of which lie in the waters. These connections appear through the inclusion of two vital characters in Acilde-Giorgio's timeline who help them acclimate to the twentieth century, Ananí and Nenuco. Located in the town of Sosúa in the late 1990s and early 2000s, Ananí and

Nenuco are descendants of the Indigenous Taíno peoples who inhabited the Caribbean long before the arrival of European colonizers.[80] Although the violence of settler colonialism decimated Indigenous populations in the Caribbean and in the Americas as a whole, these autochthonous peoples were not exterminated as is often suggested by traditional historiography. Some created subversive alliances with free Blacks and *cimarrones* (maroons) to facilitate survival, and these allegiances endure in the Indigenous currents that circulate in La 21 División. Ricourt notes:

> The few Tainos who survived diseases, abusive working conditions, and genocidal attacks interacted intimately with Africans and their spiritual conceptions of the divine, the earth, and nature. This melding of African and Taino religions has survived in [Dominican] Vodou [La 21 División] until today, affecting its adherents' valuations of such natural phenomenon [*sic*] as the sun and moon, plants, animals, bodies of water, lightning, rain, and hurricanes. (*The Dominican* 108)

The division associated with the Indigenous inhabitants of Hispaniola in La 21 División is linked to water (Davis, *La otra ciencia* 138). This spiritual reality emphasizes water's capacity for sustaining dissonance and multiplicity in the face of hegemonic history. In the context of *La mucama*, it exemplifies the reach of water's techno-resonances through the veneration of the aquatic that Anani and Nenuco enact in Indiana's novel.

Despite the continued threat of dispossession, Anani's family has been able to maintain ownership of the land that contains the sacred waters into which Giorgio will be born upon Acilde's religious contact with the sea anemone.[81] Anani and Nenuco are prepared for Acilde-Giorgio's arrival because they have been taught by their ancestors about the "hombres del agua, que venían cada cierto tiempo a ayudarlos" (*La mucama* 103).[82] While neither Anani nor Nenuco pronounces the name Olokun, they have no doubts as to the sacredness of the being that will emerge from the sea. Their disposition reflects aspects of Taíno cosmology since the culture's main spiritual deities, Atabey (Mother of the Lake Waters) and Yocahú (Yuca Lord of the Ocean), are connected to water (Oliver 237–238). Construed as mother and son, Atabey and Yocahú represent masculine and feminine energies, akin to those Olokun embodies. Yet, José R. Oliver provocatively offers that Yocahú's name might actually be "*Luku-* or *Loko-hú*, in which case it would mean 'Person (*loko*) Lord (*-hú*)'—that is, 'Person-Lord of the Ocean'"(238). This latter etymology powerfully resonates with Olokun's name in Santería/Regla de Ocha, providing a resounding though submerged connection between these systems of knowledge. Hence, it is through the epistemological and ontological techno-resonance of water that Indiana's novel blends the currents of La 21 División with those of Santería/Regla de Ocha to offer the possibility of an alternate world.

In *La mucama* there is a pivotal but brief moment of physical convergence and receptivity between the liquid knowledges of La 21 División and Santería/ Regla de Ocha. Shortly after their arrival in Sosúa, Acilde-Giorgio has a sexual encounter with Yararí. Yararí, the daughter of Ananí and Nenuco, rejects her family's spiritual practices. Yet, upon seeing Acilde-Giorgio she takes it upon herself to sexually arouse them and mount them. As they exchange bodily fluids, Acilde-Giorgio gains access to their past (or future). In a techno-resonant moment that uses consensual contact between Afro-diasporic and Indigenous bodies to repudiate centuries of (sexual) violence, the encounter between Yararí and Acilde-Giorgio is generative in multiple ways. Beyond the knowledge Acilde-Giorgio gains access to, the novel's omniscient narrator suggests that when Yararí disappears from her family's house, "estaba preñada" (*La mucama* 116).[83] No further information is given about Yararí and the sacred being she might be carrying, yet the very possibility of its existence allows hope to flourish unexpectedly. Could it be that Acilde's mission to save the ocean will be fulfilled through the inner waters of Yararí's amniotic fluid?

In *La mucama de Omicunlé*, readers never learn the fate of Ananí and Nenuco, the keepers and watchers of "la puerta a la tierra del principio" (105).[84] Though indispensable in ushering Acilde-Giorgio into the Sosúa of the 1990s, once they are thriving Ananí and Nenuco recede into the background. What will happen to Giorgio once Acilde dies likewise is not disclosed. I read these silences as moments that make legible the limits of the secular imagination. What kinds of worlds could we imagine if we conceived of communities as entities that were neither severed nor predetermined by histories of colonialism and neoliberalism? The guarding of sacred knowledges enacted by Ananí and Nenuco infuses *La mucama* with the possibility of making the world anew by affirming the techno-resonances between Afro and Indigenous worldviews. The unscripted futures of these characters in an otherwise densely populated novel presents the challenge of imagining otherwise, a process in which Afro-diasporic waters and the knowledges they carry are poised to play an instrumental role, if only we can save them from extinction.

CHAPTER THREE

Afro-Diasporic Currents in the Gloria Evangelina Anzaldúa Papers

Gloria Anzaldúa had various spiritual and out-of-body experiences throughout her life, one of which took place in the waters of South Padre Island, Texas, during her childhood. In a 1983 interview Anzaldúa declares:

> [Spirituality] connected me to the strength—to the soul and the source of power—which I can channel into myself. Part of this power is myself. It's sort of like there's an ocean out there that you call consciousness, and I have a little part of that ocean within myself. I realized this when I was about ten years old, when I almost drown[ed]. ("Within" 112)

Anzaldúa's near-drowning is not often referenced by scholars, likely because the writer herself did not underscore this experience in her publications.[1] Yet, the contents of Anzaldúa's archive reveal that this event was pivotal in transforming water into a recurrent space of communion and ceremony in her life and work.

What Anzaldúa experienced at South Padre Island sheds light on the significance of her choice to begin *Borderlands/La Frontera: The New Mestiza*, her first single-authored book, at the ocean. It also adds depth to a description found in the first chapter of her posthumously published book, *Light in the Dark/Luz en lo oscuro: Rewriting Identity, Spirituality, Reality*, where Anzaldúa processes the trauma of 9/11 and "take[s her] sorrow for a walk" by the water, where she feels that "even the sea is grieving" (10).[2] In both instances, she indicates that the ocean has a name, Yemayá, the *orisha* of saltwaters in Santería/Regla de Ocha. As early as 1981, Anzaldúa's biographical statement in *This Bridge Called My Back* identified her as a daughter of Yemayá (Moraga and Anzaldúa 277). Together, these details demonstrate that Yemayá's energies accompanied Anzaldúa throughout her life, providing her with ongoing creative and spiritual sustenance.

Despite moments of indisputable evidence, the profundity of the spiritual relationship between Anzaldúa and Yemayá cannot be gleaned solely through published material. Instead, this path must be charted with the aid of Anzaldúa's overflowing archive, the Gloria Evangelina Anzaldúa Papers (GEA Papers), located at the Nettie Lee Benson Latin American Collection at the University of Texas at Austin.[3] Every moment I spent sifting through this collection was humbling. Those who have read Anzaldúa's published work know that she was adamant about excavating every aspect of her being, no matter how painful. What is less apparent are the depths into which she plunged to develop her *conocimientos*, journeys her archive allows us to fathom.[4]

Still, the GEA Papers do not simply include a folder labeled "Yemayá" that provides all the answers. To conjure an understanding of Anzaldúa's connection to this *orisha*, I had to consider her relationship to water as a whole. To accomplish this, I found myself wading through hundreds of documents, slowly composing a story that traversed key instances of Anzaldúa's childhood in South Texas and included important moments during the late 1970s and 1980s when she lived on the West Coast and the East Coast. Anzaldúa came into contact with Caribbean diasporic communities on the East Coast, and it was there that she penned most of *Borderlands*. Furthermore, the 1980s were critical years for Anzaldúa's health, a realm of her life where Yemayá played an influential role. By reading with and through the GEA Papers, in this chapter I provide a spiritual genealogy of Anzaldúa's communion with water, one that is as cognizant of her experiences with Afro-diasporic religiosity as it is of her theorizations through and from fluidity. In doing so, I honor Anzaldúa's commitment to "bridging" as her life and work generate meaningful connections between Caribbean, Chicanx, and Latinx worlds.

The way Afro-diasporic spiritual genealogies refute the hold of borders and chronology is a productive framework from which to approach the GEA Papers. This collection eschews order as a tool for organizing, processing, and defining its contents because of its constantly shifting nature. Instead, the GEA Papers can be productively approached through Solimar Otero's concept of "archives of conjure": "work in archives of conjure disrupts the desire to create a neat timeline, to relate a linear narrative that will fall easily into recognized canons of knowledge-making in terms of the past and culture" (*Archives* 41). The GEA Papers also trouble how the establishment of an author's chronology relies on the linear organization of their works. But what happens when what an author has published does not reflect most of what they have written? This is one of the many questions researchers face as they gaze into box after box of Anzaldúa's unpublished materials. To consider Anzaldúa's published matter in light of her archive, then, is to embrace dissonance and contradiction. It is also tantamount to centering revision as praxis when we approach her work.

UNBORDERING ANZALDÚA:
NAVIGATING THE GEA PAPERS

In *The Borders of Dominicanidad*, Lorgia García-Peña introduces the concept of "bordering." While borders are typically linked to a particular space and can thus appear to be rooted, García-Peña's use of the gerund "bordering" calls attention to their incessantly shifting qualities. The term also addresses how borders become imposed upon bodies regardless of where they are located. Bordering can manifest anywhere the structures of control implicit in borders have left their indelible mark, alluding to their multiple roots and routes.[5] As a self-described border woman, Gloria Anzaldúa knew what it was like to have the US/Mexico border etched on her back, one of the many reasons the body is paramount in her work. Still, bordering makes clear that borders also exist far beyond the physical plane.

Bordering underscores how borders themselves have predetermined the parts of Anzaldúa that are visible to us and those that are not. In a letter dated August 18, 1995, Anzaldúa expresses anger at how her biography would often be "socially reconstructed" in an effort to "mainstream" her work ("Aunt Lute Books," box 7, folder 4, GEA Papers). She writes, "I don't call myself an Hispanic and use Latina and lesbian reservedly—I prefer dyke or queer." Tellingly, Anzaldúa asserts, "By erasing parts of my identity these editors are saying that we all speak and write from the same social locations" ("Aunt Lute Books," box 7, folder 4, GEA Papers). This letter demonstrates that Anzaldúa was aware of how, despite the transgressive openness of her work, attempts to market it were often confining and limiting if not explicitly violent.

Written less than a decade before her untimely passing in May 2004, Anzaldúa letter exposes the siren call of respectability politics against which she struggled throughout her career. As Juana María Rodríguez observes, queer women of color are not only called to conform to societal norms for the common good, but if they do not comply, they are "disciplined through public shame and censure, and subjected to the power of pathology and criminalization" (10). The way Anzaldúa's sexual identity was downplayed, diluted, or simply removed from view is evidence of this very censure. Nonetheless, scholars currently read Anzaldúa as a Chicana whose queerness has been recovered, documented, and asserted, challenging these initial attempts of straight-washing.[6] Anzaldúa's letter, however, should make us wonder about other aspects of her personhood that may have been sanitized in an attempt to make her legible and legitimate.

Anzaldúa's writing sought to move past limitations established by citizenship, language, race, and sexuality, among others. Yet, considering her work solely through the methodological lenses developed by disciplinary training inevitably pushes it into these molds, discarding what refuses to be boxed in. For example,

Anzaldúa has been defined as a Chicana writer, a Border writer, and a writer who unearthed significant aspects of the pre-Columbian past to infuse new life and meaning into the disjointedness she experienced throughout her life. Coyolxauhqui, the Mexica moon goddess, is a critical symbol for Anzaldúa, a fact reinforced by the posthumous publication of *Light in the Dark/Luz en lo oscuro*.[7] Picking up the pieces, moving them around, and creating meaning where previously there had only been rupture is one of the hallmarks of Anzaldúan thought. But does this understanding encompass the breadth of her writing and thinking? What do we do with the parts of Anzaldúa that flow past Coyolxauhqui? The answers to these questions position Anzaldúa as a theorist who is often cited but, according to Linda Martín Alcoff, "remains undertheorized" (256). They also suggest that while the pieces of Anzaldúa that have come to be known are important, she also had other selves that have not yet been placed in dialogue with the dominant vision of her put forth by the academy.[8]

One of the aspects of Anzaldúa's work that merits further critical attention is the development of her spirituality. For Anzaldúa, spirituality was about survival. She writes, "I would have gone stark raving mad had I not had the spirituality. Because it helped me get over everything" ("Within" 111). Anzaldúa's words are an invitation to understand her spirituality as a critical posture, one that helped her re-envision not only the world but her place in it. The connection between the ocean and spirituality manifests many times in Anzaldúa's work, a function that is more than a metaphor since for Anzaldúa "metaphors *are* gods" ("Border Arte" 180, emphasis in the original). Water's function as a bridge between the tangible and the intangible in Anzaldúa's spiritual development resonates with Omise'eke Natasha Tinsley's assertion that "we should [never] strip theory of watery metaphors but . . . we should return to the materiality of water to make its metaphors mean more complexly" (212). In Anzaldúa's work, water presents an opportunity to engage with how her multifaceted spirituality dialogues with Afro-diasporic *and* Indigenous traditions.

The intimate connection between Anzaldúa's life and her work exemplifies a central concept of feminist methodologies: the assertion of the self as a source of knowledge. A pivotal point for this epistemological turn was the 1981 publication of *This Bridge Called My Back*, edited by Cherríe Moraga and Anzaldúa. Described by Aída Hurtado as "a primordial scream of rebellion and claiming of intellectual and existential space" (215), *Bridge* proposes the concept of "theory in the flesh." Intricately linked to the now abundantly used term "intersectionality," *Bridge* defines "theory in the flesh" as one "where the physical realities of our lives—our skin color, the land or concrete we grew up on, our sexual longings—all fuse to create a politic born out of necessity" (Moraga and Anzaldúa, "Entering the Lives" 19). By mining the cacophonous intersections of race, class, gender, and sexuality, theory in the flesh transforms the body into a source from which knowledge emanates, implicitly affirming that embodiment is a gateway to other realms. Such a concept resonates with the ontological underpinnings of the corporeal in Afro-diasporic religions.[9] It also describes the role that Anzaldúa's largest textual body, the GEA Papers, plays in my analysis.

There is no one poem, short story, or *autohistoria-teoría* that can fully explain the multiple roles water played in Anzaldúa's life, but much can be surmised from navigating the contents of the GEA Papers.[10] Suzanne Bost and AnaLouise Keating, two leading Anzaldúa scholars, attest to the archive's potential to radically alter what we think we know about the author and her work. Keating goes as far as to say that "Anzaldúa's archive contains enough material to generate a small academic industry" ("Archival Alchemy" 164). The GEA Papers are an exceptional reservoir that pulsates with life, echoing the archival power of the ocean underscored by Santos-Febres's *boat people* and Indiana's *La mucama de Omicunlé*. The GEA Papers also divulge more of Anzaldúa's creative process than one would have considered possible, posing a challenge for even the most experienced researcher.

Consisting of more than two hundred boxes, the GEA Papers resist our desire to label, exemplifying Anzaldúa's lifelong struggle to defy the borders of normativity. The archive includes everything from Anzaldúa's birth certificates (yes, she had more than one) to multiple versions of published works and hundreds of unpublished ones.[11] It also contains correspondence, photographs, and many writing notes as well as "doorknob placards, ticket stubs, appointment cards, fliers [and] doodles (Bost, "Messy Archives" 616). The collection even preserves Anzaldúa's voice in hundreds of digitized recordings. The vastness of the GEA Papers precludes imposing any sense of order when working with its materials. Many documents have multiple versions, shifting titles, incomplete dates or are entirely undated and lack page numbers.[12] Others include comments by Anzaldúa and her writing *comadres*, toying with the limits of authorship.[13] The archive evinces that Anzaldúa's chronic revision process did not stop after publication, challenging notions of final versions.[14] Then there is the added hurdle of access. Several of the unpublished materials from the GEA Papers are restricted to on-site reading only; other than note taking, no reproduction is allowed.[15]

Despite the unwieldiness of the collection, various documents in the GEA Papers offer information about Anzaldúa's relationship with water. Some of these are the unpublished short story "En el hocico del mar" and two autobiographical documents, titled "Autoretratos de la artista as a Young Girl" and "Autohistoria de la artista as a Young Girl."[16] "Autoretratos" and "Autohistoria" are distinct versions of a series of autobiographical vignettes that include mention of Anzaldúa's near-drowning at South Padre Island but also speak to various other experiences. Anzaldúa describes these vignettes as "portraits of the traumas in the life of a woman writer" (Autohistoria, box 57, folder 10, p. 2, GEA

Papers). The stand-alone story "En el hocico del mar" is strictly based on her near-drowning at South Padre Island.[17] Taken together, these archival materials help plumb the origins of Anzaldúa's identification with the sea.

In each of these documents, Anzaldúa speaks of South Padre Island, a place Anzaldúa would visit with her family in the summertime. Another overlap between them is the figure of Prieta, Anzaldúa's literary alter ego.[18] Since the 1981 publication of her first *autohistoria-teoría*, "La Prieta," the author continually collapsed, rewrote, and blurred the boundaries between herself and Prieta.[19] The creation of Prieta was driven by Anzaldúa's need to establish distance from difficult life experiences in order to write about them (Anzaldúa, "Doing Gigs" 223). Given the recurrent engagement with pain, illness, and death in Anzaldúa's work, this posture is clarifying and of primordial importance.

Anzaldúa's near-drowning at South Padre Island when she was approximately 10 years old marks the second of her four living encounters with death, all of which she viewed as spiritually driven.[20] My research revealed that this moment is pivotal to understanding the spiritual origin of Anzaldúa's relationship to the ocean and Yemayá. Drowning has a distinct historical and religious charge in the Afro-diasporic world. It is also recurrently invoked in the literary renditions of initiation I discuss in this book due to the spiritual death and rebirth these ceremonies elicit. Thus, akin to the boat people's experiences in Santos-Febres's poems, Anzaldúa receives access to previously submerged spiritual knowledge while underwater.

In the summers when Anzaldúa's father was still alive, the family would sometimes travel to South Padre Island, a stretch of land in South Texas that leads into the Gulf of Mexico. When I visited South Padre in November 2017, I was jolted by how the palm trees that greeted me evoked the Puerto Rican seascapes I grew up in. Although the location is now popular with vacationers, for the Anzaldúas the trip was often tied to work. At times her father would catch shrimp off the island because "*la cosecha se había perdido*, the crops had been lost." ("Autorretratos," box 57, folder 12, p. 19, italics in the original). It was at South Padre Island that Anzaldúa first encountered the sea, and the impression this body of water made on her would have ripple effects throughout her life.

Anzaldúa writes:

> Seeing the Ocean for the first time when I was little something happened to me. I marveled [and] felt shock from my head to my toes at the sight of this moving flowing mass that breathed and had a heartbeat. It was alive, it had a personality, I'd felt this with trees, the sky, the wind but I knew with certainty that I should not tell anyone. No one talked of such things. ("Autorretratos," box 57, folder 12, p. 22)

This passage poignantly expresses how Anzaldúa had always recognized her difference from others, a difference that affected how she interacted and communicated with herself and with the natural world. The alienation she felt as a result of this difference led her to wonder if she was from another planet (Anzaldúa, "La Prieta" 199). The passage reveals the importance of understanding the prevalence of spiritual *corrientes* (currents) in initiating Anzaldúa's connection to the ocean, given that she describes a sense of shock running the length of her body upon laying eyes on the water. Similar experiences are recounted by Santería/Regla de Ocha practitioners when connecting to their *orishas* and to their ancestors (*egun*). In Marta Moreno Vega's memoir, *The Altar of My Soul: The Living Traditions of Santería*, she describes a dreamlike encounter with her ancestors as they express approval of her upcoming initiation, her *kari ocha*, to the *orisha* Obatalá.[21] Closely replicating the sensorial experience Anzaldúa encountered when looking at the ocean, Moreno Vega "felt an electrical shock rush through [her] body" as evidence of her spiritual connection (*The Altar* 139). Anzaldúa's description also aligns with Aisha M. Beliso-De Jesús's contention of spiritual *corrientes* as energies that "electrif[y] the bodies of practitioners in close proximity," leading them to "discuss [spiritual] currents in terms of bodily feeling" (*Electric Santería* 70–71). The language of Afro-diasporic religiosity thus renders Anzaldúa's experience at the water as a spiritually legible moment.

The resonance between Anzaldúa's shock and the spiritual *corrientes* of Santería/Regla de Ocha is reinforced by Anzaldúa's recollection that the first place she feels the presence of the water's energy in her body is on her head. The head is a vital bodily site and a repository for spiritual energies in *orisha* worship.[22] It is also in the head and through the head that the human body is infused with the sacred in the initiation rituals of Haitian Vodou's *kanzo*, the *bautizos* of the La 21 División, and Santería/Regla de Ocha's *kari ocha*. However, even before any act of initiation takes place, the head is a sacred node in Santería/Regla de Ocha. As Martin A. Tsang contends:

> The human body is the repository of several proto-divinities that animate the body and connect the human to the heavenly. The *orí*, or seat of destiny, resides in the physical head and is linked to its spiritual counterpart, *iponrí*. It is the combination of the spiritual and the physical *orí* that animates the body. ("Beguiling Eshu" 219)

Tsang's passage describes how epistemological and ontological synergy in Santería/Regla de Ocha can be visualized by considering the role of the head in this tradition. This framework allows readers to interpret the sensation that begins in Anzaldúa's head and runs the length of her body as the stimulation of her physical and spiritual *orí* when gazing at the sea. This reading is reinforced by the fact that Anzaldúa receives both energy and information from the water. Upon feeling this *corriente*, she affirms the aliveness of the ocean by underscoring that it breathes and has a heartbeat.[23] More than a mere moment of observation, what Anzaldúa narrates here is an experience of deep and mutual recognition. Her spirit is activated by the sight of the sea.

Of course, water is not the only aspect of nature Anzaldúa mentions in this passage. She describes similar moments of connection with the sky, the trees, and the wind, all of which are important spiritual actors in nonhegemonic spiritual traditions. As Zora Neale Hurston observes, Haitian Vodou is "a religion of creation and life. It is the worship of the sun, the water and other natural forces" (113). Moreno Vega extends Hurston's observation by identifying synergies between Afro-diasporic and Indigenous religious systems: "Native American religions worship every aspect of nature, and their affirmation that we live on sacred Mother Earth is similar to Santería's belief that all aspects of nature are divine" (*The Altar* 4). Although Anzaldúa had a profound connection to nature, water held a special place within her personal cosmology. Anzaldúa explains in an interview, "I loved being in the water. I'd go to the lake by the house, and we'd go down to the Gulf of Mexico. All the time I was with water, water, water. People thought I was water crazy" ("Within" 113). Hence, while it would be correct to identify the natural world as a significant source of energy for Anzaldúa, it is clear that she understood water to play a unique role in her life.

Although Anzaldúa had been warned by her mother not to go too far into the water because she did not know how to swim, she simply could not stay away from the shimmering ripples: "The sea called to her; she could feel ... its song surge in her bones. . . . In the sucking sound of the waves she seemed to hear her name" ("Autohistoria," box 57, folder 10, p. 8). Here, Anzaldúa reveals that what she feels toward the water is not a mere appreciation of the beauty of nature. When Anzaldúa gazes at the sea, the sea gazes back at her. The water not only looks at her, it speaks to her. The ocean knows her name. In the coming and going of the waves, she feels herself recognized and responds to its call. This moment of profound reciprocity diametrically opposes many of Anzaldúa's human interactions in South Texas, where the dominant society was set on denigrating her existence.

Anzaldúa grew up in the Rio Grande Valley, mainly in the small rural town of Hargill, Texas. Norma Alarcón notes that this region has been "notorious for its mistreatment of people of Mexican descent. Indeed, many of the narratives that emerge from that area tell of the conflictive and violent relations in the forging of an anglicized Texas" ("Anzaldúa's Frontera" 44). Indicative of this reality, in one of the vignettes of "Autohistoria" titled "Her Name Never Got Called/ Nunca llamaron su nombre," Anzaldúa describes the viciousness of the South

Texas school system.[24] Spanish was banned and English ruled, whether one could speak it or not. Anzaldúa recounts that during her second day at school she was humiliated by the teacher for not responding to the name Gloria Anzaldúa during roll call, even though this was a name she had never been called before, as everyone in her family called her Prieta: "At that moment she knew that being Mexican meant she was stupid. A dumb *tejanita* who didn't even know her own name" ("Autohistoria," box 57, folder 10, p. 3).[25] The violence of this encounter is compassionately challenged by how the sea calls out to her.

The water effortlessly speaks Anzaldúa's name in a way she viscerally understands, transcending the limits of language. That the ocean reaches out to her in this transgressively healing way attests to the importance of not imposing borders onto spirituality. This is an approach Anzaldúa lived but that led to controversial assertions regarding cultural appropriation and fetishization since, as Debra A. Castillo finds, "the common tokenizing of Anzaldúa occurs at the hands not just of her critics but also of her friends" (261).[26] These readings can be tempered by digging deeper into Anzaldúa's unpublished work, once again indicating the inordinate value of the GEA Papers for Anzaldúan scholarship.

In "Spiritual Activism: Making Altares, Making Connections," another unpublished essay from the GEA Papers, Anzaldúa discusses the difficulty of giving a name to her spiritual approach. In addition to the Mesoamerican and Catholic deities often named in the formation of Chicana spirituality, Anzaldúa explains that she blends "elements that have served me from other cultures and spiritual practices: Santería, Tibetan and Zen Buddhism, Sidha Yoga, the I-Ching and Taoism" (box 64, folder 19, p. 1). Anzaldúa elaborates on her approach to spirituality in her foreword to *Cassell's Encyclopedia of Queer Myth, Symbol and Spirit*. Published in 1996, this brief text illuminates how crucial the cultivation of spiritual consciousness was for Anzaldúa and how her understanding of *mestizaje* extended beyond racial and ethnic tenets:

> A spiritual mestizaje weaves together beliefs and practices from many cultures, perhaps including elements of Shamanism, Buddhism, Christianity, Santería, and other traditions. Spiritual mestizaje involves the crossing of borders, incessant metamorphosis. It is a spirituality that nurtures the ability to wear someone else's skin, its central myth being shapeshifting. (230)

Anzaldúa's use of the term *mestizaje* in relation to spirituality is provocative and requires us to think about the location of its enunciation. Often deployed as a signifier of a mixed racial/ethnic heritage that is primarily Indigenous and Spanish and excludes Blackness, in Latin America *mestizaje* sanctioned cultural and political processes of *blanqueamiento* (whitening). This transformed *mestizaje* into a powerful tool for maintaining the hegemony of Hispanism in the region.[27]

In the United States, however, racial identities gain their power from proximity to "purity" rather than mixture. In a US Latinx context, then, *mestizaje* becomes a double-edged sword.[28] While never devoid of its hegemonic and racist undertones, it also carries within the capacity to engender what Rafael Pérez-Torres describes as "a conscious decolonial strategy" that "indexes multiple forms of loss" (229–230). These shifts in meaning make the deployment of *mestizaje* in the United States a strategy that must be contextualized in order to be productively critiqued and questioned.

Hegemonic *mestizaje*'s erasure of African and Asian identities (Pérez-Torres 230) makes Anzaldúa's *mestizaje* potentially transgressive because her approach names these absences and places them in conversation with more visible Indigenous and European knowledges.[29] In *Borderlands*, Anzaldúa addresses the elision of Blackness in *mestizaje*, and she speaks of the need to "know . . . our afro-*mestizaje*" (108). Spiritual *mestizaje* builds on this approach by positing a life-altering, socially grounded process that re-envisions our relationship to the divine in a way that directly responds to oppression (Delgadillo, *Spiritual Mestizaje* 1). Blending the loss inherent to *mestizaje* with the recovery and survival strategies of nonhegemonic spiritual practices, Anzaldúa's spiritual *mestizaje* destabilizes the disciplinary borders built around her work. It also makes evident that she viewed *mestizaje* as "not just a mixture of bloodlines" ("Spiritual Activism," box 64, folder 19, p. 1).

The way Anzaldúa's spiritual *mestizaje* establishes a symbiosis between Mesoamerican and Afro-diasporic energies exemplifies her commitment to spiritual activism, which Aisha M. Beliso-De Jesús understands as "a frame of conjure that mobilizes cultural heritage, decolonial approaches, and queer feminist resources for survival and futurity" ("Brujx" 529).[30] In this sense, a reconsideration of key Anzaldúan concepts informed by Afro-diasporic religious thought can help revitalize Latinx studies, particularly when, as Yolanda Martínez-San Miguel finds, blind spots in the field can be attributed to "the lack of substantive collaboration between Chicanx and Puerto Rican or other Spanish Caribbean studies scholars" and "the unreadability of Afro-Latinidad" (115). In line with this revisionary thinking, engaging with Anzaldúa's work through the lens of Afro-diasporic religiosity challenges the disciplinary borders of Caribbean, Chicanx, and Latinx studies by interrogating histories and canons, an endeavor for which water is ideally suited. The possibilities of such an approach can be visualized in the image of Anzaldúa created by zine artist Eloisa Aquino, *Anzaldúa Devout*, which places Anzaldúa, Yemayá, and La Virgen de Guadalupe in communion with one another through water and the undulations of a serpent.[31]

Though it has less circulation than "spiritual *mestizaje*," Lara Medina's term "*nepantla* spirituality" is directly influenced by Anzaldúa and how the spiritual approach of many Chicanas "draws from multiple faith and spiritual

FIGURE 3.1. "Gloria was a deeply spiritual person, devoted to La Virgen de Guadalupe, Nahuatl/Toltec Divinities, and to the Yoruba orishas Yemayá and Oshún." Eloisa Aquino, *Anzaldúa Devout*, 2015. Courtesy of the artist.

traditions" (205).[32] Recognizing that the recovery of the sacred in Chicanx communities can be aided by fostering a connection with the *orishas*, Medina identifies Santería/Regla de Ocha as one of the systems that provides sustenance for Chicanas (205). Unsurprisingly, water plays a vital role in this process, particularly the ocean and the river, reiterating how these liquid bodies function as synergistic channels between distinct spiritual systems.[33] More recently,

Christina Garcia Lopez's *Calling the Soul Back* explicitly considers Anzaldúa's ties to Yemayá. Garcia Lopez's meditative study on the multiple ways "Chicanx literary narrative creatively maps vital connections between mind, body, spirit, and soul" (3) is rooted in *curanderismo,* a traditional healing system used in Mexico and throughout the Americas.[34] Garcia Lopez, however, insists that while pre-Columbian Indigenous knowledges make up a large portion of the knowledges of *curanderismo,* the system integrates other epistemologies, among them African-derived ones (9).[35] As a result, Garcia Lopez's reading of Anzaldúa's "Let us be the healing of the wound: The Coyolxauhqui imperative—la sombra y el sueño" is attentive to Yemayá's latent presence.

"Let us be the healing of the wound" addresses the negotiation of personal and collective trauma surrounding September 11, 2001. Garcia Lopez describes the piece as "a culminating work in Anzaldúa's wide and influential body of writing" (35). After establishing that the effects of trauma are epitomized by *curanderismo*'s conception of *susto* (soul fright), Garcia Lopez posits that Anzaldúa aims to heal this spiritual ailment in a *limpia* (spiritual cleansing) enacted through a ritualist walk along the ocean's edge (45). Combined with what the GEA Papers divulge about Anzaldúa's relationship to water and the sea, Garcia Lopez's interpretation takes on added epistemological and ontological power.

"Let us be the healing of the wound" closes when Anzaldúa writes, "Down on the beach, drummers serenade Yemayá, ocean mother. I'd like to think they are beating the drums of peace, calling our souls back into our bodies" (*Light* 22). Garcia Lopez's reading of this moment beautifully affirms the flows between Yemayá and Coyolxauhqui, the Mexica moon goddess, illuminating how Anzaldúa "draws together the medicinal powers of the waters . . . and the rising guiding 'light' of . . . the moon of Mesoamerican mythology" (46). Garcia Lopez's words express the power of Anzaldúa's spiritual *mestizaje* and they take on deeper meaning in the context of Santería/Regla de Ocha because the moon is one of Yemayá's signature emblems (Cabrera, *Yemayá y Ochún* 268). A close reading of this final reflection by Anzaldúa shows how seamlessly the connection between Yemayá and Coyolxauhqui can be birthed in the waters and sustained by their spiritual resonance. This convergence helps readers understand how and why Anzaldúa nurtured both relationships throughout her life. Yemayá's appearance in the last piece published during Anzaldúa's lifetime, "Let us be the healing of the wound," adds gravitas to her enduring presence in Anzaldúa's work, providing undeniable evidence of Anzaldúa's lifelong engagement with Afro-diasporic religions.

An analysis of water's spiritual undercurrents in "Let us be the healing of the wound" takes us back to Anzaldúa's near-drowning at South Padre Island. After hearing the sea call out her name, Anzaldúa writes that she decided to step into the water when, suddenly, "a tall wave, *the seventh,* knocked her off balance and swept her out to sea. She felt a tug at her ankles and then she was sucked under" ("Autohistoria," box 57, folder 10, p. 8, my emphasis). It is important to pause here and note Anzaldúa's mention of how it was the seventh wave that drew her into the sea. Earlier, Anzaldúa's emphasis on the head and the energy she felt when looking at the ocean drew attention to Afro-diasporic religions as in these traditions the head becomes the portal through which one communes with the divine. Here, a second clue regarding Anzaldúa's spiritual connection to the Afro-diasporic world emerges, leading directly toward Yemayá, whose sacred number is 7. The number 7 is also associated with las Siete Potencias Africanas, underscoring Yemayá's dual role as the mother of the *orishas* and as a gateway into the sacred world of Santería/Regla de Ocha.

Anzaldúa's choice to emphasize the number 7 is a clue for how she interpreted her encounter with the ocean. Most of the documents I analyze in this section were drafted in the 1990s, and by this time Anzaldúa had been told that she was a child of Yemayá, a fact she discloses in a footnote of *Borderlands* and in a 1982 interview.[36] Hence, although Anzaldúa does not utter Yemayá's name in these autobiographical documents, the *orisha*'s energy drives Anzaldúa's spiritual awakening. Yemayá's *aché* is in the water, and documents from the GEA Papers make clear that from an early age the energy of Yemayá's ocean was a reservoir for Anzaldúa. That all of this information is transmitted in relation to a moment of drowning strengthens the undercurrent of spirituality that frames the event as Yemayá's children are often told to have "un respeto" (respect) toward the sea. The reasoning behind this is that the attraction between Yemayá and her children can be so strong it can ultimately have fatal consequences (Teish, *Jambalaya* 133). Indeed, a handwritten note in one of Anzaldúa's autobiographical documents reads, "Don't swim when you're sad. Yemayá will take you to comfort" ("Canción," box 68, folder 7, p. 23). A similar stance exists in Haitian Vodou's conception of Agwe, the *lwa* of the seas. As detailed in Hurston's *Tell My Horse*, a copy of which is in Anzaldúa's personal library, "The belief is widespread in Haiti that Agoue' ta-Royo [Maitre L'Eau, Master of Waters] carries off people whom he chooses to a land beneath the waters" (231).[37] What these overlapping details make evident is that an awareness of the multiple Afro-diasporic deities that dwell in the waters enables readers to more deeply process the meanings of the call-and-response moment Anzaldúa recounts when looking at the sea, an event that ultimately led her to be pulled under by the currents.

In a version of "En el hocico del mar" dated September 12, 1989, Anzaldúa gives more details about what it felt like to be taken by the water:

So this big wave takes me out a little bit, but I'm not worried because I can dog paddle back. But something pulls me by my feet, an undertow. To me, it felt like someone had reached out a hand and pulled me under. I got real scared.

I'd been practicing holding my breath. But I could only hold my breath for three minutes. And in my panic I didn't even hold my breath that long. I was swallowing water through my nose and my body was resisting. My body was not accepting the water. It wanted air. And just before I lost consciousness I had the feeling that I was in the ocean and that there was an ocean inside me that had joined the "real" ocean. There was no boundary. There was no skin. The two oceans were touching. And I felt very happy. It was peaceful. I loved just being there. ("Hocico," box 70, folder 3)[38]

In this rendition of the event, Anzaldúa gradually moves from describing the water as an element ("something") to endowing it with sentience and agency ("someone"). Importantly, this shift happens before Anzaldúa speaks about the lack of boundaries between herself and the water. The way she reaches this moment of illumination is through the currents, transforming her near-drowning experience into one in which a new consciousness is birthed within her, akin to spiritual initiation. While there is fear and even rejection at the start, a common response to spiritual callings, by the end, Anzaldúa describes a feeling of communion and harmony between herself and the water. Anzaldúa is received by the ocean and notes that her internal sea and nature's ocean are now "touching," coming together in an unexpected but seamless way. At this moment, Anzaldúa is not split but connected; she is an individual and part of a spiritual collective, perhaps for the first time experiencing this kind of radical acceptance and community, one she would continue to advocate for throughout her life.

The way Anzaldúa narrates drowning as an experience of becoming aware of her own limitlessness is reminiscent of the poem that opens *Borderlands*, which is where Yemayá appears in the text. In the poem Anzaldúa writes, "But the skin of the earth is seamless. / The sea cannot be fenced / *el mar* does not stop at borders" (*Borderlands* 25). The resonance between these lines and Anzaldúa's unpublished narration of the events that transpired on South Padre Island clarify Yemayá's influence upon Anzaldúa's understanding of fluidity. Furthermore, Anzaldúa's description of the currents as "an umbilical cord tethering her to the ocean" ("Hocico" June 1997, box 70, folder 3, p. 4) attests to how the sensorial and psychic transmittal of knowledge Anzaldúa received from the ocean at a young age nurtured how she would later connect to and conceive of borders, divisions, and difference.

Anzaldúa's depiction of the ocean's ability to become a hand that pulls her under presents water as a shape-shifter, a recurrent theme in her work. Anzaldúa herself states, "I've done a lot of thinking and some writing about shifting identities, changing identities. I call it 'shapeshifting,' as in nagualismo—a type of Mexican indigenous shamanism where a person becomes an animal, becomes a different person ("Lesbian Wit" 132). The connection between shifting subjectivities and perceptions, both of which illustrate Anzaldúa's cease-less probing into the limits of the knowable, is key to grasping her concept of *la naguala* (the shape-shifter), a being that for Kelli D. Zaytoun is "situated both in and beyond the body, [and] shifts the shape and the boundaries of the subject beyond intellectual, humanist frameworks" (70). What Zaytoun's perspective makes clear is that the internal work triggered by shape-shifting is as vital as any external dimension of transformation.

The description of *la naguala* as residing inside and outside the body emulates the relationship many believers foster with their tutelary *orishas* in Santería/Regla de Ocha. Once an initiate has undergone the ceremony of *kari ocha*, that person's ruling *orisha* lives within them (in their head) and outside them (in nature). Though not often described using the term "shape-shifter," the reality is that the *orishas* do undergo this process. Yemayá is the ocean, but she is also depicted as a Black woman of various ages and as a mermaid (Fernández Olmos and Paravisini-Gebert 52; Cabrera, *Yemayá y Ochún* 32). And beyond the many *caminos* (paths) each *orisha* has, the deities are also closely connected to animals. For example, John Mason notes that "Ọ̀sun and Yẹmọja are both represented by fish and water snakes" (*Olóòkun* 54). Knowledge of the nonhuman representations of these Afro-diasporic deities adds depth to Anzaldúa's penchant for the snake, providing another point of inflection in her relationship with Yemayá.[39]

In addition to shape-shifting, the *orishas* can infuse their life force, their *aché*, into various objects or representations. Evidence of this ability is visible in how the *orishas* relate to Catholic saints, a process commonly termed "syncretism" (Abimbọla 105). More recently, Andrew Apter has noted that syncretism should be understood as an act of purposeful appropriation during which Catholic saints were transformed into Africanized "double agents," granting devotees greater freedom of worship (45). This dual flow of energies explains why, according to Ana-Maurine Lara, in La 21 División "Catholic saints are known for work-ing both hands. They can open the road to healing, but they can also open the road to great repression" (*Queer Freedom* 146). The concept of "working both hands" is often used in Haitian Vodou to describe the ethics of practitioners. As Madison Smartt Bell observes:

> Most *houngans* and *mambos* (Vodou priests and priestesses) are understood to 'work with both hands'—the beneficent right hand is applied to good works in the spirit of Ginen [underwater repository of the sacred], while the sinister left hand works to enable more culpable human desires: lust, avarice, envy, and wrath. (20)

These discussions of *lwa*, *misterios*, *orishas*, and those who serve them make clear that intention must be foregrounded when considering the use of religious imagery in the Afro-diasporic world. Such an assertion guides my reading of Anzaldúa's continued engagement with Yemayá in her published and unpublished work.

After the sea pulls her in, Anzaldúa recounts that she survived her near-drowning experience when, just as suddenly as she was swept underwater, her feet miraculously touched a sandbar. Knowing she was not a strong enough swimmer to face the ocean's currents, she managed to keep her head above water for more than three hours, waiting for the tide to recede (Anzaldúa, "Within" 112). When she was finally able to return to shore and to her family, an undeniable change had taken place within her:

> For some reason the sea had given her back. She had not fought being taken, she had not fought being given back. In the moment of her first mouthful of air she had known that she belonged to the sea and that one day water would claim her. This would later come to have great significance to her. ("Autoretratos," box 57, folder 12, p. 22)

The way Anzaldúa words the conclusion to her narrative is telling. There is an inference about her destiny and how what happened at sea will mark her for the rest of her life. She even goes as far as saying that she belonged to the sea, a statement that becomes more potent when read as an affirmation of spiritual kinship because she knew she was Yemayá's daughter. What the GEA Papers leave no doubt about is that this near-drowning experience changed Anzaldúa. After this event she became afraid of the water. She stopped venturing out by herself at sea, and even going into swimming pools became difficult (Anzaldúa, "Within" 113). Yet, those familiar with Anzaldúa's writing know that what she wrote about was often what she feared the most. Water and Yemayá incessantly influenced Anzaldúa's writing and thinking, symbolically transforming Yemayá into one of her most enduring writing *comadres*.

Anzaldúa sustained her relationship with Yemayá by purchasing a house in Santa Cruz, California, that was walking distance from the ocean. On an almost daily basis she walked to the shore to commune with the water (Reti 57). Anzaldúa describes living by the sea in the following way: "You know, to live near the ocean means that you just go there and then get another infusion of energy. All the petty problems you have fall away because of the presence of the ocean. It therefore is a real spiritual presence for me" ("Gloria" 16).[40] Combining the information Anzaldúa provides here with an awareness of her experience in the waters of South Padre Island assists readers in revisiting the multiple mentions of water in Anzaldúa's writing. Walking near the ocean allowed Anzaldúa to receive the energy of the maritime, deepening her connection to the sacred, to Yemayá, and to the fathomless realms of knowledge that lie in the saltwaters.

One of the most reproduced images of Anzaldúa depicts her knee-deep in the waters of the Pacific Ocean. It became the cover of *Bridging: How Gloria Anzaldúa's Life and Work Transformed Our Own*, a collection of essays about Anzaldúa's influence edited by AnaLouise Keating and Gloria González López. Shot sometime in the 1990s, this photo is part of a series taken by the photographer Annie F. Valva.[41] In the image, Anzaldúa displays a joyous expression on her face as the ocean waters swirl around her. The contents of the GEA Papers make clear that this was not the first time she felt the energy of the sea in her body. When Anzaldúa steps into the water, she becomes part of a larger whole, just as she does when communing with Coyolxauhqui. In both instances, spirituality flows into her life, allowing her to integrate more of her experiences. This very process is what Anzaldúa sought to transmit through her writing.

In a short piece included in the introduction to the third edition of *Borderlands*, "A Note to Gloria from the Bottom of the Sea," Sandra Cisneros uncannily speaks to Anzaldúa's experiences in South Padre Island. In this entry, Cisneros declares that while she was not able to develop a close personal relationship with Anzaldúa, as fellow writers they would forever be connected because they were both "studying the bottom of the sea":

> Because writing is like putting your head underwater. It takes great effort to go under, to push yourself to the sea bottom, a tremendous courage to withstand the pressure and pain and stay down there. Then the bobbing to the surface when a lifeline tugs you back. (242)

In this note written by Cisneros in 2007, three years after Anzaldúa's death and several decades after her near-drowning in South Padre Island, we gain one more tool for considering how, for Anzaldúa, water was always more than a metaphor. Cisneros aesthetically links the process of drowning to that of writing, but Anzaldúa lived it, both through her pen and through her body. She knew the ocean was more than an abstraction. It was a being. It breathed and had a heartbeat. It spoke to her. It was Yemayá. It was the divine. It was energy. The ocean was a place toward which Anzaldúa continually turned in her search for her roots and routes, and it is likely one of the places where we will always be able to connect with Anzaldúa's spiritual presence.

CIRCUITS OF MIGRATION:
ANZALDÚA AND YEMAYÁ

Although Yemayá's presence in Anzaldúa's archive is still very much uncharted territory, her appearance at critical moments of Anzaldúa's published writing has garnered attention. Scholars recurrently credit Luisah Teish, a Santería/Regla de Ocha priestess from New Orleans, with introducing Anzaldúa to the *orisha* (Conner 187; Díaz-Sánchez 179n21; Piña 114).[42] Anzaldúa met Teish when they were both living in California in the early 1970s, making clear that Anzaldúa's knowledge of Yemayá was generated through her personal migrations within the United States. It was also in California that *Bridge* was envisioned, reinscribing the firm connection between Anzaldúa's creative energies and her contact with Afro-diasporic religions.

Anzaldúa's relationship to Teish and Yemayá provides a valuable framework from which to consider how living in New York City in the 1980s and interacting with diasporic Caribbean communities influenced Anzaldúa's theorizing. Current scholarship addressing the Caribbean influence in Anzaldúa's published writing primarily revolves around a linguistic detail included in chapter 5 of *Borderlands*, "How to Tame a Wild Tongue."[43] Here, Anzaldúa credits Puerto Rican and Cuban women with teaching her that a group of women could use the feminine "nosotras" to refer to themselves rather than defaulting to the pronoun's masculine iteration (76). Beyond inciting a reflection on language practices, this moment in *Borderlands* invites readers to ponder how Anzaldúa's migrations within the United States transformed her worldview. It also underscores the fundamental way(s) internal migration shaped Anzaldúa's overall life; as Norma Elia Cantú and Aída Hurtado observe, "her family worked as farm workers requiring them to migrate between Texas and the Midwest" (Cantú and Hurtado 4). Anzaldúa's relationship to borders, then, was always fluid, setting the stage for how water would come to play a significant role in her conception of borders and borderlands.

The 1981 publication of *This Bridge Called My Back* was a pivotal moment in Anzaldúa's career; Li Yun Alvarado notes that its publication opened "important professional, creative, and spiritual opportunities" for Anzaldúa (73). Yet, this text was years in the making. In the 2001 foreword to the third edition of *Bridge*, "Counsels from the Firing . . . past, present, future," Anzaldúa recounts that the idea for this anthology came to her in the mid-1970s when she was a doctoral student at the University of Texas at Austin. Although Anzaldúa dropped out of the university due to the overt racism she experienced within it, her experience as both student and instructor at UT Austin planted the seed for *Bridge*.[44] For example, when Anzaldúa taught the course "La Mujer Chicana," she struggled to find texts to include in her syllabus.[45]

After leaving Austin in 1977, Anzaldúa traveled to California, spending time in San Francisco, Oakland, and Berkeley. It was there that she met Moraga, who would soon become coeditor for *Bridge* due to the health challenges Anzaldúa faced in the early 1980s. It was also in California and through her work on *Bridge* that Anzaldúa connected with Teish, a Santería/Regla de Ocha priestess initiated to the *orisha* Ochún and also knowledgeable about the traditions of New

Orleans Vodou. I read the encounter between Anzaldúa and Teish as a meeting of the waters (ocean and river) in that "crossing boundaries and borderlands, especially in terms of kinds of water (salty/sweet) ... challenges fixed notions of subjectivity (Otero, "Yemayá y Ochún: Queering" 86). Anzaldúa's relationship with Teish was transformative. That Anzaldúa learned about Yemayá and the spiritual tradition of Santería/Regla de Ocha from a Black woman from the US South initiated to another water deity of this Afro-diasporic religion reaffirms the role migration and diaspora played in Anzaldúa's life and writing.

Bridge includes an interview Anzaldúa conducted with Teish discussing the santera's approach to spirituality (Teish, "O.K. Momma"). The interview appears in the last section of Bridge, "El Mundo Zurdo" (The Left-Handed World), another of Anzaldúa's key concepts.[46] The inclusion of the interview in this section of the anthology evidences the epistemological resonance between Anzaldúa and Teish, especially since "El Mundo Zurdo" also features Anzaldúa's autohistoria-teoría "La Prieta." During the interview Teish declares, "What we've got to do is feed that which has survived, build on that which has survived" ("O.K. Momma" 230, emphasis in the original). This statement subtly gestures toward the rituals of Santería/Regla de Ocha in which offerings to the orishas are commonly referred to as "feedings" (Cabrera, Yemayá y Ochún 27; D. H. Brown 135). Upon hearing this comment, Anzaldúa adds that she sees a direct connection between Teish's statement and the subversive power of La Virgen de Guadalupe, exemplifying the openness and flows her spirituality sought to create among seemingly disparate traditions. Years later, Teish herself professed that Anzaldúa "consistently made connections between African and Indian-based spiritual practices and addressed both with the utmost respect and reverence" (quoted in Piña 114). These moments of spiritual resonance underscore the need to reread Anzaldúa with a sensibility for how her life and work were continually traversed by diverse knowledges.

In their interview, Teish shares that she is working on a book centered "on women's spirituality that would be a combination of my own personal experiences and certain historical information, but mostly a book of charms" ("O.K. Momma" 225). Teish's book was published in 1985 as Jambalaya: The Natural Woman's Book of Personal Charms and Practical Rituals, a text that presents readers with "a way (not the way) to responsibly cultivate and utilize spiritual power" (Teish x, emphasis in the original). Focused on accessibly explaining rituals and practices inspired by New Orleans Vodou and Santería/Regla de Ocha, Jambalaya is Teish's response to the women's movement's need for a spirit-infused vision of the world that revered the feminine. Teish's title, Jambalaya, refers to a dish from New Orleans in which various ingredients are stewed together. For Teish, jambalaya is an apt metaphor for New Orleans Vodou because this system "blends the practices of three continents into one tradition. It contains African ancestor reverence, Native American earth worship, and European Christian occultism" (*Jambalaya* x). Teish's use of jambalaya connects to the Caribbean, given its resonances with Fernando Ortiz's use of the *ajiaco*, a Cuban stew that brings together various ingredients. In "Los factores humanos de la cubanidad" (The Human Factors of Cubanidad), a lecture given in 1939 and published in 1940, Ortiz declares that Cuban culture is an *ajiaco*. He then describes how the island became the cauldron in which the hot sun of the tropics cooked ingredients associated with the various ethnic identities of the land (African, Asian, Indigenous, and European).[47] In both dishes, water plays the distinct role of conjoining disparate elements to create a new whole.[48] Afro-diasporic religions, however, are a constant yet always controversial "seasoning" in the elaboration of this national plate.[49]

Like *Borderlands*, *Jambalaya* is a multigenre text that is simultaneously autobiographical, didactic, and creative. Teish dedicates the book to her three mothers, one of whom is Yemayá (*Jambalaya* iv). Although this might seem to indicate that Yemayá is her titular *orisha*, Teish is a daughter of Ochún, the *orisha* primarily associated with rivers and sweetwaters who is often considered Yemayá's sister. Through her dedication, Teish displays the intimate connection that exists between *orishas* associated with the same natural element. In *Jambalaya*, Teish discloses that during a reading a Vodou priest told her that she was Ochún's daughter (40). This moment is another visible sign of rebellion against orthodoxy, as it goes against the dominant practice in Santería/Regla de Ocha in which only *babalawos* (male priests who have been initiated into Ifá and serve Orula, the deity of divination) are authorized to disclose this information. This unruly transfer of knowledge would be replicated in Anzaldúa's life in the early 1980s when during a reading Teish would tell Anzaldúa she was Yemayá's daughter (Conner 187).[50] Later in life Teish would be called to become an *iyanifa* (mother of secrets), who in the Nigerian Ifá tradition is equal to a *babalawo* in Cuba (Conner 187). In this way Teish continues to disrupt the male hegemony that can often undergird Afro-diasporic traditions.[51]

That Anzaldúa came to know Yemayá through Teish, a Black priestess from the United States who also sought the recovery of sacred knowledges, is an integral part of understanding this *orisha*'s presence in Anzaldúa's life. Although Anzaldúa never became formally initiated, it is in *Bridge* that she first makes public her connection to Yemayá.[52] Anzaldúa's biographical statement describes her as "a Tejana Chicana poet, hija de [daughter of] Amalia, Hecate y Yemaya" (277).[53] Anzaldúa's biography transforms Yemayá into a bridge, reflecting the work of *Bridge* itself, a text that created cross-cultural/racial/ethnic conversations among women. In this triad of the divine feminine, Yemayá is the sole representative of non-European epistemologies.

In 1981, the same year *Bridge* was published, Anzaldúa moved from the West

Coast to the East Coast. She spent most of her time in New York City, where she lived from 1982 to 1985 (L. Y. Alvarado 72). Anzaldúa describes her move from west to east as one in which she went "del mar pacifico al mar atlantico," from the Pacific to the Atlantic Ocean, underscoring the significance of water as a marker of her sense of place and being ("La serpiente" 1982–1983, box 78, folder 10). Though not often emphasized in current scholarship, Anzaldúa's time on the East Coast was pivotal to her writing because it set the foundation for what would become *Borderlands*, the bulk of which she wrote from 1984 to 1986 (Anzaldúa, "Gloria" 4).[54] In "On the Process of Writing *Borderlands/La Frontera*," a posthumously published essay, Anzaldúa discloses that her feeling of homesickness for South Texas during her travels on the West Coast and East Coast spurred her to write the text because "you are closer to home when you're further away" (187). This admission reiterates the significance of travel and migration in Anzaldúa's evolving perception of the world. As a Chicana on the East Coast in the 1980s, when Mexican and Mexican American communities were much smaller than they are now, she gained a new appreciation of difference and otherness, particularly concerning other Latinx communities (L. Y. Alvarado 73). Anzaldúa herself recounts:

> When I lived in Brooklyn (or Boston, or New Haven, or South Bend) both whites and some Latinas/os would often ask, "Well, when did you come from Mexico?" Or "Are you Latin American from—like, South America or Central America?" I heard these questions from people who thought they were in tune with the Latino community and Latina identity, but didn't know how to distinguish between Puerto Ricans, Cubans, Chicanas, or Mexican immigrants. ("On the Process" 188)

The illegibility of Chicanx identity on the East Coast was shocking to Anzaldúa, particularly when it came from self-identified Latinx people. Undoubtedly, this experience added impetus for her to write *Borderlands*, a text that stems from the US/Mexico divide in order to speak to broader issues of Latinx displacement.

Spirituality was also at the forefront of Anzaldúa's time on the East Coast. She quickly realized that the move would force her to develop her spirituality on her own terms. In a 1983 interview Anzaldúa elaborates on how one could easily seek all kinds of spiritual services on the West Coast, which, though convenient, could also foster dependency on outside providers ("Within" 107). On the East Coast, in contrast, Anzaldúa had to develop her spirituality on her own since "there's nothing readily visible; you have to hunt for it. Of course . . . there's Santería. But they don't give information to just anyone who goes in and asks" ("Within" 107). Here, Anzaldúa rightly references the guarded nature of Santería/Regla de Ocha. Some knowledge about this religion circulates publicly, but most teachings are reserved only for initiates. It is possible that in this comment Anzaldúa is addressing the lack of access that she as a non-initiate, an *aleya*, experienced when seeking to learn more about the *orishas*.

In the ever-growing Caribbean diaspora on the East Coast Anzaldúa witnessed a community's sustained engagement with Santería/Regla de Ocha for the first time. She was primed to learn about these processes because she arrived in New York knowing her tutelary *orisha* was Yemayá. Anzaldúa's interest in Afro-diasporic spirituality is in line with David Hatfield Sparks's contention that in the 1980s he, Anzaldúa, and his partner, Randy P. Conner, were "on a spiritual path that was both African-focused and woman-led" (368). Sparks also mentions the impact of a 1981 interview Anzaldúa conducted with a Santería/Regla de Ocha devotee from New York, a conversation that included discussion not only of Yemayá but also about the possibilities for nonheteronormative gender expression within the religion (Sparks 379). It is likely that the fluid embodiments of Santería/Regla de Ocha drew Anzaldúa to this tradition, for "Santería is a religion that has historically emerged as a solution to problems for marginalized subjects" (Beliso-De Jesús, *Electric Santería* 104).[55] Anzaldúa's relationship to Yemayá thus reflects her personal spiritual evolution, a process that took place alongside her search for epistemological lenses that could transcend hegemonic societal norms.

The GEA Papers provide evidence of Anzaldúa's research on Afro-diasporic religions. While not easy to locate given their dispersed nature within the archive, many of these instances can be found in an autobiographical document from the early 1980s titled "Esperando la serpiente con plumas/Waiting for the Feathered Serpent." The text from which several of Anzaldúa's notes on Santería/Regla de Ocha come is Migene González-Wippler's 1982 book *The Santería Experience*, which is in her personal library. Anzaldúa's notes reveal a primary interest in the origins of Santería/Regla de Ocha. She is drawn to the tradition's survival despite the imposition of Catholicism, the way the religion centered ritual knowledge, and the connection the *orishas* have to nature. One of her notes reads, "The Orisha religion as well as those of Native American[s] is based on the understanding that an interaction exists between humans and nature. Both give great respect to the forces of nature. The Orisha are forces of this universe" ("Esperando," box 78, folder 9). Though stated differently, Cabrera purports this vision on the first page of her 1954 path-opening work, *El monte*, where she writes that the *orishas* are more present on earth than in the heavens and that nature is the temple of many practitioners (13–15). These notes make evident that the role of the natural world within Santería/Regla de Ocha resonated with Anzaldúa's visceral connection to the earth, creating a vibrant point of contact between herself and the *orishas*, a resonance that is also on display in her narrations about South Padre Island.

By this same token, the detachment Anzaldúa perceived between people and nature on the East Coast deeply affected her. Anzaldúa's initial reaction to the concrete jungle of New York City was overwhelmingly negative. She writes that in the city, she found "people who never see soil, dirt. Who only know unyielding pavement.... No grass grows here, just steel and glass and concrete" ("Esperando," box 78, folder 9, p. 90). Then, one day, her connection to New York shifted:

I suddenly felt the City *pulsating* like a live animal. The buildings became watchful trees rooted deep in the bowels of the Earth. Even the subways felt like huge artieries [*sic*] of the Earth's *blood* system. I rode the underground *rivers* inside their roar, swaying to the stops and starts.... I had stopped fighting the City. ("Esperando," box 78, folder 9, p. 91, my emphasis)

Anzaldúa's description of the subway system as pulsating arteries and rivers overlaps with her awareness of the ocean's aliveness on South Padre Island and with the transformative experience she had when the waters pulled her in. Just as Anzaldúa spoke about drowning becoming peaceful once she surrendered to the water, here she states that she stopped fighting the city and was able to see it anew after becoming submerged in it. This depiction reveals that what is transformed is neither the city nor Anzaldúa but their relationship to each other. Though certainly more abstractly than in South Padre, this transformation is facilitated by water and fluidity as well as by Anzaldúa's memory of her initial aquatic experience. Her new way of seeing New York City encourages reflection on how the *orishas* themselves came to New York and other urban centers. Accustomed to having a deep connection with nature's elements, they too had to acclimate to a life dominated by concrete and high-rises.[56]

Still, Anzaldúa's contact with the Afro-diasporic world did not begin on the East Coast, though it did evolve there. This assertion strengthens the fluidity and movement that distinguish Afro-diasporic traditions and their growth in the United States while calling attention to materials in the GEA Papers. Drafts of her posthumously published poem "Yemayá" stem from 1980 through 2001.[57] Yemayá's presence thus spans the length of Anzaldúa's career. This timeframe is particularly significant because in 1981 Anzaldúa had not yet aligned herself with either Coatlicue or Coyolxauhqui, both of whom scholars identify as key figures in her work. In the genealogy of the divine feminine of Anzaldúa's work, Yemayá appears before any Mexica deity, emphasizing water's role as gateway and activator of knowledge in Anzaldúa's oeuvre. Yemayá's connection to Anzaldúa elucidates how the *orishas*, as well as the ancestors, "assisted [Anzaldúa], by way of the deployment of certain sacred technologies, in learning to recognize, contact, and invoke Mesoamerican divinities and ancestral spirits"

(Conner 187). And a critical moment for witnessing this kind of spiritual chan-neling took place in 1980.

THE WOMB AS OFFERING: ANZALDÚA'S WRITERLY *EBÓ*

Afro-diasporic waters are as important in death as they are in life. This fluid understanding informs how and why Yemayá played a pivotal role in sev-eral of Anzaldúa's living death experiences. Contrary to the overall silence that surrounds her near-drowning at South Padre Island, the last of these precarious crossings is repeatedly discussed in Anzaldúa's published writing.[58] In 1980, after months of suffering from undiagnosed pain and just prior to her move to the East Coast, Anzaldúa was informed that she had several tumors in her uterus that were becoming dangerously infected. She had to undergo an emergency hysterectomy, and she flatlined during the operation. Anzaldúa directly refer-ences this moment in *Borderlands* when she declares that she was pronounced dead on the operating table (56). Upon waking from the surgery, Anzaldúa felt that she had stepped outside her body in a dreamlike state. Her medical chart revealed that her heart had stopped beating due to "complications" ("La ser-piente" June–July 1984, box 68, folder 3, p. 29).[59] The doctors never discussed the incident with Anzaldúa, so she turned to writing to process it. Box 68 of the GEA Papers contains a series of variously titled unpublished autobiographical materials related to this event. Many of them are from the 1980s and show shifts in the narrative point of view as well as varying degrees of detail; some initial versions are written in a more journal-like fashion, while other versions are more fictionalized. Here, as in Anzaldúa's experience at South Padre Island, the bor-ders between Anzaldúa and Prieta disappear.

In much of the GEA Papers' unpublished autobiographical material the body takes center stage, a detail heightened in accounts of Anzaldúa's hysterectomy. She describes one of her initial interactions with the hospital's medical staff as follows:

> "One more day," [the doctor] was saying, "and the *thing* would have exploded in your beely [*sic*]. You'd be dead right now. Didn't you *know*? You must have been in awful pain for months" ("La serpiente" June–July 1984, box 68, folder 3, p. 7, emphasis in the original)

What the doctor's comment does not take into account is that for Anzaldúa pain had become a way of life due to the medical system's constant refusal to address her symptoms. "How could she have known whom to believe, the doctors or her body? Hadn't her body always betrayed her? Si, desde chiquita la había traicionado" (Yes, since she was a little girl it had betrayed her) ("La serpiente" June–July 1984, box 68, folder 3, p. 7).[60] This statement discloses the primordial role Anzaldúa's reproductive system played in determining her health, another way of considering Yemayá's constant presence in Anzaldúa's life. Although Ochún is the *orisha* linked to pregnancy, in Santería/Regla de Ocha mythology the ocean is the place from which life emanates, making the sea the world's womb.[61] Yemayá's role as the creator of life is also reflected in how the womb is laden with amniotic fluid, and it is often when its water breaks that the birthing process begins.

Despite its life-giving qualities, for Anzaldúa the womb is a source of trauma. When she began suffering from painfully debilitating periods in her childhood, doctors told her the pain was all in her head and that the solution was to get married and have children ("La Prieta" 200). Then, when this new pain started, she sought medical advice and was prescribed antibiotics that had been unable to bring her fever down for more than two months ("La serpiente" June–July 1984, box 68, folder 3, p. 7). Given her encounters with the medical system and its disregard for women's bodies in general and especially the bodies of women of color, Anzaldúa presents herself as haunted by the disease in her womb.[62] This haunting begins on a literal level when she describes the infected tumors as monsters growing inside her and ultimately manifests as intergenerational trauma. During her first night in the hospital, Anzaldúa begins menstruating. As the blood flows, so do the memories. She remembers the last time she saw her grandmother, Mamagrande Ramoncita, dying on a hospital bed and coughing up blood. She thinks of her brother wounded in the Vietnam War and drowning in a pool of blood where his own mixes with that of his fallen comrades.[63] Last, she sees her father lying on the ground in a pool of his own blood ("La serpiente" June–July 1984, box 68, folder 3, p. 6). Anzaldúa's understanding of her illness, then, is that it is not just rooted in her own body; it encompasses the collective trauma passed down to her through generations.

Identifying and revering one's ancestors is an essential element of Afro-diasporic religions. In Santería/Regla de Ocha, there is a saying, "Ikú lo bi ocha/El muerto parió al santo," which translates to "the dead, the ancestors, give birth to the saint" (the *orisha*).[64] Hence, the dead must be as respected as the *orishas* (Cabrera, *El monte* 62). This belief dictates that before any ritual for the *orishas* can take place the spirits of the querent must be consulted and appeased. Oftentimes, this consultation is conducted by means of a *misa espiritual* (spiritual mass) in which the querent's *egun* (dead) are invited to speak and make their opinions and desires known.[65] Although *egun* and *orishas* are distinct entities, they work together to create an individual's spiritual cosmology. Collaboratively, they determine how and when any ritual activity should occur. These processes elucidate that in the Afro-diasporic world, the dead are not only not gone but require constant attention.[66] The dead can still receive healing once they have crossed over, an aspect that signals how assuaging ancestral wounds can allow the living to find peace, contesting linear notions of time imposed by secular structures. In depictions of her hysterectomy, Anzaldúa's body functions as a node of ancestral pain, a festering wound that is once again opened before her operation through the shedding of (menstrual) blood. As Anzaldúa's spirits speak to her in this dreamlike, pain-induced state, her ancestors communicate the need to perform a healing ritual that will address her current physical condition and the generational memories lodged within her cells.[67]

Anzaldúa's understanding of the womb as a place where life and death gestate as well as her spiritual encounter with the pain of her ancestors provides critical context for her intention to offer her removed uterus to Yemayá, a desire not disclosed in her published work but documented in her archive. After learning about her impending operation Anzaldúa explains that "Teish, a practicing Santeria priestess, phoned offering to do a healing ritual to Yemaya by the ocean" ("Canción," box 68, folder 7, p. 12).[68] Before going into surgery, Anzaldúa requests that the doctors save her uterus for her. When she wakes up after the procedure, she receives some unwelcome news:

> "Can I have my uterus?" she said. "Did you save it for me like I asked you?"
> "I forgot."
> Prieta's breath hitched. "Oh, but I wanted to do a ritual." She and Teish had planned to walk to the edge of the sea and offer Yemaya a watermelon or molasses. ("Canción," box 68, folder 7, p. 23)[69]

Anzaldúa's intention displays a profound knowledge of Yemayá's energies. Her request asserts the spiritual resonance between womb and ocean, and shows her familiarity with Yemayá's favorite offerings. Every *orisha* has sacred foods; for Yemayá, two of them are watermelon and molasses, and Anzaldúa would often go to the ocean and offer them to her (Conner 187). Furthermore, in another document from her archive she describes being on a writing retreat and notes the following:

> The surge of the sea of leaves in her head—she can ask for no better music. . . . Behind white pine she squats bestowing to the Earth and the forest the pale yellow waters from her body, a token she never fails to give her mother—Yemaya, the ocean. ("Autoretratos" May 1991, box 57, folder 12, p. 43)

By constantly seeking small ways to make offerings to the *orisha*, including offerings from her own body, Anzaldúa quotidianly nurtured her sacred connection to Yemayá. An awareness of these personal practices makes Anzaldúa's desire to bring her uterus to the ocean not an exception but rather a moment of inflection in a lifelong relationship.

Anzaldúa's request for her uterus also demonstrates her growing knowledge of Santería/Regla de Ocha rituals. Had the doctor complied with the request to save her uterus after the surgery, Anzaldúa would have been able to take part in the practice of *ebó*. Although Santería/Regla de Ocha does not uphold a strict binary system, within its epistemological framework it is understood that at any given moment, every person and situation is influenced by one of two opposing energies, *osogbo* (negativity) or *iré* (positivity). Moving between these energies is part of the ebb and flow of life. However, those who find themselves unduly under the influence of *osogbo* may choose to perform an *ebó* (sacrificial offering) to change this energy. The purifying and strengthening qualities an *ebó* bestows upon an individual bring them closer into alignment with *iré*. *Ebó* is about transformation and evolution. The practice reminds us that we can influence many aspects of our lives through intentional action.

An *ebó* can be as simple as lighting a candle or as complex as a ceremony necessitating the assistance of several trained practitioners.[70] In orthodox communities, the mandate to perform an *ebó* often comes directly from the *orishas* when they are consulted on the querent's behalf by a diviner.[71] In line with Anzaldúa's independently crafted relationship with Yemayá, which she sustained through her ongoing connection to Teish, Anzaldúa decides to offer an *ebó* to her tutelary *orisha* guided by her spirits and her own volition. By making this choice, Anzaldúa demonstrates an unwavering commitment to nurturing Yemayá's energies in her life. She also acknowledges the power of the *orishas* and *egun* to facilitate ancestral healing, as this *ebó* would have been performed for herself and her lineage. In the end, however, Anzaldúa is unable to complete the ritual due to the doctor's dismissal of her request.

The doubled grief of losing her womb and the opportunity to perform an *ebó* for Yemayá provides a framework from which to consider the poem "Matriz sin tumba o 'el baño de la basura ajena'" ("Womb Without Tomb, or 'The Bath of Other People's Trash'"), in *Borderlands*. To be sure, the poetry in *Borderlands* is severely underread, and even the text as a whole is largely consumed in excerpts.[72] This particular poem has an added layer of inaccessibility for English-dominant readers because it is written solely in Spanish.[73] George Hartley observes that the poem "concerns Anzaldúa's struggle against the mainstream patriarchal Anglo-American conversion of the mestiza's womb/matrix (in all its implications) into mere trash" ("The Trash" 41). In making this assertion, Hartley is guided by the poetic presence of Tlazolteotl, whom he defines as "the goddess of lust and filth who figures as one of Coatlicue's aspects or manifestations" (41).[74] Hartley also notes that the verses appear to recount a hysterectomy, an experience he rightly connects to Anzaldúa's narrative in "La Prieta" (50). How Anzaldúa's womb wound up in the trash, however, is not legible to him, nor to anyone without access to Anzaldúa's archive because that information lies in the submerged story of Anzaldúa and Yemayá archived in the GEA Papers.

"Matriz sin tumba" presents a poetic rendition of the pain before Anzaldúa's hysterectomy and of the operation itself, although the verses are largely devoid of medical imagery. Instead, Anzaldúa weaves together images of night, blood, and pain, all of which abound in her autobiographical writings on this event. The exception to these metaphors is the substance to which the persona in the poem surrenders, "éter" (ether) (Anzaldúa, "Matriz" 158). Yet, "éter" triggers a double reading. "Ether" is a spiritual term that refers to the boundless heavens, and it is a colorless liquid still used as an anesthetic in several countries due to its low cost.[75] In Anzaldúa's poem this word powerfully combines the spiritual and the medical, an approach that aligns with how Anzaldúa viewed this moment of simultaneous birth and death in her life. Such a combination is also common in Santería/Regla de Ocha, as this and other Afro-diasporic religious systems often provide medical care for their faith communities.[76]

In the poem, Anzaldúa gives dangerous power to the night.[77] It is the night who comes to her, armed with knives (scalpels), and, while Anzaldúa watches, "me saca las entrañas, / que avienta la matriz en la basura—matriz sin tumba" ("Matriz" 158).[78] As Anzaldúa's autobiographical renditions of this event show, when she flatlined on the table she had an out-of-body experience. This perception is replicated in the poem when the poetic voice watches as the night guts her and throws her womb in the trash. The depiction of these actions parallels what happened when, during Anzaldúa's surgery, the request to save her womb was disregarded by her doctors. In this way, "Matriz sin tumba" becomes Anzaldúa's writerly *ebó*.

The connection between *ebó* and writing is strengthened by another detail found in the GEA Papers. Here, Anzaldúa describes the actions taking place just before entering the operating room:

> The nurse stripped her, shaved her abdomen, cut off her pubic hair, washed her lower body. Bautismo, ritual bath, thought Prieta watching another nurse drawing blue lines on her belly. Another priestess in regulation white dressed her in a wrinkled gown, then stretched her across the bed-on-wheels. . . . She descended into the abyss called OR-B on the second floor. ("La serpiente" June–July 1984, box 68, folder 3, p. 17)

The preparation for Anzaldúa's operation triggers a reconsideration of the intertwining of Afro-diasporic spiritual initiations and secular medical interventions.

The ultimate purpose of both is to heal, and they both require depurative measures such as those indicated here (bathing, shaving). Even the color white,
associated with sterility in hospital spaces, has strong religious meaning in the
Afro-diasporic world. These connections are reinforced by Anzaldúa's use of
the word "priestess" to describe the nurses and "baptism" to refer to the general
procedure.

The above extract from the GEA Papers exemplifies how access to the archive
enables readers to witness Anzaldúa's channeling of spiritual knowledge into
written accounts of her hysterectomy. As Ricardo F. Vivancos-Pérez and Norma
Elia Cantú point out, the second part of the poem's title, "Matriz sin tumba"
('el baño de la basura ajena'), "refers to the negativity cast upon specific people
and communities by others, especially in colonization contexts" (*Borderlands,
Critical Edition* 207). Read through Santería/Regla de Ocha's understanding
of *osogbo* and *iré*, this connection reinforces Anzaldúa's need and desire to perform an *ebó*, a ceremony capable of dislodging negative energies and ushering
in positive ones.

Deprived of the opportunity to physically perform her *ebó*, Anzaldúa instead
pens "Matriz sin tumba," a literary offering that hinges on the resonances
between Afro and Indigenous spiritual traditions. Anzaldúa's poem surreptitiously merges the pre-Columbian spiritual world, embodied by Coatlicue/
Tlazolteotl, with the Afro-diasporic one, enabling her to fulfill her promise to
Yemayá. This reading is aided by Hartley's avowal that "Tlazolteotl is the goddess
of the crossroads" ("The Trash" 55). Such a depiction generates a provocative
parallel between this goddess and Eshu/Elegguá, the *orisha* of the crossroads,
who also has a strong association with discarded things, such as trash. As the
traveling and messaging *orisha* par excellence, Eshu/Elegguá, channeled into
"Matriz sin tumba" through the figure of Tlazolteotl, allows Anzaldúa to fulfill
her spiritual mission despite the nightmare of the operation. Though her physical womb may ultimately lack a tomb, its loss generates a poem she can offer
Yemayá in lieu of what the allopathic medical world denied her. "Matriz sin
tumba" is potent evidence of the seamless flow between spiritual traditions in
Anzaldúa's life and her innately cultivated spiritual *mestizaje*.

Anzaldúa's hysterectomy altered her day-to-day life dramatically; she no
longer suffered from debilitating periods, but she was thrust into the grip of
menopause. This final encounter with death during her lifetime also changed
her in ways that extended far beyond the physical. Anzaldúa believed that each
of her deaths had been an initiation of sorts, a spiritual process by which she
was profoundly altered each time. Her near-fatal operation left her with an
eternal reminder of the changes she experienced, etched on her skin through
a "snake-like scar that undulated from waist to clit" ("Canción" 2001, box 68,

folder 6, p. 27). The scar came to represent Anzaldúa's simultaneous death and (re)birth, two aspects of her life marked by blood. She writes:

> From the beginning of the blood to the end of the blood. She felt like she was now someone else. She had been replaced but not deposed. She had given birth to herself and the new self was very familiar. She no longer felt alien. ("La serpiente" 1980, box 78, folder 11, p. 244b)

Discarding the feelings of alienation she had felt since childhood, Anzaldúa's final death before her ultimate passing in May 2004 from diabetes complications left her with a new perspective on herself and the world. After emerging from surgery, she found that she "knew secret things she should not have known. . . . She knew the answers to questions that she had never asked having been scared to hear the ansers [sic]" ("La serpiente" June–July, box 68, folder 3, p. 25). These brief mentions of the ability to know beyond the limits of everyday comprehension appear to herald the coming of Anzaldúa's theory of la facultad (the faculty), which she first discusses in Borderlands and describes as "a quick perception arrived at without conscious reasoning" (60).[79] This comment reflects how Anzaldúa's theoretical concepts flowed from the processing of her bodily experiences, making her work a living expression of theory in the flesh. And throughout this process, Yemayá accompanied and sheltered her, serving as a gateway to understanding how sacred energy could be used to seek knowledge, to heal, and to transform.

Water enabled Anzaldúa to travel through time, space, and belief systems. Her life experiences gave Anzaldúa the knowledge that water knew her name and that water itself had a name, Yemayá. As a living and breathing entity, water sustained Anzaldúa through countless experiences, replenished her sense of self when she needed refuge, and continually served as a portal through which she could connect to numinous energy and fathom healing for herself and for others. In this manner, Anzaldúa learned from Santería/Regla de Ocha to venerate water and the sacredness it holds. She then used that teaching to develop her own conocimientos, fueling her search for change and transformation. Such an understanding of the aquatic primes readers to look to the presence of this life-affirming liquid in her most cited work, Borderlands/La Frontera: The New Mestiza.

CHAPTER FOUR

Orishas in the Borderlands

*B*orderlands/*La Frontera: The New Mestiza*, Gloria Anzaldúa's first single-authored full-length work, can be read as the text in which the writer births herself through the crossing of borders: cultural, emotional, geopolitical, and psychic. Yet, it is far from a definitive work. As she declares in a posthumously published piece, "As a mestiza, I have many true faces, depending upon the kind of audience or the area I find myself in" ("The New Mestiza Nation" 211). Anzaldúa's expansive understanding of truth calls to mind her earlier claim that "'making faces' is my metaphor for constructing one's identity" ("Haciendo caras" xvi). Like much of Anzaldúa's writing, these proclamations underscore how the constantly shifting nature of her work can sustain what might appear to be contradictory readings.

Originally published in 1987, *Borderlands* displays many of the nuances of Anzaldúa's identity. The title of its first chapter, "The Homeland, Aztlán/*El otro México*," emphasizes the importance of Mesoamerican and Chicanx culture in Anzaldúa's writing. It also demonstrates her investment in making the construct of Aztlán, the mythological home of the Mexica/Aztecs, inclusive to more than those who identify as cisgendered men.[1] An equally important part of *Borderlands* lies in its untitled opening poem, where Anzaldúa describes seeing "*el mar atacar / la cerca en* Border Field Park" (the sea attacking / the fence at Border Field Park) (*Borderlands* 24). The tension between land (Aztlán and the border) and water (the sea and the river) suggests that the flows between solidity and fluidity encompass the theoretical epicenter of *Borderlands*. Soon, Anzaldúa provides a pivotal detail: her sea has a name. It is Yemayá, the Santería/Regla de Ocha *orisha* of saltwaters, whom Anzaldúa scripts as brazenly tearing down the border fence between the United States and Mexico. Anzaldúa's inclusion of Yemayá at such a crucial moment confirms her awareness of the emancipatory power of Afro-diasporic religious knowledges. Current scholarship on *Borderlands*, however, has largely glossed over the spiritual presence of Afro-Latinidad in the text, a gap this chapter seeks to fill.

It is striking that even as Yemayá appears in *Borderlands* before Coatlicue and Coyolxauhqui and right before La Virgen de Guadalupe, these three figures are heavily researched by Anzaldúan scholars while the *orisha* remains largely untouched.[2] Rather than suggest a hierarchy between these deities, I propose that Yemayá's early mention in *Borderlands* attests to Anzaldúa's awareness of the resonance between Afro and Indigenous spiritual systems. By reading *Borderlands* as a text suffused with the energies of Afro-diasporic waters, this chapter addresses how Anzaldúa's work productively engages with Blackness. Following M. Jacqui Alexander's assertion that sacred waters are "unrelated on the surface only, for down in that abyss their currents reach for each other and fold, without the slightest tinge of resentment" (258), I propose that the waters in *Borderlands* are unbounded by secular cartographies. While the Rio Grande/Río Bravo and the Pacific Ocean are not often placed in conversation with the Atlantic Ocean and the Caribbean Sea, I work from the premise that the energies that inhabit bodies of water are always already in communion with each other.

The submerged connections sustained by Afro-diasporic waters in *Borderlands* become evident if we read water as a place and a nonhuman actor that enables Anzaldúa to channel Yemayá and other *orishas* from the Santería/Regla de Ocha pantheon such as Eshu/Elegguá and Oyá into the text. Their presence aids Anzaldúa in blurring the boundaries between worlds, spiritual and otherwise. In this chapter, I identify key moments in *Borderlands* where the *orishas* appear to uncover the epistemological weight of water in the text. My analysis is guided by Aisha M. Beliso-De Jesús's observation that "Santería copresences speak to the power of silence. They caution those who listen that not everything can or should be fully articulated, disclosed, or transparent" (*Electric Santería* 103). Such a portrayal makes evident that the silence that has largely shrouded the Afro-diasporic knowledges in *Borderlands* is reflective of their very essence. By reading at the junctures between the legible and the illegible, I show how incorporating a Caribbean-infused Afro-diasporic theoretical framework when considering the work of Gloria Anzaldúa, a Chicana from the Rio Grande Valley, productively challenges our understandings of disciplines and knowledges and opens us to multiple readings of her work.

THE BORDERWATERS OF *BORDERLANDS*

In Chicanx and Latinx studies, the word "borderlands" has become synonymous with Anzaldúa's eponymous text. Nonetheless, C. J. Alvarez, a historian of the US Southwest, advises that this word be used with caution because it "tends to ignore 'borderwaters'" and is rarely used by the inhabitants of border spaces (241n1). Although he rightly addresses Anzaldúa's writing on the borderlands and, notably, the inflection of race and gender her work brought to the term, C. J. Alvarez's analysis does not take into account that for Anzaldúa, the borderlands *did* encompass borderwaters. Though rarely spoken of in this way, *Borderlands* is a text that opens and closes with water. The first body of water it presents is the sea, and the last one it references is the Rio Grande/Río Bravo. Yet, why would a text that explores the histories, cultures, and lived experiences of Chicanx communities in the US Southwest be bookended by water in this way?

One answer for this question is that the sea and the river are part of the US/Mexico border, even though bodies of water are often absent in discussions of this space.[3] One need only think of the pejorative term *mojado*, "wetback," to realize how water becomes both hypervisible and invisible in border spaces.[4] Anzaldúa's decision to frame *Borderlands* with water makes evident that the United States has more aqueous borders than terrestrial ones (Roberts 5). Spirituality, however, is another part of the answer, especially when considering the role that water and particularly the ocean played in Anzaldúa's spiritual awakening and evolution. As a sacred element that can traverse the borders of time, geographies, and cultures, Anzaldúa's invocation of Afro-diasporic waters at the start of *Borderlands* affirms the nonheterogeneous nature of her narrative and enables her to visualize a way through the intense moments of pain and suffering discussed in the text.

In the preface to the first edition of *Borderlands*, Anzaldúa beseeches the reader to avoid anchoring her work to a particular physical space. Although she acknowledges that she is writing about experiences that emanate from the Texas-US Southwest/Mexican border, she contends that "the psychological borderlands, the sexual borderlands and the spiritual borderlands are not particular to the Southwest" (*Borderlands* 19). This self-dislodging of *Borderlands* reflects Mary Pat Brady's observation that "Chicana considerations of the border render the border much more ambivalent and complex than the simple, alluring metaphor cultural theory imagines, and more revealing than the national political imaginary might wish" (173). Anzaldúa's decision to begin and end *Borderlands* with water can thus be considered an aesthetic manifestation of her desire to broaden the reach of her text; in *Borderlands*, water repeatedly moves beyond and even tears down borders, tempering tensions between the particular and the universal.

Water is the conduit by which Anzaldúa channels Yemayá and other *orishas* into *Borderlands*. The element's centrality in the text reflects her penchant for the maritime as well as her knowledge of the lived experiences of the *orishas*, all of whom arrived in the Americas due to the forceful crossing of waters imposed by the transatlantic slave trade. Yemayá's origin story reverberates with Anzaldúa's in that the latter's identity as a Chicana was dictated by shifts in bodies of water that took place when "*los norteamericanos* pushed the Texas border down 100 miles, from *el río Nueces* to *el río Grande*" (*Borderlands* 29). Anzaldúa and Yemayá are both border crossers. The violence of (neo)colonialism cannot be divested from their life stories or from their waters. In this context, Anzaldúa's inclusion of water and the sea in her work, particularly regarding the correlation between its physical and spiritual dimensions, is pivotal to understanding the relevance of rippling borders in *Borderlands*.

My concept of rippling borders emerges from the need to address the particularities that arise when water is made to serve as a border.[5] To be sure, the current global reality scripts borders as static spaces that can be opened, closed, and patrolled. Rippling borders, however, render visible the futility of these measures, as they are constantly moving and sometimes even violently changing. A prime example of the actions and consequences of a rippling border is the Chamizal dispute between El Paso and Ciudad Juárez on the US/Mexico border. In this controversial incident "a piece of Mexican territory [was] accidentally ceded to the United States by an out-of-control river," the Rio Grande/Río Bravo (C. J. Alvarez 144). After almost a century of conflict, in the 1960s the Chamizal dispute was rectified through various methods of control. Forever altering the border between El Paso and Ciudad Juárez, the river was "shortened, straightened, canalized, channelized, and immobilized to the specifications of border builders" (C. J. Alvarez 156).[6] The severity of the response to the Chamizal dispute illustrates how the dilemma was ultimately about "the failure to control water" (C. J. Alvarez 151).

Knowledge of the historical legacy of the Rio Grande/Río Bravo as a rippling border adds power to Anzaldúa's evocation of this forcefully contained river at the end of *Borderlands*, augmenting the unfettered energy of the ocean, Yemayá, evoked at the book's beginning. Rather than consider the Chamizal dispute an example of futility, I read the Rio Grande/Río Bravo in *Borderlands* as a rippling border whose power is preserved by its ties to the boundless ocean, intensifying water's noncompliance to hegemonic power in the text. Rippling borders continue to resist control, unleashing their potential to become sites and metaphors for territorial, ideological, and spiritual contestation. By bookending *Borderlands*, water heightens the text's own indomitable nature.

The resistant fluidity that permeates *Borderlands* drives the book's constant repudiation of the borders of genre. Blending prose, poetry, history, memoir, and many others, Anzaldúa's work textually personifies the title of its first section, "*Atravesando Fronteras*/Crossing Borders." The use of the gerund here connotes incessant movement, directly contesting the presumed fixity of geopolitical borders and heralding the role ascribed to water in the opening poem. The title also resonates with the Afro-diasporic religious world, where no crossing is ever final

(Alexander 6). Emphasizing the importance of focusing on process rather than product, the title of the opening section of Borderlands speaks to the experiences of migration and diaspora taking place across the waters throughout centuries. The repetition of slashed/bilingual titles in the text suggests the interplay between borders and borderlands, mirroring the role of the Rio Grande/Río Bravo, one of the most visible borders of the Global South. Consistently playing more than one role and holding more than one meaning, water's presence at the start of Borderlands signals the necessity of avoiding Manichean understandings of borders and divisions. Instead, Anzaldúa's text offers a profound reflection on the various ways borders simultaneously sever and generate new channels of engagement.

Borderlands opens with a poem that literally and spiritually depicts a powerful rippling border, the Pacific Ocean. Its verses infuse Borderlands with Yemayá's energy, marking the text as one in dialogue with the Afro-diasporic world through its engagement with water. The poem's transformative power begins with its visual depiction on the page. The first stanza is printed in a way that roughly resembles the shape of the United States, and the second suggests that of Mexico. The rest of the poem undulates back and forth, snakelike, flowing like ocean and river water.[7] Most of the poem appears in the fluid pattern, giving credence to water's often disregarded presence as part of the US/Mexico border. Additionally, it underscores Anzaldúa's recurrent communion with the aquatic, evident in rituals such as her almost daily walks along the ocean during her time in Santa Cruz, California. Anzaldúa visited the sea to spiritually recharge and reconnect; by beginning Borderlands in this space, she invites readers to do the same.

The opening poem is written in the first person, setting the stage for the confessional tone that distinguishes Borderlands. The power of the first person collapses the boundaries between Anzaldúa the narrator and Anzaldúa the writer. As she explains, "Here we all are: Gloria the author, the I who's the narrator who's immersed in the writing of the poem—often the boundary between author and narrator gets erased so that I become the I of the poem" ("On the Process" 195–196). Inspired by this intentional permeability, in my analysis I refer to the "I" in the poem interchangeably as Anzaldúa and as the poetic voice. In the first stanza, the one shaped like the United States, Anzaldúa situates readers in time and place. She divulges that the poetic voice is "at the edge where earth touches ocean," a mercurial place where energies quickly shift from "a gentle coming together" to "a violent clash" (Borderlands 23). This portrayal hints at one of Anzaldúa's most widely recognized concepts, that of nepantla, the space in between.

It is in Borderlands that Anzaldúa first speaks of nepantla, one of her best-known theories.[8] Nepantla surfaces as Anzaldúa describes the new mestiza, a new subjectivity that is "in a constant state of mental nepantilism, an Aztec word meaning torn between ways" (*Borderlands* 100). Although Anzaldúa only names *nepantla* toward the end of the prose section of *Borderlands*, readers aware of Anzaldúa's theories will note that they have entered *nepantla* upon picking up the text. The poetic voice's location at the lip of the ocean is another example of this precarious location. Early on in her career, Anzaldúa defined *nepantla* as "the space between two bodies of water, the space between two worlds" ("Gloria" 13). In *Borderlands*, she conceives her trademark concept as a watery site and portal, one she will continually evoke in her writings, underscoring the importance of reading water in her work. Water, then, plays a multifaceted role in the development of Anzaldúan thought, quietly infusing her visionary outlook with radical possibilities for connection in the face of rupture. Such a fluid understanding of *nepantla* explains why scholarship on Afro-diasporic religions has begun to incorporate the term, creating epistemic bridges that acknowledge Anzaldúa's geopolitical and spiritual transgressiveness.[9]

The role afforded to water in the initial poem in *Borderlands* tempers the hegemony of Aztlán within the Chicano imaginary. Although Anzaldúa views Aztlán as a homeland for Chicanx peoples, her rendition of this mythical place is not solely land-based, evident in how the first place she visits upon invoking it is the ocean. From the start, water broadens the reach of the text, echoing Anzaldúa's own actions when she questioned the exclusionary facets of Aztlán. In 1989 Rudolfo Anaya and Francisco Lomelí excerpted the first chapter of *Borderlands* for their edited anthology, *Aztlán: Essays on the Chicano Homeland*. Although the revised and expanded version of this collection published in 2017 increased the diversity of the original contributors, out of the twelve essays in the first edition, Anzaldúa's is the only one authored by a woman. When Anzaldúa raised this issue with Anaya, he responded by stating that he and Lomelí had "looked far and wide for women writers who have written on the subject. Yours was it" (Anzaldúa, Correspondence with Anaya, box 6, folder 11). The lack of inclusion in the original version of this landmark text for Chicano studies attests to how violence can be perpetuated by alternative constructs, even mythical ones such as Aztlán. In *Borderlands*, water and Yemayá enable Anzaldúa to bring this fissure to the surface. As the sea battles against the border wall, it erodes Aztlán's predetermined limits.

In contrast to the presumably fixed nature of land, mythical or otherwise, water encourages the confluence of contradiction. In *Borderlands*, this leads to a provocative juxtaposition of the subject and the border/borderland in the opening poem. Anzaldúa, as the subject, is called in many directions: "wind tugging at my sleeve," enacts a horizontal movement, and "feet sinking into the sand," signals a vertical pull (*Borderlands* 23). In her interaction with the natural elements, then, Anzaldúa is at a crux: "I stand at the edge where earth touches ocean" (*Borderlands* 23). The poetic voice embodies vulnerability here because they are not on solid ground. But marginality affords a tenuous privilege. From her liminal position, Anzaldúa has a panoramic view that allows her to witness what those immersed in the clearly delineated world cannot. Performatively standing on the borderlands, in *nepantla*, the poetic voice can see everything on either side of the border.[10] That all of this happens by inhabiting an amphibian location that is neither fully land nor fully aquatic illustrates how quickly water begins to epistemologically function in the text.

The crossroads of land and water where Anzaldúa stands in the initial poem is a prologue to the space invoked in the book's last chapter, "*La conciencia de la mestiza*/Towards a New Consciousness" (*Borderlands* 102). This chapter contains another pivotal point regarding the text's engagement with the Afro-diasporic world, although it is likely even more overlooked than the mention of Yemayá at the start of *Borderlands*.[11] The section titled "*La encrucijada*/The Crossroads" begins with the following poem:

> A chicken is being sacrificed
>   at a crossroads, a simple mound of earth
> a mud shrine for *Eshu*,
>   *Yoruba* god of indeterminacy,
>   who blesses her choice of path.
>   She begins her journey.
>   (*Borderlands* 102)

This poem is printed on the page in a way that conveys walking or moving forward step-by-step. In Santería/Regla de Ocha, the action of moving forward is associated with Eshu/Elegguá, also known as Legba in Haitian Vodou and La 21 División.[12] Since Eshu/Elegguá is known as the doorman of these traditions, his invocation by Anzaldúa displays her understanding of and appreciation for Afro-diasporic worldviews. Eshu/Elegguá's inclusion in *Borderlands* strengthens Suzanne Bost's contention that Anzaldúa's "*conciencia de la mestiza* is built on a foundation of violence, cross-cultural penetration, and internal fragmentation" ("Gloria Anzaldúa's Mestiza Pain" 7). Such a portrayal creates bonds between Anzaldúa's new *mestiza* and the processes by which the knowledges of Afro-diasporic religiosity were generated in the Americas, presenting another valuable point of contact between Anzaldúa's engagement with Indigeneity and Blackness.

A multifaceted and complex deity, Eshu/Elegguá is tasked with maintaining what Rowland Abiodun describes as "the precarious balance between the malevolent and the benevolent powers of the universe" ("Who Was the First to Speak?" 56). An embodiment of dynamic duality, he is the path opener as well as the path closer, and one of the most repeated prayers to him asks that he "abra camino" (open the path). Eshu/Elegguá's penchant for movement links him to the feet, which Martin A. Tsang finds are "closest to the earth, maintain a connection with the earthly plane and with the ancestors, and are tools of movement, bringing forward motion to the body" ("Beguiling Eshu" 219). Eshu/Elegguá presides over all crossroads, earthly and otherwise, leading Solimar Otero to describe this *orisha* as a translator between the physically tangible world and the spiritual one ("Èṣù" 202). His presence at the crossroads adds nuance to how Anzaldúa's predilection for this space in her writing exemplifies her investment in "making the structures of the world themselves mobile" (Bost, *Shared Selves* 112). Eshu/Elegguá's extraordinary expansiveness enables him to be everywhere at all times, defying the confines of time and space. A mediator by nature, his natural habitat is *nepantla*, making him an integral guide and companion for the new *mestiza's* journey.

Eshu/Elegguá also relates to speech; his ability to understand all languages grants him access to infinite knowledge, a quality that explains the interpretive role he plays in Ifá rituals of divination.[13] His capacity for fluency in the face of linguistic multiplicity is a clear repudiation of the ruptures upheld by biblical stories such as that of the Tower of Babel, in which language variance becomes a tool of division and control. This quality places the *orisha's* presence in *Borderlands* in sync with the multilingual nature of the text. Finally, since Eshu/Elegguá is believed to have witnessed the creation of the world, he is "able to advise and counsel humanity regarding their destinies" (Tsang, "Beguiling Eshu" 217). Given his importance in path opening and path blessing, it is not surprising that Anzaldúa's new *mestiza* pays homage to him through a literary *addimú*, an offering, which expresses the energies of Afro-diasporic ceremony surrounding *Borderlands*.[14]

Anzaldúa's invocation of Eshu/Elegguá aligns with Toyin Falola's view of the *orisha* as "a force of goodness that makes a new beginning possible" (13). Through her poem, Anzaldúa asks Eshu/Elegguá to bless the journey the new *mestiza* is about to undertake. To gain his favor she offers him a chicken, demonstrating her familiarity with the functions of ritual sacrifice in Santería/Regla de Ocha. The verses to Eshu/Elegguá are thus more than a poem; they are a prayer.[15] The intersection between water and land in the opening poem of *Borderlands* presages the appearance of Eshu/Elegguá because the crossroads are his domain. Attention to these subtleties enables readers to witness how Afro-diasporic religiosity creates a fluid gateway through which Anzaldúa epistemologically births her new *mestiza*. At this point, we would do well to remember that engagement with Afro-diasporic knowledges is far ranging. Throughout history, these spiritual *corrientes* have been accessed by diverse groups of people who, as Vanessa

K. Valdés finds, "have been touched culturally by the contributions of those of African descent" (*Oshun's Daughters* 165). By paying attention to the role of the *orishas* in *Borderlands*, readers can trace how Anzaldúa's new *mestiza* dialogues with the realities of Afro-diasporic peoples and with Afro-Latinidad. True to his role as witness to the creation of the world and harbinger of new opportunities, Eshu/Elegguá is the deity who opens the door to this path.

Anzaldúa's decision to address Eshu/Elegguá at the end of the book rather than at the beginning is perhaps perplexing at first. Yet, this *orisha* revels in contradiction and surprise. He has no regard for the linearity of time or the limitations of space, a reality evident in how his appearance in *Borderlands* relates to what is happening at this precise juncture. Anzaldúa writes that "*la mestiza* has gone from being the sacrificial goat to becoming the officiating priestess at the crossroads" (*Borderlands* 102). This verse serves as an apt description of the transformation the author herself has undergone throughout the text, one that can be read as an act of spiritual initiation due to the power of water in Afro-diasporic religions. Read through this framework, the way *Borderlands* opens and closes with the mention of two Santería/Regla de Ocha *orishas* (Yemayá and Eshu/Elegguá) deepens the book's engagement with spiritual death and rebirth as it proposes a reconfiguration of the self.[16]

GUTTED, CRUMBLED, AND GASHED: THE RAGING WATERS OF BORDERLANDS/LA FRONTERA

Beyond providing a complex rendition of the relationship between water and borders, the opening poem in *Borderlands* establishes water's agency and strength in the text. This becomes particularly apparent in the second stanza:

Across the border in Mexico
    stark silhouette of houses gutted by waves,
        cliffs crumbling into the sea,
            silver waves marbled with spume
                gashing a hole under the border fence.
                    (*Borderlands* 23)

The words employed by the narrative voice to describe the effect of water on land-based structures are revelatory. Water guts, crumbles, and gashes, all forceful actions that are ongoing. The verses leave no doubt of the power Anzaldúa attributes to the aquatic. Though it may be life-giving, it is very much capable of destruction.

Beyond having a shape that alludes to the landmass of Mexico, the way these verses are set on the page suggests erosion. Erosion is a crisis of land, a dilution of its presumed solidity by elements of the natural world such as wind and, tellingly here, water. In addition to the "houses gutted by waves," even naturally occurring structures such as the cliff are crumbling under the transformative power of water. Erosion may also allude to the loss of territory Mexico experienced in 1848 when it was forced to cede a large portion of its territory to the United States, an experience Anzaldúa addresses in the first chapter of *Borderlands*.[17] In this manner, water's forceful movement traces and surpasses the sanctioned histories of these spaces, augmenting its ability to sustain contradiction.

At this point in the poem, the water's actions are concentrated in the comings and goings of the waves. Waves are border products; they result from the dynamic interaction between two natural elements, water and wind. This confluence is visible in concepts such as Karin Amimoto Ingersoll's "seascape epistemology," in which water and wind operate as interconnected beings (6). Furthermore, the formidable combination of water and wind in the poem evokes the relationship between Yemayá (water, sea) and Oyá (wind), both of whom Anzaldúa claimed as spiritual mothers. The emphasis on waves in the opening poem of *Borderlands* thus provides another entry point into Anzaldúa's engagement with Afro-diasporic religions.

There is another verse in this stanza that points to Yemayá's presence, even though the *orisha* has not yet been named. Anzaldúa describes the color of the waves as silver, one of Yemayá's colors.[18] Blue is considered Yemayá's primary color, but silver is also associated with her, and her hair is sometimes depicted in this hue (Cabrera, *Yemayá y Ochún* 32). Silver signals the wealth attributed to this *orisha* and her waters, and it is the material of many of her sacred tools (Cabrera, *Yemayá y Ochún* 268).[19] In addition, silver is the color associated with the moon, a celestial body intimately connected to the tides and hence to Yemayá.[20] As early as the second stanza of the opening poem, Anzaldúa threads water, Yemayá, and resistance together. By portraying the ocean and Yemayá in this manner, Anzaldúa proclaims the power of water to withstand and surpass painful experiences of border imposition. Her choice to allude to Yemayá as she looks at the Mexican side of the border is a nod to the existence and marginalization of Afro-diasporic spirituality on both sides of the divide, another vital detail gleaned from examining the presence of the *orishas* in *Borderlands*.[21] For, if Yemayá is present in Mexico and the United States, why would she not be a deity revered by Anzaldúa? What does the elision of the *orishas* in scholarship on *Borderlands* say about the invisibility of Afro-Latinx epistemologies in Chicanx and Latinx studies?

The third stanza of the poem is the first one set to replicate the flows of water. Now moving past the presumably familiar space of land, the fury of the sea increases:

> *Miro el mar atacar*
> *la cerca en* Border Field Park
> *con sus buchones de agua,*
> an Easter Sunday resurrection
> of the brown blood in my veins.
>
> *Oigo el llorido del mar, el respiro del aire,*
> my heart surges to the beat of the sea.
>   In the gray haze of the sun
>   the gull's shrill cry of hunger
>   the tangy smell of the sea seeping into me.
>   (*Borderlands* 24, italics in the original)[22]

The movement of the verses on the page reflects the ocean's undulating currents and resistant fluidity. The sea refuses to conform to the linear, rigid border fence that intends to cut across it. Moreover, water and wind are anthropomorphized; the ocean wails and the air breathes, hinting at the presence of the *orishas* Yemayá and Oyá.

In this stanza Anzaldúa discloses her exact physical location: Border Field Park, a place with a distinct history within the US/Mexico borderlands and borderwaters. In 1971 a part of Border Field Park was christened Friendship Park by the Nixon administration. This name was meant to allude to the presumably cordial relationship that could be cultivated between the United States and Mexico, countries divided by an iron veil ("Families Resuming Tradition"). The creation of Friendship Park was a moment of temporary respite in the border's complicated history. The park provided a space where families from both sides could come together on neutral ground, even though it also included Boundary Monument 258, which marks the line established in 1848 between the United States and Mexico (Holslin 140; Tocilovac 178). Epitomizing a particularly violent rendition of *nepantla*, for Marko Tocilovac, Friendship Park is "both a park and a part of the border fence, [a] place of meeting and of division" (178). The contradictory meanings of Border Field Park and Friendship Park in the San Diego/Tijuana borderlands add nuance to the opening verses of Anzaldúa's poem, where she writes of "a gentle coming together / at other times and places a violent clash" (*Borderlands* 23).

When Anzaldúa published *Borderlands* in 1987, Friendship Park was only surrounded by barbed wire (Tocilovac 178). Yet, the book presciently foretells what would come with the erection of a new border wall in the 1990s, followed by the imposition of post-9/11 policies such as the Secure Fence Act of 2006, which led to the increasing militarization, policing, and barricading of the US side of the border (C. J. Alvarez 212). As a result, between 2008 and 2010 the

US government erected a second border fence in Border Field Park (Tocilovac 181). This new wall cut directly through Friendship Park, making impossible the family gatherings that had served as a healing balm for many torn communities. Jill M. Holslin observes that where families had been able to sit down together, touch, hug, and share a meal, now "a thick mesh covers the bars, and visitors can get up close but can only put their fingertips through to touch loved ones" (146).[23] Although I was unable to visit Friendship Park due to the many access restrictions that govern this space, I visited Border Field Park in 2018.[24] I could not get within several feet of the border wall on the beach. The moment anyone moved too close, the ever-present Border Patrol would sound an alarm, a warning to move back.

Border Field Park is located on an estuary "situated directly on top of the international boundary, near the delta and lagoon where the Tijuana River drains into the sparkling Pacific Ocean" (Holslin 139–140).[25] The meeting of salty and sweet waters adds depth to this site's selection as the beginning for *Borderlands*, as the power of the sea described in the initial poem is never separate from that of the river. In Santería/Regla de Ocha, estuaries are potent spiritual sites that house the energies of Yemayá (sea) and Ochún (river).[26] The diversity of the waters in Border Field Park points to how in *Borderlands* the river and sea are implicitly joined from the start. Anzaldúa's choice to begin the text at an estuary reflects how the borderwaters of the Tijuana River, the Colorado River, and the Rio Grande "have been dammed, channelized, canalized, straightened, relocated, pumped, and, in some places, lined with concrete" (C. J. Alvarez 3). The borderwaters of these rivers bear the wounds of colonization and empire in distinct ways. Such a realization underscores the relevance of Anzaldúa's decision to feature water in the beginning and end of *Borderlands*. The omnipresence of the aquatic transforms the text itself into a literary estuary where the confluence of knowledges and histories fuels Anzaldúa's search for new ways of being in the world.

Beyond inviting reflection on the location of where *Borderlands* begins, the watery stanzas of the initial poem mention a spiritual ritual: Easter. In Catholicism, Easter is a moment of joy and celebration as the resurrection of Christ is believed to provide assurance of salvation for the faithful. Easter can thus be read as a powerful moment of death and rebirth, continuing with the ongoing discussion of Afro-diasporic religious initiations. Anzaldúa's invocation of Easter is infused with the power of Afro-diasporic waters. She becomes energized as she watches the ocean "attack" the fence at Border Field Park, a process that evokes the resurrection she viscerally experienced in the waters of South Padre Island as a child. The way Anzaldúa describes the "brown blood in my veins" and "the tangy smell of the sea seeping into me" generates an irrevocable bond between the currents of the ocean, a Catholic feast, and the body of the woman of color. At the same time, Anzaldúa's mention of Easter signals how this religious ceremony has become one that she acknowledges despite her dissociation from the Church.[27]

In a recorded discussion on *Borderlands* that took place September 16, 1987, Anzaldúa declares that she only remembers going to church on three occasions: for her first communion, when her father died, and when her grandmother died (box 155, folder 1, MP3 #101, GEA Papers). This view is supported by her mention in "La serpiente que se come su cola," her never-published autobiography, that "la Iglesia [the Church] felt like a cage" (1982–1983, box 78, folder 10, p. 14). In *Borderlands*, Anzaldúa recalls that her family "did not practice Roman Catholicism but a folk Catholicism with many pagan elements" (49). This view elucidates how for many people the adoption of Catholicism became a vehicle for ensuring the survival of Indigenous ways of knowing (Broyles-González 121). For this reason, Anzaldúa's religious and spiritual upbringing fostered an openness to the multiple faces of Catholicism in the Americas, faces that are also a part of the histories of Afro-diasporic religions in the hemisphere.

In Cuba, Santería/Regla de Ocha developed alongside Catholicism, often creating significant spiritual bridges and reciprocities between African and Western deities. A common representation of Yemayá is La Virgen de Regla (The Virgin of Regla), the patroness of the port of Regla, in Havana (Cabrera, *Yemayá y Ochún* 19). Rómulo Lachatañeré contends that La Virgen de Regla was originally white but became Black when she voyaged across the Black Sea (387); Elizabeth Pérez maintains that this Virgin is "the only Marian icon in Cuba considered to be of direct African descent" ("Nobody's Mammy" 10). In *Borderlands*, Catholicism's allusion to Yemayá and La Virgen de Regla flows into Anzaldúa's discussion of La Virgen de Guadalupe in the book's third chapter, "Entering into the Serpent," when Anzaldúa writes that "the *indio* and the *mestizo* continue to worship the old spirit entities . . . and their supernatural power, under the guise of Christian saints" (*Borderlands* 53). This statement is accompanied by a footnote in which Anzaldúa uses her discussion of La Virgen de Guadalupe to refer to other sacred feminine deities, including Yemayá. She states, "*La Virgen María* is often equated with the Aztec *Teleoinam*, the Maya *Ixchel*, the Inca *Mamacocha* and the Yoruba *Yemayá*" (*Borderlands* 116n17). By disclosing that when she invokes La Virgen she is simultaneously honoring Yemayá, Anzaldúa invites readers to see her recurrent mention of Guadalupe in her life and work as an act of Afro-Indigenous spiritual avowal.

To be sure, the sacred exchanges in Anzaldúa's life flowed in multiple directions. Luisah Teish brought the *orishas* to Anzaldúa's consciousness, but Anzaldúa also taught Teish, who explains, "It was Gloria that made me realize that

Our Lady of Tonantzin and consequently La Guadalupe holds a place of honor on my shrines" (quoted in Piña 114).[28] It is also noteworthy that Anzaldúa's collapsing of La Virgen de Guadalupe and Yemayá precedes *Borderlands*. The melding first appeared in "El Mundo Zurdo: The Vision" in *Bridge*, the very text that brought Anzaldúa and Teish together. Teish also wrote a preface to this particular section of the anthology. In "El Mundo Zurdo" Moraga and Anzaldúa declare:

> We, the women here, take a trip back into the self, travel to the deep core of our roots to discover and reclaim our colored souls, our rituals, our religion. We reach a spirituality that has been hidden in the hearts of oppressed people under layers of centuries of traditional god-worship. It emerges from under the veils of La Virgen de Guadalupe and unrolls from Yemaya's ocean waves whenever we need to be uplifted from or need the courage to face the tribulations of a racist patriarchal world where there is no relief. Our spirituality does not come from outside ourselves. (195)

This passage illustrates how Anzaldúa's spiritual framework recognized the affinity between Indigenous and Afro-diasporic epistemologies. The specific naming of Yemayá alongside La Virgen solidifies the bond between these deities, declaring it a touchstone of Anzaldúa's personal cosmology. The attention to secrecy in this passage also suggests why Yemayá is ever-present though sublimated in *Borderlands* and in much of Anzaldúa's oeuvre. By allowing her to shape-shift, Anzaldúa honors the survival strategies of the *orishas* and their practitioners, all of whom have mastered the practice of hiding in plain sight.

FIERCE WINDS: ANZALDÚA AND OYÁ

The opening poem in *Borderlands* continues with the poetic voice crossing from Border Field Park into Mexican territory. To accomplish this, they pass through the opening in the fence that the water has created.[29] As this action takes place, Anzaldúa notes that the wire has rusted due to "the salty breath of the sea" (*Borderlands* 24). Presenting yet another forceful action by Border Field Park's waterscape, this verse reinforces the intertwining of water and wind by uniting salt and breath. In the initial stanza, the wind was tugging at the narrator's sleeve as it helped create the waves that were eroding the landscape. Here, the wind helps dismantle the border fence through corrosion. Wind and breath are vital elements in the Afro-diasporic religious world and are associated with the *orisha* Oyá. Judith Gleason finds that Oyá "has the habit of becoming invisible, only to reappear somewhere else where you least expect her" (*Oya: In Praise* 1), an apt description of this *orisha*'s role in *Borderlands*.[30] Gleason's book, *Oya: In Praise of an African Goddess*, was originally published in 1987 and is part of Anzaldúa's personal library, evidencing her interest in learning more about this *orisha*. Moreover, Anzaldúa was fascinated with how *remolinos*, whirlwinds, are manifestations of Oyá in the natural world (Conner 187).

Oyá's energy is fiercely feminine, so much so that she helps warriors triumph in seemingly impossible battles.[31] Echoing the strength and fearlessness Anzaldúa ascribes to Oyá's winds in the initial poem of *Borderlands*, in Yoruba the *orisha*'s name means "she tore" (Gleason, *Oya: In Praise* 5). Unlike Yemayá, who despite having many sides is recurrently depicted as maternal, Oyá is unquestionably a fighter. Associated with fire, lightning, storms, tornadoes, and whirlwinds, Oyá is linked to transformation, primarily as it pertains to the transition between life and death: "As shape-shifter she [Oyá] is the River Niger, buffalo woman, dual symbol of the carrier of fire and mother of the cemetery, and mother of nine" (Alexander 304). There is a strong link between Oyá and shape-shifting but also between Oyá and the cemetery, one of the places in which her energy resides given her visceral association to *egun* (the dead, the ancestors).

An understanding of Oyá's energies bestows added meaning to Norma Alarcón's contribution to the introduction to the third edition of *Borderlands*, "Encuentros en la Encrucijada" (Encounters in the Crossroads). Given the importance of crossroads within the Afro-diasporic spiritual world, the very title of the piece presents a framework from which to interpret Alarcón's words. In this short reflection, Alarcón recounts a dream she had about Anzaldúa shortly after her death in 2004. In it, Alarcón was talking to Anzaldúa, who was standing between herself and a door to a cemetery. Alarcón shared this dream in a memorial for Anzaldúa held in September 2004 where Teish was in attendance. After the talk, Teish came up to Alarcón in a concerned manner and told her she needed to go to the cemetery and speak to Anzaldúa. She explicitly said Alarcón needed to "tell her [Anzaldúa] that you are not ready to leave" (Alarcón, "Encuentros" 231). Alarcón complied, visiting a cemetery on December 12, the day of La Virgen de Guadalupe. Alarcón's choice to speak to Anzaldúa in Oyá's dwelling place on the day of La Virgen de Guadalupe reinforces the multivalent spiritual currents of Anzaldúa's life.

Teish's attention to Alarcón's dream underscores how the dream world functions as a significant source of information in Afro-diasporic and Indigenous traditions. Due to Anzaldúa's ties to Oyá and the fact that she appeared to Alarcón at the threshold to a cemetery, Teish read Alarcon's dream as one in which Anzaldúa's spirit manifested through Oyá's energy to transmit a message. The energetic fusion between Anzaldúa's essence and that of the *orishas* reflects the enduring connection between them. It also supports the Santería/Regla de Ocha and Ifá death and memorial rites Teish and other practitioners conducted in memory of Anzaldúa after her passing (Conner 187). Because her domain is the cemetery, death rites in Santería/Regla de Ocha always invoke Oyá, adding power to the last line of Alarcón's entry, where she wishes that Anzaldúa's "spirit-breath dance to the rhythms of the cosmos" ("Encuentros" 232). As the *orisha* associated with the wind and the air, Oyá is present in every breath we take, from the first to the last (Alexander 304). In these closing lines, Alarcón honors the ties between Oyá and Anzaldúa while simultaneously freeing them of all restrictions and boundaries.

Borderlands provides additional textual evidence of the reciprocity between Oyá and Anzaldúa. While Yemayá and Eshu/Elegguá are directly invoked in *Borderlands*, to find Oyá readers must turn to the endnotes.[32] In the book's fourth chapter, "*La herencia de Coatlicue*/The *Coatlicue* State," the subsection entitled "The *Coatlicue* State" includes an endnote attached to the word "whirlwind":

> For me, *la Coatlicue* is the consuming internal whirlwind,[7] the symbol of the underground aspects of the psyche.... Goddess of birth and death, *Coatlicue* gives and takes away life. (*Borderlands* 68, italics in the original)

Endnote 7 reads as follows: "*Yemayá* is also known as the wind, *Oyá* as the whirlwind. According to Luisah Teish, I am the daughter of *Yemayá*, with *Oyá* being the mother who raised me" (*Borderlands* 118n7, italics in the original).[33] Anzaldúa's revelation is fascinating because orthodox Santería/Regla de Ocha tradition construes Yemayá and Oyá as enemies, so much so that they cannot be in the same room when a ceremony takes place (Cabrera, *Yemayá y Ochún* 277–278). As a result, Anzaldúa's spiritual genealogy defies convention, intimating a more collaborative nature. Some *orisha* devotees attest to this possibility: "Oya will call upon Yemayá to help her children . . . I know that some stories talk about the enmity between the two of them, but that is not what I experience" (Alexander 305, ellipsis in the original). *Borderlands* presents Yemayá and Oyá as having an unbreakable bond that manifests in the powerful waves comprised of Yemayá's waters and Oyá's winds.[34] Theirs is a union capable of dismantling the border wall.

Even though the *orishas* contributed to Anzaldúa's understanding of the sacred as an inherent tool for survival, academic scholarship has largely focused on the centrality of Coatlicue (Serpent Skirt) in Anzaldúan thought. Acknowledging the flows between Coatlicue and *orishas* such as Yemayá and Oyá thus becomes generatively disruptive work. Coatlicue's attributes, as depicted in the passage above, are a blend of many of the characterizations afforded to Yemayá and Oyá. This resonance shows how Anzaldúa uses her evolving spirituality to channel Mexica and Afro-diasporic knowledges into her writing. The existence of this energetic transmittal is pivotal to understanding how in an earlier draft of *Borderlands* Anzaldúa referred to the now-iconic "Coatlicue State" as "the Medusa State" (Keating, "Archival Alchemy" 166). Although Medusa and Coatlicue are affiliated with the serpent and with creation and destruction, Medusa hails from Europe and Coatlicue is Mesoamerican. Moreover, Oyá is present in this invocation of female divinity, as her energy is often likened to that of Medusa and Hecate, both of whom Anzaldúa identified with early in her career (Fernández Olmos and Paravisini-Gebert 55; Gleason, *Oya: In Praise* 14). Careful attention to these movements and shifts by Anzaldúa discloses how the presence of the *orishas* in *Borderlands* signals moments of resonance and growth in Anzaldúa's spiritual and creative process.

Reading the opening poem of *Borderlands* through the lens of water continues to reveal elements connected with the Afro-diasporic religious world. Once the poetic voice crosses the border represented by the fence (through the hole created by the conjoined forces of Yemayá's water and Oyá's wind), they see children playing soccer on the Mexican side able to kick the ball from Mexico to the United States without hindrance (*Borderlands* 24). Given the poetic voice's position in an ambiguous spiritual plane that lies beyond the confines of borders (*nepantla*), here the poem gestures toward Eshu/Elegguá. His presence is signaled by the mention of children, as this *orisha* has a strong association with their innocence and playfulness. Eshu/Elegguá's complete disregard for borders and limitations explains the ease with which the children's game surpasses borders. As the master of ceremonies, Eshu/Elegguá is the *orisha* who must be honored before any ceremony begins, and his appearance at this moment heralds Yemayá's spectacular entrance into *Borderlands*.

WIRE CROWNS AND BLOWN WALLS: ANZALDÚA'S YEMAYÁ

Once the poetic voice traverses the fence, the border wall becomes a "chainlink fence crowned with rolled barbed wire" (*Borderlands* 24). This portrayal creates another moment of polysemic spiritual meaning, bringing to mind Catholicism through the allusion to a crown of thorns. At the same time, when one is initiated into Santería/Regla de Ocha the person is said to be "crowned."[35] To become crowned, initiates must undergo *kari ocha*, the complex ceremony that transforms the human body into a receptacle for the sacred. Once the ritual is completed, the newly birthed *iyawo* (a genderless term that implies one who is wedded to the *orishas*) is rendered an embodiment of their titular *orisha* on earth.[36] In this sense, the crown symbolizes new life, a resurrection or rebirth, as an initiate's life is thought to begin anew after coronation (Cabrera, *Yemayá y Ochún* 128). In contrast with how Catholicism's crown of thorns construes physical suffering as a gateway toward spiritual salvation, Santería/Regla de Ocha's crown protects the physical body from harm, spiritual and otherwise. These clashing meanings parallel the competing images of the fence and the sea as sites of both violence and regeneration in *Borderlands*.

Soon after these verses the climax of the poem arrives:

> The sea cannot be fenced,
> *el mar* does not stop at borders.
> To show the white man what she thought of his
> arrogance,
> *Yemayá* blew that wire fence down.
> (*Borderlands* 25)

Through these verses Yemayá finally makes her stunning though often over-looked entrance into *Borderlands*.[37] Micaela Díaz-Sánchez argues that it is not only the mention of Yemayá that should capture the reader's attention but the placement of her presence in the poem (156). The stanzas above come directly after Anzaldúa indelibly describes how the US/Mexico border violently cuts through her body. Hence, Yemayá's dismissal and removal of the border fence that is "staking fence rods" (*Borderlands* 24) into Anzaldúa's flesh can be read as an act of subversive and submerged healing. It is also a repudiation of the violence enacted upon the *orisha*'s own liquid body, as the border wall is simultaneously piercing Yemayá's "skin."

In the context of the double meaning of the barbwire crown, the potent healing enacted by the ocean responds to the psychic wounds of dogma. This reading reconnects with Anzaldúa's uneasy relationship with Catholicism and the image of the crucified Christ, whose pierced body is healed through his resurrection on Easter.[38] Anzaldúa's inclusion of the *orishas* Yemayá, Eshu/Eleggúa, and Oyá in *Borderlands* is thus aligned with the overall psychic, physical, and historical healing enacted by the text. Rather than compete with the many forces and deities invoked throughout its pages, the presence of the *orishas* in *Borderlands* demonstrates that for Anzaldúa the sacred is "a praxis of resistance and methodology: not a grand mythical or disembodied notion of transcendence" (Díaz-Sánchez 155). The book's complex epistemic backbone, which signals various and sometimes contradictory traditions, exemplifies Anzaldúa's profound understanding of what Afro-diasporic waters have to offer.

The way Anzaldúa chooses to depict Yemayá is noteworthy. *Borderlands* actively rejects the white, heterosexual, male adjudication of power and desire, represented here through the erection of the border wall. Rather than exalt Yemayá's motherly, nurturing qualities, which could be read as potentially docile, Anzaldúa focuses on the anger and power that lie just below the surface. These are the forces that enable Yemayá to "blow that wire fence down." The focus on Yemayá's motherly rage places the *orisha* in conversation with Anzaldúa's investment in unearthing chthonic representations of femininity. This quality of Anzaldúa's spiritual activism is often asserted in her recovery of Coatlicue and Coyolxauhqui, the subversive mother-and-daughter team that challenges the phallic primacy of Huitzilopochtli, the Aztec god of war, but it is also applicable to her entanglements with the Afro-diasporic religious world.

Anzaldúa's scripting of Yemayá and of the ocean itself challenges patriarchy's representations of water. In *Water and Dreams: An Essay on the Imagination of Matter*, Gaston Bachelard claims that when water is nurturing, it is female; when it becomes aggressive, it is male (14–15). Yet, this binary and heteronormative understanding of a nonconforming and ever-transforming element such as water is severely limiting. It also distorts how Afro-diasporic religious epistemologies conceive of balance. Western hegemony has created a world where male and female energies are two opposing ends of a rigid spectrum. Nature, however, does not follow these strict constructs. Neither do the *orishas*. In their world, the feminine and the masculine often seek balance in each other, and androgyny is in abundance.

Due to how *Borderlands* insists on proposing worlds, histories, and spiritualities in which complex representations of femininity, fluidity, and queerness exist, the presence of Yemayá in this poem takes on an edifying dimension. Although she is often understood as female, Yemayá has masculine iterations and *caminos*, paths. Like Oyá, she can be considered a fierce warrior, "una amazona temible" (a fearsome Amazon) (Cabrera, *Yemayá y Ochún* 29). Yemayá is also associated with Olokun, the *orisha* of the ocean's depths. Olokun, who is both male and female, unleashed such fury upon the earth that they had to be chained to the bottom of the ocean to prevent total annihilation (Cabrera, *Yemayá y Ochún* 25–28). The energy of Yemayá-Olokun is present in Anzaldúa's opening poem when water tears down the fence and frees the currents. As a result of her breadth, Yemayá is best understood as gender-fluid, a quality visible in how the word for sea, *mar*, can be gendered male or female in Spanish. In her poem Anzaldúa uses the definite male article (*el*) to introduce the sea and follows it with her insertion of Yemayá in a feminized though fully activated form. The two are complementary, akin to how Coatlicue's power to give birth does not invalidate her capacity for death and destruction.

Finally, in presenting Yemayá as a mother who moves beyond the socially prescribed role of submissive motherhood, Anzaldúa's understanding of this *orisha* seeps into another border-crossing aquatic mythical figure, La Llorona.[39] Sometimes known as Cihuacoatl and as Serpent Woman, La Llorona is introduced in the third chapter of *Borderlands*, "Entering into the Serpent," in the subsection titled "The Presences."[40] Sonia Saldívar-Hull explains, "*La Llorona* is another part of the *virgin*/whore dyad the New Mestiza reclaims" (256). Before naming La Llorona, Anzaldúa evokes the space from which she emanates: "On the gulf where I was raised, *en el Valle del Río Grande* in South Texas—that triangular piece of land wedged between the river y *el golfo* which serves as the Texas-U.S./Mexican Border—is a Mexican *pueblito* called Hargill" (*Borderlands* 57). This passage is notable because it constructs Hargill, Texas, as an island, giving context for La Llorona's presence in its waters. It also shows how water shapes Anzaldúa's configuration of her hometown, accentuating her reliance on this life-giving liquid. Anzaldúa's mention of La Llorona recognizes that both Yemayá and La Llorona lost children to the waters, and these narratives surface how Anzaldúa channels traumatic memory into *Borderlands*. The rage and grief of loss drive Yemayá's capacity to resist and topple structures of oppression, represented in the poem by the border fence. The echoes between Yemayá and La Llorona reaffirm the urgency of underscoring the spiritual energy of water in Anzaldúa's physical and theoretical borderlands and borderwaters.

Of course, the fence Yemayá blows down is not only that of the border wall. Yemayá and the multiple spiritualities she infuses into *Borderlands* challenge us to tear down the boundaries of our own inner *desconocimientos* (willful ignorance). Only when these walls come down can we begin to cultivate the tools to understand and transform our world. This call is the driving force behind *Borderlands/La Frontera: The New Mestiza*. To read this foundational Chicanx/Latinx text as one that communes with the Afro-diasporic religious world extends the reach of Anzaldúa's visionary outlook. It also strengthens the conviction, evident in all of Anzaldúa's work, that people of color, queer people, colonized people, and all marginalized people have historically sought and will continue to seek possibilities and alternative spaces from which to craft visions of the world not dictated by those in power. And given that for Anzaldúa the Rio Grande Valley was always a water-laden place, a "borderlands between the Nueces and the Rio Grande" (*Borderlands* 112), looking to water in her work provides a deeper rendition of her vision.

Borderlands begins and ends with Anzaldúa gazing at the water. This decision suggests a larger pattern in Anzaldúa's single-authored work because *Borderlands*, her first book, and *Light in the Dark*, her last, begin at the water, at the sea, to be exact. At the end of *Borderlands*, however, Anzaldúa is gazing at the Rio Grande/Río Bravo. She writes, "I stand at the river, watch the curving, twisting serpent, a serpent nailed to the fence where the mouth of the Rio Grande empties into the Gulf" (*Borderlands* 111). She notes the river's pain at being controlled and stifled by the border, by the fence, and by the various constructions that have attempted to tame it. Yet, this sentence echoes a verse in the text's opening poem where Anzaldúa portrays "*el río Grande* / flowing down to the flatlands / of the Magic Valley of South Texas / its mouth emptying into the Gulf" (*Borderlands* 24). The sustained connection and generative movement between river and sea in *Borderlands* reinforces the power of the estuary embodied in the text itself and how water, be it salty or sweet, was a place of ceremony and communion for Anzaldúa.

ANZALDÚAN WATERS BEYOND *BORDERLANDS*

I would like to close this chapter by going back to Anzaldúa's poetry, the first genre of writing she cultivated.[41] "The water doesn't breath [*sic*]" is one of many unpublished poems found in the Gloria Evangelina Anzaldúa Papers. Located in box 88, folder 40, the earliest draft of this text is from 1980, with revisions dating from 1990. This poem displays Anzaldúa's understanding of water as the lifeblood of the planet, a position that aligns with how Afro-diasporic religions view water as the blood of the earth, the lifeblood of all creatures, and the place from which life springs (Cabrera, *Yemayá y Ochún* 20–22). Written simply and directly, the poem depicts a world where life has ceased due to the disappearance of living water. The natural world teems with an overwhelming sense of loss and deathly stillness; the wind no longer rustles the leaves of trees, and animals, from birds to crocodiles to fishes, have died or disappeared. When "the sea makes no waves" there is "no heartbeat in the planet earth" (Anzaldúa, box 88, folder 40). Provocatively, this text describes an ocean in diametrical opposition to the one that opens *Borderlands*, underscoring the liquid's vitality and strength and how its loss precludes life itself.

In Anzaldúa's life, water most certainly breathed. The Afro-diasporic waters in *Borderlands* crystallize this through the author's representation of a rebellious ocean activated by the *aché* of Oyá (breath) and Yemayá (life). In her personal life, Anzaldúa continually turned to the aquatic for inspiration. Beyond her walks by the ocean, a section of the archival document "Autohistoria de la artista as a Young Girl" titled "The Woman Writer/La escritora" reveals the role of water in Anzaldúa's writing rituals:

> There are times I'm writing when I reach an edge I can't get past. I feel like a caged animal flinging itself against the walls until I'm dizzy with exhaustion. I wash my white t-shirts, white undies. I mop the floor, I do the dishes. I run more water and take a shower, unstopping the spigot all the way. Water almost always helps me move into the writing. But sometimes nothing works. I can't seem to reach my cenote, my well of images and sounds. ("Autohistoria," box 57, folder 10, p. 33)

The tension between constraint and creativity in this passage is palpable. In her attempt to dissolve writing obstacles, Anzaldúa mentions various activities that, while appearing to signal quotidian actions, can also be read through the frameworks of Santería/Regla de Ocha to identify additional meaning. The emphasis on washing white clothing triggers an association with Obatalá, the ruler of all heads, associated with peace, clear thinking, cleanliness, and the color white. White is also the color of ritual ceremony in Haitian Vodou, La 21 División, and Santería/Regla de Ocha. Finally, white is the color that new initiates, *iyawos*, are meant to wear for a year and seven days after their *kari ocha* due to the color's association with spiritual protection and purification. The multiple sacred energies attributed to this hue help explain why Anzaldúa would dress in white when she wrote, because writing was a numinous process for her.

Additionally, Anzaldúa discusses the ritual cleaning or cleansing of the house, an essential aspect of bringing beneficial energies into one's space and dispelling harmful ones. The presence of negativity here is foregrounded when she states that she begins to clean because there is an edge she "can't get past." In this case, water is used to refresh, to transform. Then, as a conclusion to these rituals of purification and alignment, Anzaldúa takes a shower. In Santería/Regla de Ocha, practitioners often use *baños* (ritual baths) to promote harmony and balance within their physical and spiritual bodies, a role that mimics, to a less intense degree, the role of the *omiero*, the sacred herbal water that is intrinsic to the ceremonies of Santería/Regla de Ocha. In this passage about Anzaldúa's writing rituals readers can see her attempt to move from *osogbo* (negativity) to *iré* (positivity), paralleling the *ebó* she wanted to offer Yemayá after her hysterectomy.

A consideration of the processes Anzaldúa performs in this passage (washing, cleaning, bathing) through the lens of Afro-diasporic religions facilitates a connection with another water-laden Anzaldúan space: the *cenote*. *Cenotes* are subterranean pools of sweetwater often found in caves and are considered sacred nodes in Mesoamerican cultures. For the Maya, *cenotes* are a representation and embodiment of connection. Nicholas P. Dunning observes that *cenotes* are simultaneously an "opening in the sky and earth, a place of dynastic origin, [and] a home of gods and deified ancestors" (55). As a point of convergence between meaning and memory, Anzaldúa's *cenote* is "the creative reservoir where earth, female, and water energies merge" ("Border Arte" 182). The *cenote* is a repository of submerged knowledges, "an inner, underground river of information" (Anzaldúa, *Light* 28). Anzaldúa's mission to reach her *cenote* through writing evinces the ontological and epistemological power of water in her cosmovision. That she attempts to reach it by engaging in acts of cleansing that reverberate in the Afro-diasporic religious world provides yet another example of how, for Anzaldúa, the valence of water facilitates the flow of knowledges between Afro and Indigenous traditions.

In the GEA Papers I could only find one piece of writing solely dedicated to Yemayá. Filed in box 88 along with many other poems, the text is titled simply

"Yemaya." Although a version of this poem was published posthumously in *The Gloria Anzaldúa Reader*, the earliest drafts are from the 1980s, and Anzaldúa continued to revise it throughout the decades.[42] That Anzaldúa returned to this poem again and again points to the continuous presence of the *orisha* in her spiritual and intellectual life, even if that presence in her published material was not always apparent. Written in the first person, the poem displays an effortless intimacy with Yemayá. It evokes feelings Anzaldúa might have often had when walking near the ocean, feelings that likely began that fateful day on South Padre Island.

In the version published in *The Gloria Anzaldúa Reader*, Anzaldúa writes:

Yemayá, your tongues lick me,
your green mouths nibble my feet.
With your brine I inhale the beginnings of life.
Your silver tongues hiss and then retreat
leaving hieroglyphs and silence on the sand.
("Yemayá" 242)

These verses bridge a traditional understanding of Yemayá with Anzaldúa's strong Mexica influences. Anzaldúa discretely acknowledges Yemayá's role as the mother of the *orishas* by stating that through the salt in the air she "inhale[s] the beginnings of life." This phrasing, however, also surreptitiously references Oyá due to her association with the air, the wind, and breathing. In this manner, the poem reiterates the incessant circulations between Yemayá and Oyá inscribed into *Borderlands*. Moreover, the mention of Yemayá's "silver tongues" crafts a resonance between the serpent and the ocean, two natural elements with strong spiritual undercurrents that repeatedly appear in her writing and that bridge Afro and Indigenous worldviews.[43] As in *Borderlands*, Anzaldúa associates the snake with the Rio Grande/Río Bravo, which she considers serpentine. The similitudes between the *orishas*, salty and sweet waters, and the snake flow into each other, maintaining their singular importance even as they overlap through the convergence of physical and mythical energies.

Among the multiple drafts found in the GEA Papers, there is a 1980 version of "Yemaya" that displays a growing interest in this *orisha's* conception within Santería/Regla de Ocha. This version explicitly mentions Olokun, the *orisha* of the depths of the ocean often associated with Yemayá. A note scribbled on the side of this version is one of the proverbs about Olokun: "No one knows what lies at the bottom of the sea."[44] This statement speaks to the depth and vastness of the ocean's profundity, Olokun's lair, a space of infinite possibility that lies beyond the reach of the secularly knowable. Another note states that the tonality of blue associated with Yemayá-Olokun is the deepest blue, indigo, and adds a series of blue tonalities to the poem. While there is no way to know when these notes and changes were made, I am left wondering: If this version of the poem had been published, what reaction would it have elicited from readers? What would it have communicated about Anzaldúa's lifelong engagement with Afro-diasporic waters?

The mysterious appearance of Olokun's proverb in Anzaldúa's poem to Yemayá is an apt ending to this chapter, as we will never fully know the depths of Anzaldúa's communion with Afro-diasporic knowledges. Rather than provide a definitive reading, I set out to trace how the power of water in Anzaldúa's literary production is connected to the epistemological importance of this element in the Afro-diasporic religious world. By dwelling on the moments in *Borderlands* when the *orishas* appear we can read beyond what we have come to know about Anzaldúa. We can also make remarkable observations about how water infuses critical Anzaldúan theories. An avowal of the spiritual tributaries that come together in *Borderlands* reveals that water is an energetic, aesthetic, methodological, and theoretical presence in Anzaldúa's writing. Its capacity for traversing cultures, languages, and borders shows that there are, in fact, many true faces to consider when encountering the work of this Rio Grande Valley Chicana.

Water and Light

THE *BÓVEDA* AS COUNTER-ARCHIVE

In chapter after chapter of *Channeling Knowledges* I have shown that reading with a sensibility for the religious currents of Afro-diasporic waters can surface submerged histories and create unexpected openings. What I have not said is that this book truly began to come into existence after my active witnessing of and participation in the Border of Lights (BOL) in 2018. As I stood at the banks of the Massacre River/Dajabón River in the town of Dajabón on the northwestern border between the Dominican Republic and Haiti, I viscerally understood that water is alive. More than a backdrop, it is an active nonhuman participant in the generation of material and spiritual realities. Looking to remember but also to heal, BOL recognizes that the Massacre River/ Dajabón River is "a border between two geographies of grief" (Gay 32).[1] As a transnational and transgenerational act of collective memory, BOL's commemoration epitomizes how important cultural work occurs in unexpected places.[2]

BOL was initiated in 2012 by activists, artists, and scholars from Hispaniola and its diaspora.[3] The group organizes non-government-sanctioned acts of remembrance of the 1937 Massacre, a gruesome episode in Hispaniola's history that, as Ginetta E. B. Candelario asserts, primarily targeted women and children ("La ciguapa" 109–110).[4] BOL's activities vary yearly due to its grassroots organization, but its main event consists of a candlelight vigil held on both sides of the river to honor and remember the lives lost in the Massacre.[5] Scholars estimate that close to 20,000 were killed in October 1937 when Trujillo authorized Dominican soldiers to kill Haitians and Dominicans of Haitian descent on the border (Turits, "A World" 590). Historians have noted the lack of evidence and personal testimonies of the event (Paulino 56–57), a fact reflected in the Massacre's overall suppression in the Dominican Republic's national memory (Myers and Paulino 2). Beyond baring the (neo)colonial wounds between the two nations, the 1937 Massacre exemplifies the unceasing global assaults on

FIGURE 5.1. Border of Lights, October 2018. Dajabón, Dominican Republic. Photo by the author.

Blackness that continue to this day.[6] Epitomizing Terry Rey's and Alex Stepick's contention that Afro-diasporic religious currents are "invested deeply with pain, passage, and memory" ("Visual Culture" 237), in this epilogue I read BOL's candlelight vigil as edifying a spiritual *bóveda* (altar) at the banks of the Massacre River/Dajabón River. BOL's candlelight vigil seeks to honor the dead in ways not legible through secular documentary means, demonstrating the curative potential of Afro-diasporic religions in the face of violence.

THE DIASPORIC ORIGINS OF THE BORDER OF LIGHTS

It was Julia Alvarez, the most established female writer of the Dominican diaspora, who first dreamed BOL into being (Myers, "Dos rayanos" 177).[7] When she shared her idea with the historian Edward Paulino in 2011, they began to manifest the idea of "literally lighting up the border, raising candles alongside the Massacre River" (Paulino and García 113). This move was fueled by two intentions: their wish to publicly acknowledge what had happened in 1937 and their desire to honor the passing of Sonia Pierre, a Dominican activist of Haitian descent and founder of MUDHA, the Movimiento de Mujeres

Dominico-Haitianas (Movement of Dominican-Haitian Women) (Paulino and García 113). BOL's gestation in the diaspora attests to how knowledge about the Massacre often circulates most freely outside the boundaries of the nation. It also reflects the event's openness; anyone who wishes can join in the act of remembrance.

Alvarez's instrumental role in setting BOL into motion gained new significance for me when, in a 2021 virtual interview, the author discussed her personal connection to a Catholic saint.[8] This disclosure was prompted by an attendee's comment regarding an image of La Virgen de la Altagracia that was visible on the screen in the space immediately to Alvarez's left. The attendee described it as "a powerful image for all Dominicans" and thanked the author for including it in her space (J. Alvarez and Pérez-Rosario). In response, Alvarez pointed to a small medallion she was wearing and said, "She's also on my little medallion because my name is actually Julia Altagracia, so she is my saint. And, you know, don't meddle with your saint!" (J. Alvarez and Pérez-Rosario).[9] This exchange immediately transported me to the Afro-diasporic spiritual world as it exemplifies Solimar Otero's observation that "Catholic hagiography, symbols, and rituals are recontextualized physically and ritually in Afrolatinx vernacular practice" (*Archives* 173). In addition, La Virgen de la Altagracia's origin story in Hispaniola is intrinsically linked to Blackness and healing.[10]

As the patron saint of the Dominican Republic, La Virgen de la Altagracia is a key figure of La 21 División.[11] La 21 División is deeply enmeshed with Catholicism, so much so that practitioners use Catholic images as representations for many *misterios* (deities).[12] This connection is one of the reasons researchers have often referred to La 21 División as "folk Catholicism."[13] Cristina Sánchez-Carretero finds that "the syncretism with Catholicism in the Dominican Republic is higher than in Cuban Santería or Haitian Vodou, where there is a more structured religious system already in place" (309). The role of La Virgen de la Altagracia is comparable to that of La Virgen de la Caridad del Cobre in Cuba, Ochún's Catholic counterpart.[14] As patron saints with Afro-diasporic spiritual iterations, La Virgen de la Altagracia and La Virgen de la Caridad del Cobre offer refuge to island-based and diasporic communities.[15] By enabling displaced communities to express what Thomas A. Tweed terms "diasporic nationalism" (10), these religious icons defy the limits of geography and citizenship.[16]

La Virgen de la Altagracia's guiding presence in Julia Alvarez's life transforms the deity into a charged religious node that opens a path to a spiritualized reading of BOL. This reading is strengthened by evidence that during the unification of Hispaniola (1822–1844) pilgrimages to La Virgen de la Altagracia's shrine in Higüey were common from all parts of the island (Rey, *Our Lady* 139).[17] The deity's role in the creation of a healing ritual that takes place on the shared currents of the Massacre River/Dajabón River thus evinces how Afro-diasporic religious systems abound on both sides of Hispaniola, transforming spirituality into a fluid emblem of continuity in the face of the 1937 Massacre's violent truncations.[18] Moreover, the presence of La Virgen de la Altagracia in BOL's gestation attests to the urgency of the spiritual work that needs to be done regarding the Massacre. Neglected by governments and state agencies, this work lies in the hands of the *lwa*, the *misterios*, the *orishas*, the dead, and their descendants.

ESPIRITISMO'S *BÓVEDA* AND THE BORDER OF LIGHTS

Multiple religions commemorate the dead using candlelight.[19] Growing up in a Catholic community, I was always drawn to the Easter vigil, in which glimmers of candlelight in the dark become embers that fuel new life cycles. Hence, it is perhaps not coincidental that in Dajabón, a Catholic Mass at Nuestra Señora del Rosario, a local church led by Jesuit priests, precedes BOL's candlelight vigil. In 2018, immediately after the mass, all attendees were given candles that were lit communally in preparation for the procession toward the riverbank. Though solemn, the atmosphere at the event was not of sadness or remorse but rather of awakening and responsibility. Edward Paulino and Scherezade García's recollection of the initial vigil echoes this feeling:

> On the border of this very river in October of 2012, (a river originally named for an eighteenth century colonial battle between French and Spanish forces), there was an eerie sense among those present that night of the initial stages of closure, a closure allowing for the thousands of dead spirits who wandered for decades throughout the Dominican-Haitian borderlands to finally rest. At last their lives—and deaths—would be acknowledged; their spirits responding as if to say "Despite being poor and black I, too, existed! We did not die in vain. They, the living, remember (us)." (117)

The felt transmission of the message of the dead is a spiritual confirmation of how, in Afro-diasporic rituals, healing is an active process that engages spiritual and secular actors (McCarthy Brown 349). Understood as a collaborative effort and as a form of coalition-building, healing is a critical point of connection between BOL and the Afro-diasporic religious world. It also reflects how "the dead understand and engage in struggles for different kinds of justice" (Otero, *Archives* 125), infusing a public act of commemoration with transcendental power.

Nonetheless, what the dead respond to at BOL, what enables them to communicate with the living and receive respite and healing despite the pain they have endured, is light. Here, Diana Espírito Santo's description of Espiritismo's practice of *darle luz al muerto* (to give light to the dead) is elucidating:

> Giving light wishes the dead well and aids the ascension or elevation of the departed to 'higher' spaces, through song, prayer, and thought. But it also empowers, ennobles, aggrandizes, and enhances the potency and vision of the dead in assisting and guiding the living. (219)

Read through the lens of Espiritismo, BOL's candlelight vigil is a veritable act of giving light to the dead and to the river that holds them. Light is literally and figuratively brought to the Massacre River/Dajabón River by those seeking to acknowledge, remember, and honor the victims of the 1937 Massacre. The following scene Paulino and García describe from 2012 puts this process into words:

> Everyone held their candles toward the Massacre River and on the Dominican side someone climbed down to the river bank and placed in the water several paper boats, each with a lit candle in the middle; everyone watched as they floated down the river. At the same time, Haitians on the other side of the river alongside the Columbian nuns, Las Jaunistas de St. Jean Evangeliste, were doing the same thing: holding their lit candles to the sky, singing, praying, and remembering. (116)

As this passage recounts, at BOL, light is an offering, an affirmation, and an activator of the loaded reservoirs of the Massacre River. This sacred commemoration enables the river to momentarily release streams of the grief stored in its currents, soothing the dead and their descendants. Like the Atlantic and Pacific Oceans, the Caribbean Sea, and the Rio Grande/Río Bravo, the Massacre River/Dajabón River is a wound that also contains curative powers. For in the Afro-diasporic religious world, wounds have always been a conduit for healing.[20]

Yet, healing is a process of unceasing spiritual transactions. It becomes an inheritance, a responsibility the living must assume to ensure the cycles of release and integration continue. An understanding of Afro-diasporic healing reveals that the word "closure" in Paulino and García's testimony refers to how the candlelight vigil treats the wound of the Massacre River/Dajabón River. By suffusing the river with light, some of the pain archived in the water is released.[21] This process closes at the end of the ceremony, illustrating Régine Michelle Jean-Charles's contention that throughout the vigil "the Dajabón River becomes a place where an experience other than death can take place, if only briefly, although it does not supplant or deny the tragic loss of life" (83). BOL's candlelight vigil exemplifies how light's function in the Afro-diasporic religious world is enmeshed with that of water. As Martha Ellen Davis finds, in La 21 División, candlelight is integral to channeling knowledge in spiritual consults during which a practitioner may read "una copa llena de agua limpia, iluminada por una velita; otros usan una vela en sí, cuya llama indica el estado de salud del paciente" (a glass of clean water, illuminated by a candle; others only use a candle, whose flame indicates the state of the patient's health) (*La otra ciencia* 235). Both water and light sustain the ongoing connection and transmission of spiritual *corrientes* (currents) between the living, the dead, and the sacred.

Water and light are also essential components of the spiritual *bóveda*. The *bóveda* is one of the key technologies of Espiritismo, a tradition that hinges on communication with the dead. Although Espiritismo's roots are European, its practice is often integrated into the rituals of Afro-diasporic religions, most notably documented in relation to Santería/Regla de Ocha though certainly not exclusive to it.[22] The transnational currents intrinsic to Espiritismo create a fluid space where "a diasporic *afrolatinidad* specifically emerges from fissures created by cultural convergence" (Otero, *Archives* 82). Espiritismo is likely the most permeable of the spiritual systems I discuss in this book, a testament to how its unruliness ushers in inclusivity. As Ysamur Flores-Peña finds, Espiritismo also gives "voice to diverse spiritual forces regardless of their origins" (96), an assertion supported by how formal initiation is not a prerequisite for access in this tradition.

Espiritismo exemplifies the power of communal embodiment, endowing practitioners with the tools needed to disrupt the historical narratives of hegemonic memory. Spirits channeled into being in Espiritismo often enact "a replaying of the past with a flipped script" since those who were stripped from power during their lifetime now command it (E. Pérez, "Spiritist" 353). In contrast to instances of spiritual possession in Afro-diasporic religions in which a *misterio, lwa,* or *orisha* takes temporary control of a devotee, a practice commonly referred to as "riding their horse," in Espiritismo, many of the spirits that commune with the living are of everyday people who were silenced in life and now speak in death. These democratizing aspects of Espiritismo elucidate an ongoing communication between the living and the dead that erodes the border between self and other and between individuals and their communities. This quality parallels the functions of social memory, an intrinsic aspect of this kind of channeling (Moreno Vega, "Espiritismo" 340). Espiritismo is thus a site where Afro-diasporic subjectivities are fashioned and refashioned through ritual (Beliso-De Jesús, *Electric Santería;* Espírito Santo; Otero, *Archives;* E. Pérez, "Spiritist").

A powerful practice in Espiritismo is the elaboration of a *bóveda,* an altar consecrated to a person's ancestors and guiding spirits. A *bóveda* often consists of the following:

seven glasses of water (as well as a *copa*—larger cup—representing the Almighty) each dedicated to a spirit guide or a *comisión* of guides, along with Catholic items such as crosses and rosaries and other identificatory parapher-nalia such as images and spirit representations. (Espírito Santo 57)

Individuals may incorporate the use of a *bóveda* in their private practice because "the presence of a *bóveda* in the home spiritually charges the environment with the memory of those who are no longer on this Earth" (Moreno Vega, *Altar* 40). In the *bóveda*, water functions as an essential carrier and container of energetic currents. The spiritual labor of water is aided by light, two elements that when combined attract spiritual entities (Moreno Vega, "Espiritismo" 349). A *bóveda*'s water is an active body cohabited by the living and the dead, transforming this site into one of the most quotidian ways ancestral knowledge and influence can be accessed and honored.

The word *bóveda* in Spanish can refer to a tomb or a vault, insinuating the depths of this spiritual technology, especially in the context of BOL's candlelight vigil. As Elizabeth Pérez explains:

In Spanish, *bóveda* usually refers to a sepulcher or burial vault, and as in the case of tombs arrayed with the favorite items of the deceased, bóvedas give practitioners a place to remember the spirits of the dead and piece together aspects of their pasts. ("Spiritist" 350)

Dajabón's history primes it to become a *bóveda*. During the 1937 Massacre, bodies were thrown not only into the river but into several unmarked graves (Strongman, "Reading" 40; Paulino and García 111).[23] With physical bodies violently cast aside and unable to be ritually mourned, lives lost during the 1937 Massacre engendered spirits that, viewed through the lens of Afro-diasporic religiosity, are in acute need of appeasement and attention.[24] Bringing light to the dead is both an acknowledgment and a contestation of their trauma. Cooling the violence of the Massacre soothes the living and the dead; when spirits who have deeply suffered in their lifetime receive light, they become empowered to facilitate the most profound moments of healing (E. Pérez, "Spir-itist" 351).

Combining BOL's origin story with the power of the dead in Afro-diasporic religions and Espiritismo transforms BOL's candlelight vigil into the enactment of a binational spiritual *bóveda* that gives visibility to the historical trauma of the 1937 Massacre and seeks to appease the souls of the victims and their descen-dants. It is no surprise, then, that "many who were there that night [in 2012] confess the sea of candles on both sides of the border was emotionally over-whelming" (Paulino and García 116). BOL harnesses the transgenerational potential for healing conjured through both Espiritismo and Afro-diasporic religions, processes channeled by the spiritual currencies of water and light. The candlelight vigil also reflects the revisionary ethos of Espiritismo, where an engagement with the past is capable of producing "'countermemories' that [go] against the grand narratives of religious and secular colonial authorities" (E. Pérez, "Spiritist" 336). By bringing the events of 1937 to the surface and attempting to attenuate and reinscribe them into the social and spiritual consciousness of Hispaniola's variegated communities, the spiritual *bóveda* created by BOL's candlelight vigil elucidates water's power to connect and transform past, present, and future.

THE MASSACRE RIVER/DAJABÓN RIVER AND HISPANIOLA'S BORDERS IN THE TWENTY-FIRST CENTURY

The vital work undertaken by BOL has continued unabated since 2012. Despite the global lockdowns of the COVID-19 pandemic, BOL persisted. They organized a virtual candlelight vigil on October 10, 2020, a feat that was aided by the technology that has been a critical part of BOL's grassroots organizing from the very start (Myers, "A Promise" 176). But the wound embodied by the Massacre River/Dajabón River is far from healed, not because BOL's actions are ineffective but because much work remains to be done. The 1937 Massacre continues to shape the binational and diasporic consciousnesses of Hispaniola, a fact documented in the island's literature and reflected in current events on the ground.

Nelly Rosario's *Song of the Water Saints* is a multigenerational family saga that has become a cornerstone of Dominican studies. Though it only briefly engages with the 1937 Massacre, this traumatic moment in Hispaniola's history is narrated through the water.[25] Rosario writes, "The month of October opened with thirty-six hours of carnage in which drunken Dominican soldiers, on orders from Trujillo, took their machetes and built a dam of human bodies in the western Dajabón River" (181). Rosario's rendition emphasizes how violence was inflicted upon those targeted by machetes and upon the river itself.[26] Through the evocation of a dam, Rosario asserts that violence forcibly conscripted bodies, waters, and knowledges. What does it mean, then, that in 2021 tensions were once again high at the Massacre River/Dajabón River?

When the Haitian state began building an irrigation canal alongside the Massacre River/Dajabón River, tempers flared on the Dominican side of the border. On May 27, 2021, in a meeting of the Mixed Binational Committee between the Dominican Republic and Haiti, Dominican Foreign Minister Roberto Álvarez exhorted the countries to work together to resolve the situation. Despite this official messaging, on June 4, 2021, Dominican nationalists took to the streets, proclaiming that Haiti's construction of the canal was a declaration of war and that "podría correr la sangre" (blood could flow) if its building continued ("Haiti Warning"). The image of a dam in the river also circulated, evident in the words of a Dajabón official: "They, the Haitians, can take their water, but in an equitable way, so that they do not dam the river, because that would affect us a lot" (quoted in "At Full Steam"). More than 80 years later, the mention of a dam and blood along the Massacre River/Dajabón River is enough to unleash the traumas lodged in Hispaniola's most notorious aquatic body. Still, the nationalistic rhetoric surrounding the irrigation canal pales in comparison to Dominican President Luis Abinader's announcement of his administration's plan to build a border fence meant to "curb illegal immigration" from Haiti ("Dominican Republic"). In response, on March 17, 2021, several human-rights organizations, among which were BOL, MUDHA, and entities from around the world, wrote to Abinader condemning the wall's construction ("Concern").[27] A dam and a wall. Water and light. The work continues. The Massacre River/Dajabón River, a wound that has never fully closed, has once again been torn open.

Although rivers can be forcibly contained, they always remember where they used to flow. As Toni Morrison writes about the Mississippi River: "All water has a perfect memory" (99). When a river overflows, it shows its disregard for borders and all methods of control, an action evident in the Spanish word *desbordar*.[28] The undoing (*des-*) of limits (*-bordar*) is both an insurgent and reparative action enacted by water. This posture brings to mind another critical fluid body in Hispaniola, the Artibonite River, which flows through the central region of the borderlands. While the Massacre River/Dajabón River marks a point of violent truncation in Hispaniola's border history, the Artibonite River is the island's largest shared aquatic body. Ralph R. Frerichs notes that "the long, grand Artibonite River originates in the mountains of neighboring Dominican Republic and flows west 240 kilometers (150 miles) through central Haiti and on to the ocean waters of the Gulf of La Gonâve" (7). Despite the hundreds of bodies of water that exist in Hispaniola, Patrick Bellegarde-Smith observes that "the longest river is the Artibonite, which has ten times the flow of any other river in the country [Haiti]" (14–15). The Artibonite conjoins multiple worlds: the island nations of Hispaniola, the sweetwaters of rivers, and the salty currents of the sea. The Artibonite's breadth endows it with the power to channel alternate narratives between the Dominican Republic and Haiti. This trait helps explain why this aquatic body plays a central role in the work of Firelei Báez, a visual artist from Hispaniola.

FIGURE 5.2. Firelei Báez, *TC/0168.13 (Anthropophagist wading in the Artibonite River)*, 2014. Gouache, acrylic polymer, and ink on paper. 84 x 74 in (213.4 x 188 cm). Photo © Scott McCrossen/FIVE65 Desi. Courtesy of the artist and James Cohan, New York.

Báez's 2014 painting *TC/0168.13 (Anthropophagist wading in the Artibonite River)* is a haunting image whose spectral qualities flow from its title. "TC/0168.13" refers to the 2013 ruling by the Dominican Constitutional Tribunal, popularly called "La Sentencia" (the Sentence), that stripped Dominicans of Haitian descent of their Dominican citizenship. The crux of this ruling is rooted in a punishing understanding of movement and migration. Retroactively applied to 1929, the passing of La Sentencia deemed those born to Haitian parents in the Dominican Republic to be "in transit" and thus exempt from the constitutional right to citizenship.[29] This context informs the audience's understanding of the second part of the painting's title, "(Anthropophagist wading in the Artibonite River)." Since anthropophagism evokes cannibalism, Báez's painting suggests that TC/0168.13 itself is a flesh-eating entity.[30] The law consumes thousands of lives by denying citizens the state-sanctioned documentation that makes their existence institutionally legible. The cannibalistic tendencies of La Sentencia are also evoked through the dominant color in the painting, a rust-colored tone reminiscent of dried, spilled blood.

However, the scripts of blood cannot contain the movement of water. Báez's choice to address La Sentencia by representing the Artibonite River and not the Massacre River/Dajabón River, which is so often associated with blood, hinges on water's power for contestation. As a point of suture between nations, the waters of the Artibonite River can carry energies that the overly inscribed Massacre River/Dajabón River cannot. The Artibonite's movement toward the sea suggests a grand picture where water diminishes the soldierlike figures the artist depicts at the center of the painting. Moreover, Báez's painting anthropomorphizes the river through the emergence of what appears to be a woman's face in the water. The existence of this aquatic being is a stark challenge to the inhumanity of the laws created by governments. To be sure, *TC/0168.13* incorporates signature aspects of Báez's work such as chains, combs, and fists. In contrast to other creations, however, this painting renders these details in color. Blending water and blood with the colors yellow and blue, Báez presents an unnamed but tempering depiction of the spiritualities that inhabit Afro-diasporic waters. Given Báez's knowledge of Afro-diasporic entities, I read her inclusion of yellow and blue as a subtle invocation of Ochún and Yemayá, two *orishas* that represent the spiritual power of water, specifically the river and the sea. Ochún's and Yemayá's intimate connections with the dead (Palmié, *Wizards* 165) also lend credence to their presence in *TC/0168.13*.

Movement is one of Ochún's innate qualities, leading Isabel Castellanos to emphasize that "like the river, she is constantly moving, eternally pursuing a path. Ochún represents the constant flow of human life" (39). Though often associated with beauty and love, Ochún embodies these virtues precisely because she knows, profoundly and in her own skin, that the world is full of sorrow.[31] Even honey, one of Ochún's key attributes, is as linked to sweetness as it is to pain, as it can heal but also cause illnesses such as "stomach ailments, dysentery, hepatitis, and diabetes" (E. Pérez, "Crystallizing" 185). In Haitian Vodou, the *lwa* Erzulie is associated with many of Ochún's attributes, including her knowledge of suffering (Desmangles 19), a fact that explains why, for Maya Deren, "the wound of Erzulie is perpetual: she is the dream impaled eternally upon the cosmic cross-roads" (145). A visual representation of Erzulie's

pain appears in the pierced heart that distinguishes her *vèvè* (sacred symbol).
The same pierced heart accompanies Metresilí, a *misterio* of La 21 División
who manifests in the body of her *servidores* (devotees) by crying (A.-M. Lara,
Queer Freedom 84). These shared spiritual resonances are a potent reminder
that while the *lwa*, *misterios*, and *orishas* exist beyond the physical world, they
intimately know its positive and negative aspects. In Báez's art, Ochún, Erzulie,
and Metresilí condemn the viciousness of La Sentencia because they, too, have
lived through the horrors of this world.

As the Artibonite River, Ochún's currents lead to the sea, a journey suggested
through the inclusion of the color blue toward the margins of Báez's canvas.
The connection between salty and sweet waters in *TC/0168.13* is reminiscent of a *pataki* that recounts the stinging nature of water's sacred knowledges.
When Yemayá finds her sister Ochún sickly, alone, and hurt, she cures Ochún's
wounds with saltwater.[32] This process causes Ochún an indescribable amount
of pain even as it ensures her healing and survival. Having witnessed her sister's
pain, Yemayá transforms the saltwater into sweetwater in an attempt to protect
Ochún from further suffering (Cabrera, *Yemayá y Ochún* 83–84). What this
sacred story exemplifies is that as both witnesses and actors in the Border of
Lights and beyond, the ancestors, the *lwa*, the *misterios*, and the *orishas* teach us
that while pain's memory cannot be erased, it can be cooled, and as it cools, new
possibilities for being can emerge.

The message imparted by this *pataki* of Santería/Regla de Ocha reverberates with the texts analyzed in *Channeling Knowledges*. In Mayra Santos-Febres's
boat people the sea embraces centuries of undocumented maritime migrants
and offers them spiritual sanctuary. Rita Indiana's *La mucama de Omicunlé* suggests how the subtle yet powerful techno-resonances between Afro-diasporic
knowledges and secular technologies transmitted through the water are intrinsic
to survival. And the multiple ways in which Afro-diasporic waters seep into
and unsettle disciplinary-bound conversations surrounding the life and work
of Gloria Evangelina Anzaldúa illustrate the regenerative qualities of these
currents. Undeniably, the overflows of water create points of contact between
Afro-diasporic religious traditions and throughout time, cultural works, and
even worlds.

The role of saltwater in the *pataki* of Yemayá and Ochún demonstrates the
various ways this liquid "cures," a complex action that drives the readings of
water I offer in this study. For "to cure" is "to heal," but it is also "to preserve."[33] In
Afro-diasporic religions, saltwater cures by both healing and preserving, making
this *pataki* one that is enacted repeatedly in the works I examine in this book.
Furthermore, Yemayá's caretaking of Ochún emulates the experiences of the
survivors of the Middle Passage, communities whose injuries were healed by
saltwaters as they spread across the Americas.[34] Centuries later, we continue to

live through this *pataki* when the salty tears that flow from our eyes release and soothe the pain stored in our emotional, physical, and spiritual bodies. While science may not be able to explain why we cry, the spiritual currents of the Afro-diasporic world attest to how even human biology recognizes water as an energetic channel. Yemayá, Ochún, and all of the ancestors, *lwa*, *misterios*, and *orishas* whose energies pulsate in the Afro-diasporic waters within and around us will always be with us, because water never forgets.

Notes

1. I quote Hernandez directly because almost every source describes Báez solely as Dominican.
2. This moment appears at 0:25 of the video. The *orishas* are the deities of Santería/Regla de Ocha, an Afro-Cuban-born spiritual tradition that is now practiced worldwide.
3. Throughout my analysis I employ the Kreyòl spelling for the names of the *lwa* and other aspects of Haitian religious life. At times, however, different spellings appear as they are present in other sources, such as the title of Báez's painting. A full-color reproduction of *Ode to la Sirène* is included in *Firelei Báez: Bloodlines,* edited by M. E. Ortiz.
4. The *lwa* are the deities of Haitian Vodou. The term is both singular and plural (Hebblethwaite, *Vodou* 321n2). For a thorough discussion of the *lwa,* including their various names, see Hebblethwaite's *Vodou Songs in Haitian Creole and English.* I refer to Vodou regularly as "Haitian Vodou" to avoid confusion with New Orleans Vodou or Voodoo, a related yet distinct system. Although La 21 División was born in the Dominican Republic and Santería/Regla de Ocha emerged in Cuba, I refrain from identifying them by their places of origin due to their current spread across the globe. All of these traditions are practiced by people of various races, ethnicities, and nationalities.
5. Diminishingly, the vital force of nature in Afro-diasporic religions is regularly used to justify the classification of these traditions as "primitive" (Ricourt, *The Dominican* 108).
6. By "official," I mean an initiation that takes place according to the extensive ethnographic work conducted on these ceremonies. See, for example, chapter 7 of Lydia Cabrera's *Yemayá y Ochún.*
7. Secrecy is intrinsic to these traditions because of the dangers faced by Afro-diasporic religious practitioners. Persecution against them is often perpetrated by dominant institutions such as the Catholic Church (A.-M. Lara, *Queer Freedom* 143n7). As

a result, Ana-Maurine Lara explains, "the majority of these ceremonies, rites, and rituals are held in secret" (*Queer Freedom* 145). Solimar Otero finds that "these traditions of secrecy also resemble queer strategies of evading categorization of knowledge and the self through performances that code, mimic, and keep hidden key aspects of recognition" ("Yemayá y Ochún: Queering" 90–91).

8. This fluid approach to scholarship works in multiple directions. Aisha M. Beliso-De Jesús finds that practitioners engaged in "Afro-Latinx activist magic and warfare . . . dialogue with scholarly 'sources' that is, the writings (and spirits) of academic scholars—dead and alive—who are activated and whose scholarship is animated in spiritual ways" ("Brujx" 529). Gloria Anzaldúa is one such scholar.

9. For a recent example of this approach see Martin A. Tsang's discussion of Lydia Cabrera in his 2021 essay "Write into Being."

10. For an editorial perspective on the term see Milian's "Extremely Latin, XOXO" and Torres's "Latinx?" Other positions on the term that inform its presence in this book are DeGuzmán's "Latinx: ¡Estamos aquí!" and Overmyer-Velázquez's "Global Latin(X) AmericanXs."

11. For more on the debates surrounding "diaspora" see Butler's "Defining Diaspora, Refining a Discourse."

12. A recent exception is Theresa Delgadillo's discussion of Espiritismo and Santería/Regla de Ocha in Marta Moreno Vega's memoir *When the Spirits Dance Mambo*, a text that for Delgadillo "reveals a unique form of Latina feminisms that emerges from the experiences of Afro-Latinas" ("African, Latina" 158).

13. Latinidad thus functions in tandem with *mestizaje*, a term I discuss in chapter 3 in relation to Anzaldúa's work.

14. For a discussion of Latinidad in this context see R. Ortiz's "Edwidge Danticat's *Latinidad*."

15. Torres-Saillant also notes the importance of considering terms such as "Afro-Latin Americans" and "Afro-Hispanic" (279).

16. As John D. Ribó points out, the exclusion of Haiti has multiple historical precedents in Latin American history (477).

17. Jiménez Román and Flores state that "the Brazilian presence in the United States has been relatively small and the Afro-Brazilian negligible" ("Introduction" 3).

18. There are important exceptions to Haiti's elision in the context of Afro-Latinidad. Three interventions worth noting are Myriam J. A. Chancy's *From Sugar to Revolution*, Ana Sabau's *Riot and Rebellion in Mexico*, and Vanessa K. Valdés's edited collection *Racialized Visions*. All three texts offer valuable readings that foster a critique of disciplinary constraints.

19. For more on the uses of "diaspora" and "dyaspora" see Clitandre (20–23) and Hyppolite's personal essay "Dyaspora."

20. These limitations extend into the reception of Danticat's work. While she has become "'the voice' of the Haitian diaspora" (Clitandre xi), the Afro-diasporic religious elements in her work are understudied. Two notable exceptions are Brüske and Beushausen's "Writing from Lòt Bò Dlo" and Daniels's "Sea, Stone, Sky, and Cemetery."

21. For example, Marlene L. Daut finds that although largely unacknowledged, "nineteenth-century Haitian historians . . . contributed to many of the political and cultural theories that govern contemporary historical and literary study" (136). For a sustained discussion of Haiti's invisibility in intellectual scholarship see Trouillot's *Silencing the Past*.

22. All translations are my own unless otherwise attributed.

23. Although this move was preceded by the formal recognition of the Asociación Cultural Yoruba de Cuba by the Cuban state in 1991, Paul Christopher Johnson and Stephan Palmié note the power of secularization in the replacement of "religion" with "culture" in the association's name (458).

24. In the Dominican Republic, Law 391, established during the Trujillo dictatorship, criminalized the practice of "voudou" or "luá" worship (Tejeda Ortiz 96).

25. Joseph M. Murphy also refers to Santería/Regla de Ocha as "the religion" in his preface to the 1992 edition of *Santería*. Tsang, however, provides a more expansive definition: "In Cuba, *la religion* is understood to signify the conglomeration of collaborative and entwined practices of Lukumi/Santería, Palo Mayombe, *espiritismo* as well as the Calabar Abakuá presence" ("¿Tienes memoria?").

26. These divisions refer to communal groupings of deities. Davis includes a possible list of them in *La otra ciencia* (125). Nonetheless, she also notes that there is a great deal of fluctuation between these groups depending on the practitioners. Ricourt also discusses the tradition's name (*The Dominican* 116).

27. In the case of Haitian Vodou, Ramsey notes that while academics often refer to "Afro-Haitian spiritual belief and ritual practices" as Vodou, practitioners rarely use the term and instead speak of "*sèvi lwa* (serve the spirits)" (6). La 21 División is often referred to as "Dominican Vodou," a term that emphasizes its connection to Haitian Vodou (Deive), or simply as "Afro-religious practice" (García-Peña). Santería/Regla de Ocha is also known as Lucumí/Lukumí, the Afro-Cuban language associated with the religion.

28. For a thorough description of religious life in Little Haiti see Rey and Stepick, *Crossing the Water*.

29. Báez discusses navigating her identity in the art world in her interview with the Dominican American writer Angie Cruz ("Firelei Báez on Generosity").

30. María Elena Ortiz notes, "Firelei Báez is a Caribbean hybrid. She was born in the [*sic*] Santiago de los Caballeros, Dominican Republic to a Dominican mother and father of Haitian descent" (11).

31. Deive identifies a direct link between the functions of blood and water in the rituals of La 21 División as both are connected to vitality and life (200).

32. For further discussion on this aspect of Firelei Báez's work see L. Alvarado's "Flora and Fauna Otherwise."

33. Alourdes, the *manbo* (priestess) whose life Karen McCarthy Brown documents, describes Lasirèn as a *lwa* who "always got a comb, to comb her hair" (223). Hair is also linked with spiritual power, Rowland Abiodun observes, because "the hair-plaiter (hairdresser) is seen as one who honors and beautifies *orí* (*orí-inú*), the 'inner-head,' the 'divinity' of the head" ("Hidden Power" 10–11).

34. This assertion is particularly evident in discussions of the Haitian Revolution and the ceremony at Bwa Kayiman. For more see Hebblethwaite's *A Transatlantic History of Haitian Vodou* 24–25.
35. These *lwa* and others appear in later paintings by Báez, such as *Becoming New (a tignon for Mami Wata)*, which is figure 1.2 of this book.
36. In 2018 Báez continued to expand her repertoire of muses with the piece *For Améthyste and Athénaire (Exiled Muses Beyond Jean Luc Nancy's Canon), Anacaonas*, created for the Museum of Modern Art (MoMA) in New York. Améthyste and Athénaire are the daughters of Henry Christophe, the first king of Haiti. Báez's piece recovers these women from history because no photographs of them exist (Báez "Studio Visit").
37. According to Tiffany Ruby Patterson and Robin D. G. Kelley, "One reason that New World black cultures appear 'counter' to European narratives of history is that Europe exorcized blackness in order to create its own invented traditions, empires, and fictions of superiority and racial purity" (13).
38. Rey and Stepick find that "people everywhere have long found water to be a powerful sacrament or symbol, thus making it essential to religion" ("Visual Culture" 237). For a conversation that places Haitian and Peruvian sacred waters in conversation see Daniels's "The Coolness of Cleansing."
39. The introduction to Thompson's book is titled "The Rise of the Black Atlantic Visual Tradition."
40. For more, see Murphy's *Botánicas*.
41. Tsang addresses the presence of *botánicas* in Europe ("Beguiling Eshu" 216).
42. *Vèvè* are discussed further in chapter 2.
43. Scholars have afforded both Santería/Regla de Ocha and Haitian Vodou a robust bibliography from which I draw in my writing. By comparison, work on the Dominican Republic's La 21 División is scarce, and of what exists, a great deal has only been published in Spanish and is in limited circulation. I seek to make this tradition accessible to a wider audience through its inclusion in my book.
44. The *misterios* are the deities of La 21 División.
45. In her discussion of La 21 División, Davis states, "La palabra 'nación' indica acertadamente que cada categoría de misterios proviene de un diferente origen étnico en Africa" (The word "nation" aptly indicates that each category of *misterios* comes from a different ethnic origin in Africa) (*La otra ciencia* 116).
46. For a discussion of the nations in Haitian Vodou and La 21 División see Ricourt, *The Dominican Racial Imaginary* 115–116.
47. A recent example is Strongman's *Queering Black Atlantic Religions*.
48. "Because Dominican vodú is so intertwined with Haitian Vodou, I have deemed it worthwhile to study both systems of worship together, establishing their relationships to one another, as well as their differences and influences.... For comparison's sake, correspondences with other Afro-American syncretic systems such as Santería and Afro-Brazilian cults are also indicated, as well as the existent symbiosis between vodú and Catholicism."
49. While Spiritism (Espiritismo) is not an Afro-diasporic religion, it coexists with

Afro-diasporic spiritual practices. A more thorough discussion of Espiritismo can be found in the epilogue.

50. For an overview of the role of the ancestors in these traditions see Rey, "The Life of the Dead in African and African Diasporic Religion."

51. Kristina Wirtz lists four primary reasons a person becomes initiated in Santería/ Regla de Ocha: "because of family tradition; because of irresolvable problems; because of serious illness; or purely because of affinity for the religion" (89).

52. Though less common, in Haitian Vodou there are those who claim to have received initiation directly from the lwa. When this occurs, their instruction is said to have taken place "below the water" because the lwa reside there (McCarthy Brown 224).

53. For the testimonies see Deive 193–199. The inheritance of lwa and orishas is also common.

54. Informal initiations were also common in Santería/Regla de Ocha, but in the 1950s formal initiations became the norm, a change driven by the growing desire to transform Santería/Regla de Ocha into an economically viable product (Sandoval, Worldview 93).

55. In Migration and Vodou, Karen E. Richman states, "Colonial Haiti produced such basic raw products as sugar and coffee. Neocolonial Haiti today produces raw, or unskilled, peasant labor for export" (39). Richman's observation denotes the twentieth-century connections between Haitian braceros working in US agribusiness in the Caribbean and the imported Mexican braceros who worked on the US mainland. Such a realization uncovers the understated history that the bracero program was piloted in the Caribbean before it was implemented on the mainland. As noted by García-Peña, the program was established during the US intervention in Hispaniola, from 1915 to 1934 in Haiti and from 1916 to 1924 in the Dominican Republic (207).

56. Carr's narrative begins with the experience of exiting the spiritual "womb" of the trono (throne), one of the words used to describe Santería/Regla de Ocha's initiation chamber (1).

57. Richman documents it as "a ten-day rite of passage" (130). Hebblethwaite supports both views (Vodou Songs 27; A Transatlantic History 31).

58. In El monte Cabrera describes the omiero as "el agua bendita y regeneradora de todas las consagraciones en la Regla de Ocha, la de 'lavar y hacer Santo'" (the holy and regeneradora water of all consecrations in Regla de Ocha, of "washing and making the Saint") (105). This comment emphasizes the omiero's critical function within and beyond initiation rituals.

59. In her discussion of the preparation of the omiero in "Matanzas-style" Santería, Beliso-De Jesús notes that "the waters seem to turn the hues of the saint" (Electric Santería 134), adding a visual dimension to the spiritual potency of this fluid.

60. Deive indicates that initiation into La 21 División consists of a triple baptism: "el lavado de cabeza, el refresco, y el bautismo de sangre" (the washing of the head, the refreshing of the head, and the blood baptism) (199).

61. Although not distinguished by its use of water, in the context of these rituals we must consider Santería/Regla de Ocha's "head rogation." A succinct explanation by

Elizabeth Pérez defines the *"rogación de cabeza*, or 'feeding of the head'" as a process "that employs disposable 'white' substances associated with the *orisha* Obatalá [ruler of all heads], such as cocoa butter, cotton, eggshell powder, and coconut" ("Portable" 45). For more details about the head rogation see Cabrera, *El monte* 394–396.

62. The metaphor of the bridge has been present in Anzaldúa's work since the 1981 publication of her coedited anthology *This Bridge Called My Back*. For Anzaldúa, to become a bridge one must assert the need to create connection but also recognize that many times this bond comes from a place of mutual pain and sacrifice.

CHAPTER 1. CHANNELING THE UNDOCUMENTED IN MAYRA SANTOS-FEBRES'S *BOAT PEOPLE*

1. The title of Santos-Febres's text is purposefully not capitalized. An earlier version of this chapter was published in the Spring 2021 issue of *Chicana/Latina Studies* under the title "'Por el mar que nos une': *boat people*'s Living Waters."

2. In her translator's note for the 2021 bilingual edition of *boat people*, Vanessa Pérez-Rosario also describes the collection as an elegy (78).

3. The Mona Passage is an eighty-mile strait that lies between the island of Hispaniola and Puerto Rico. It also connects the Atlantic Ocean to the Caribbean Sea. Another text that depicts this migratory experience is A.-M. Lara's novel *Erzulie's Skirt*.

4. In "Transformative Currents," I discuss the figure of Don Chan in Angie Cruz's *Let It Rain Coffee*. Cruz's inclusion of Don Chan indicates the importance of addressing undocumented Asian migration to the Dominican Republic, echoing *boat people*'s invitation to move beyond strict historical and geographical constructs. For a panoramic take on these migrations see Hu-DeHart and López's "Asian Diasporas in Latin America and the Caribbean."

5. While "tanto" is associated with quantity and would typically be translated as "much," I employ "vast" in my translation to call attention to the notion of space. The vastness of the ocean, vertically and horizontally, renders this aquatic body as one that will never be fully comprehensible, a view that resonates with Glissant's portrayal of opacity in *Poetics of Relation*.

6. The use of diminutives in the collection also contributes to this challenge (J. P. Rivera 181). In addition, diminutives express intimacy, an affect that defies documentation in a private rather than public way.

7. An English translation of Vega's story appears in *Her True-True Name: An Anthology of Women's Writing from the Caribbean*, 105–111.

8. The trope of the boat in "Encancaranublado" has overtaken the presence of water in the text. As Mariana Past notes, "Critics of Vega's story have repeatedly wrestled with the matter of the boat at the center of the tale" (163).

9. The US/Mexico border has a rich and complex literary legacy in which the physical presence and symbolic power of the Rio Grande/Río Bravo, the fence, and/or the wall abound. Some notable contemporary authors who engage with these elements

are Norma Elia Cantú, Reyna Grande, Emmy Pérez, Jenny Torres Sanchez, and Luis Alberto Urrea.

10. The establishment of Little Haiti in Tijuana is but one recent example of the importance of understanding the growing Caribbean presence seeping into US/Mexico patterns of migration. Scholars are avidly working to document these stories, as discussed in Mayes's November 5, 2020, virtual talk "To Be Haitian Means to Leave."

11. For more on "theory in the flesh" see chapter 3.

12. For some of these *patakís* see Cabrera, *Yemayá y Ochún* 20–22.

13. In Haitian Vodou, Agwe is the *lwa* most often associated with the ocean. He is also known as the "Maitre L'Eau (Master of Waters)" (Hurston 231), a title that asserts his dominion beyond the sea and into other liquid bodies.

14. Cabrera's connection to Yemayá is reinforced in her correspondence with Pierre Verger, another scholar of Afro-diasporic religions. For more see Cañete Ochoa, *Cartas de Yemayá a Changó.*

15. While the presence of Caribbean women writers in the twentieth century cannot be denied, many theorists of the region are male: the Martiniquais Édouard Glissant, the Bajan Edward Kamau Brathwaite, and the Cuban Antonio Benítez Rojo are some of the names with most resonance, representing the region's various linguistic currents. In many of their literary and critical works, while the feminine and the sea are pivotal players, they are often used illustratively rather than given agency. For example, Benítez-Rojo states that the Atlantic Ocean is what it is today, a space of economic and political power, "because it was the painfully delivered child of the Caribbean, whose vagina was stretched between continental clamps" (5).

16. The "Periodo especial en tiempos de paz" (Special period in times of peace) took place in Cuba in the 1990s. It marks a time of extreme scarcity on the island following the collapse of the Soviet Union, upon which the island heavily relied for trade.

17. Jennine Capó Crucet's debut novel, *Make Your Home among Strangers*, depicts the emotional toll of the Elián González case on Miami's Cuban American community.

18. Although Elián was rescued by fishermen, narratives of his survival have often replaced the fishermen with dolphins (Banet-Weiser 149).

19. Others saw Elián as an embodiment of the *orisha* Eleggúa, the path opener, who is often associated with children (Acosta 56–61).

20. Shakespeare presents Sycorax and Caliban as less than human due to the presumed primitiveness of their culture and spirituality as well as their race. While Sycorax never speaks in the play and is depicted as a "hag" and a "witch," Shakespeare discloses that she was originally from Algiers, establishing her African roots.

21. I was able to locate one narrative written by a female *balsera*, Carmen Vázquez-Fernández, titled *Balseros cubanos* (1999). Yet even in her story (which, though based on real life events, is fictional) the dominant actors are male. Her main female character, Ana, spends her time at sea ill, tacitly turning into a passive passenger.

22. By only invoking Elisabet as the mother who sacrificed herself to give her son a better life in the United States, the media perpetuates long-established Latina archetypes of socially acceptable femininity and domesticity: the self-sacrificing, almost

virginal ethnic mother who gives her happiness and in this instance her own life so her child may achieve the American dream of upward mobility (Molina Guzmán).

23. Danticat's short story "Children of the Sea" describes one such journey.

24. Even the 2005 cover of the book reinforces this reading, as it shows a fish being used as bait.

25. The connection between water, voice, and divination drives the understanding that when an initiate receives the combination 7-7 (Yemayá's number) through divination with the *diloggún* they are believed to have the potential of becoming exceptional diviners (Fernández 55).

26. "Transculturation" is a term proposed by Fernando Ortiz, Lydia Cabrera's brother-in-law, in the 1940s. Eugenio Matibag describes it as "the process by which a culture constitutes itself as a crossing, combination, fusion, and mutual transformation of two or more preexisting cultures. In the process, cultures are uprooted and new cultures are formed" (*Afro-Cuban* 24).

27. Rey served as an interpreter of Haitian Kreyòl during rescue missions for migrants at sea in the summer of 1994 (Rey, "Vodou" 205).

28. Beyond water, the *lwa* also live in natural sites such as mountains, rocks, caves, and trees (Métraux 92).

29. In her ethnography of Afro-diasporic religiosity in the Dominican Republic, Wendalina Rodríguez Vélez presents the case of Antero, a healer of La 21 División who works with a mirror for divination (216).

30. For a thorough discussion of this complex *lwa* with multiple names see Hebblethwaite, *Vodou Songs* 254–256.

31. "The crossroads is a *lwa* and also a symbol for the intersection between worlds, and thus for change" (McAlister, *Rara!* 92).

32. In 1975 Edward Kamau Brathwaite wrote the infamous line "The unity is submarine" when speaking about the future of Caribbean thought and cultures (1). Jenny Sharpe notes that this line was inspired by the poet's visit to Haiti in the late 1960s and the "pleasurable shock of recognition" he experienced there (60).

33. For more on this in relation to Cuban history see Palmié, *Wizards*.

34. For a discussion of the violence of the US occupation on the Dominican Republic's Afro-religious practices see chapter 2 of García-Peña, *The Borders of Dominicanidad*.

35. Duvalier's choice to embody the Gede is telling, as these *lwa* are associated with male dominance (McCarthy Brown 380).

36. This terror also extended to "Papa Doc's" secret police, the *tonton makout*, who were "named after a childhood bogeyman" (Ramsey 251).

37. Although *boat people* was published in 2005, the collection painfully anticipates what would happen to Dominicans of Haitian descent in the Dominican Republic in 2013 when the Dominican Constitutional Tribunal violently stripped them of their citizenship. Additional discussion on this law is included in the epilogue.

38. For a thorough description of how divination is performed with the *diloggún* (cowrie shells), see Wirtz 144–146.

39. In her research on Caribbean Indigeneity, Sherina Feliciano-Santos discusses the process of receiving her Taíno name, Anajuke (110–111), identifying a fruitful

point of connection between Indigenous and Afro-diasporic spiritual practices in the Americas.

40. Tsang translates *ofeicitá* as "one who makes the itá" ("Write" 14).

41. Fernández's scholarship includes details of his conversations with Natalie Hernández Cubilla, Omi Lai, a daughter of Yemayá who became a renowned *ofeicitá* (55–59).

42. The troubling connection between writing *by* practitioners and writing *about* practitioners by academics is a source of tension. In Cabrera's work, Tsang notes that "the lack of proper citations, whether purposeful or not, upheld the assumptions that Cubans of African descent were without a rich textual history" ("Write" 250). Scholarship on Afro-diasporic religions has thus been complicit in rendering these practices illiterate and undocumented, a portrayal that is currently being challenged.

43. Pointedly, at the end of *boat people* Santos-Febres's sea has bewitched (*embrujado*) the drowned migrants. This proclamation strengthens the volition and initiatory power of the water by insinuating that it has access to the names of the boat people.

44. A similar tactic exists in La 21 División through the use of *el nombre prestado* (the borrowed name), a process by which a practitioner keeps their given name hidden and instead uses an alias to shield themselves from spiritual harm (Deive 285).

45. In the 2005 version, "aqui" appears without an accent mark; in the 2021 edition the accent mark has been added. The title of this poem may resonate with readers of "En el fondo del caño hay un negrito" (At the bottom of the bayou there is a Black boy) by José Luis González. Initially published in 1954, this story narrates the tragic death by drowning of Melodía, a young Black boy living in "El fanguito," one of the *arrabales* (slums) that resulted from the mass migration of Puerto Ricans from the countryside to the San Juan region during the government's push for industrial development, which began in the 1940s. Santos-Febres's poems re-engage with the abysmal connection between water, drowning, migration, and the Black body presented by González, although *boat people*'s inclusion of Afro-diasporic spirituality counters the unyielding realism that distinguishes González's prose.

46. Though largely depicted as female, Mami Wata has male avatars known as *papi wata* (Drewal, "Charting the Voyage" 1).

47. Drewal asserts that even the name Mami Wata, "which may be translated as 'Mother Water' or 'Mistress Water,' is pidgin English, a language developed to lubricate trade" ("Sources and Currents" 23).

48. Drewal contends that Mami Wata is not visible in Yoruba culture (and by extension in its diaspora) because this tradition has an array of water deities such as Ochún, Olokun, and Yemayá "whose powers encompass those of *Mami Wata*" ("Charting the Voyage" 3).

49. For more on Santa Marta see Giovanni Savino's 2005 documentary *Misterios*.

50. Santa Marta does not have a Catholic counterpart. She is believed to come directly from Africa, strengthening her connection with Mami Wata (Tejeda Ortiz 131).

51. For a description of a Haitian Vodou ritual that incorporates the use of water and Indigenous technologies see McAlister, *Rara!* 93–97.

52. "La división de agua se llama también india" (the water division is also called the Indian division) (Deive 179).

53. José R. Oliver describes *ciboney* as "a term that the Spaniards claimed was given to a people from central to eastern Cuba who, to the Spaniard's eyes, were less developed than those originating from Hispaniola" (7).

54. While I recognize that the term "Taíno" is contested, I employ it due to its continued circulation in academic and communal settings. The inclusion of the Taíno in *boat people* extends the reach of the collection, as some community activists in Puerto Rico connect the island's Indigenous language to Mayan (Feliciano-Santos 114–118). This claim is supported by evidence of contact with South and Central America (Anderson-Córdova 17–18).

55. The square brackets are part of Lara's original text.

56. Elsewhere I have argued that in Puerto Rican literature, Blackness is often displaced from national land-based discourses and finds its place in the water (Hey-Colón, "Toward a Genealogy" 187). This stance is also applicable to the presence of Blackness and Indigeneity in La 21 División.

57. Drewal points out that Lasirèn is one of the multiple faces of Mami Wata in the Americas ("Sources and Currents" 25).

58. A nuanced discussion of Olokun is provided in chapter 2.

CHAPTER 2. THE TECHNO-RESONANCES OF RITA INDIANA'S
LA MUCAMA DE OMICUNLÉ

1. In *La mucama de Omicunlé*, Acilde is a transgender man for whom Indiana initially uses feminine pronouns. After Acilde undergoes a gender-affirming transition coupled with an Afro-diasporic religious initiation, Indiana switches to using masculine pronouns for Acilde. At no point are readers directly informed about Acilde's chosen pronouns. Guided by the spiritual multiplicity that characterizes Acilde's presence in the novel, I consistently use "they" and "them" in my discussion of this character. This decision also underscores the importance of paying attention to the Santería/Regla de Ocha copresences that surround Acilde.

2. "One of the many Haitians who've crossed the border, fleeing from the quarantine declared on the other half of the island" (*Tentacle* 9). Achy Obejas translated Indiana's novel under the title *Tentacle*. Although my chapter uses Indiana's original text, I provide Obejas's translation for access. At times I add words to the translation to ensure clarity.

3. "To help ease the terrible circumstances affecting the islands of the Caribbean after the March 19 disaster" (*Tentacle* 10). The disaster referenced here is the destruction of the Caribbean Sea.

4. Aisha M. Beliso-De Jesús discusses Espiritismo in the Cuban context and asserts that it is "a central component of Santería formations for black communities in the United States" (*Electric Santería* 205). Despite its European roots, Espiritismo has been absorbed by Afro-diasporic communities because, in the words of Elizabeth Pérez, it "reconstitutes their 'Blackness' within the sociocultural framework of a

global African Diaspora" ("Spiritist" 333). Additional discussion of Espiritismo is provided in the epilogue.

5. For a thorough discussion of this see chapter 1 of *Electric Santería*. Palmié also addresses the "Virtual Atlantic" in chapter 5 of *The Cooking of History: How Not to Study Afro-Cuban Religion*.

6. In a 2021 virtual event, Indiana recounted that her openness to Santería/Regla de Ocha came from growing up surrounded by the energies of La 21 División in the Dominican Republic. She was later drawn to Santería/Regla de Ocha because it offered life-affirming models for nonbinary ways of being and living ("A Conversation").

7. In "Soundscapes of Disaster" McAlister notes that the collapsing of linear time is also evident in how digital technology mediates the experience of events such as the 2010 earthquake in Haiti.

8. Discussion of time in the novel also appears in Hamilton, "Another Shape."

9. Acilde lives in the years 2027–2037; in 1991–2001 the story follows Giorgio, and in 1606 it centers on Roque.

10. As Stephan Palmié declares: "Whatever else Afro-Cuban religion is, it is as modern as nuclear thermodynamics, or the suppositions about the nature of our world that underlie DNA sequencing, or structural adjustment policies, or on-line banking" (*Wizards* 15–16).

11. "The doorbell at Esther Escudero's house has been programmed to sound like a wave" (*Tentacle* 9).

12. For a summary of the various ways in which the relationship between Yemayá and Olokun is conceived see Ferrer Castro and Acosta Alegre 19–20.

13. "The cloak that covers the sea" (*Tentacle* 17).

14. Cabrera's informants state that Yemayá is "una y siete a la vez" (one and seven at the same time) (*Yemayá y Ochún* 21). Cabrera asserts that Yemayá is the ocean from which life emanates, and she also indicates that Olokun was there from the beginning (25). This is supported by other practitioners who say that Olokun is one of the oldest manifestations of Yemayá (Ferrer Castro and Acosta Alegre 15).

15. Gómez's religious name means "Òrìṣà is Born" (Mason, *Olóòkun* 26).

16. Cabrera writes that the tumultuous relationship between Orula (the deity of divination associated with male *babalawos*) and Yemayá ended badly because "Yemayá sabía demasiado" (Yemayá knew too much) (*Yemayá y Ochún* 42–45). Beliso-De Jesús finds that this *pataki* indicates why, at times, a *santera* must request assistance from a *babalawo* for interpretation of the *diloggún* (*Electric Santería* 190–191).

17. This reading is enhanced by Esther's last name, Escudero, since *escudo* means "shield" in Spanish.

18. "The 21 Divisions, with its blend of African deities and Catholic saints, as the official religion" (*Tentacle* 44).

19. "According to the media, President Bona's victory and continued power via the presidency are the work of this gray-haired woman who shuffles along in her blue silk slippers into the kitchen and pours herself a cup of the coffee Acilde has prepared for her moments before" (*Tentacle* 10).

20. For more on these networks see pp. 211–213 of Palmié's *The Cooking of History*.

21. "Her father had stayed by her mother's side just long enough to get her pregnant. Jennifer, her mother, a brunette [*trigueña*] with good hair who'd gone to Milan with a modeling contract, had gotten hooked on heroin and ended up selling her ass on the metro in Rome. She'd had six abortions when she decided to go through with *the seventh* pregnancy, returning to her country so she could dump the baby on her parents, two bitter peasants from Moca who'd moved to the city after La Llorona and its two years of rain that had destroyed their homestead forever" (*Tentacle* 14, my emphasis).

22. Hoffnung-Garskof also emphasizes the importance of the color/racial description entailed by the word *trigueño*, which he translates as "wheaten" (27).

23. See Sánchez-Carretero's 2005 article "*Santos y Misterios* as Channels of Communication in the Diaspora." Tsang's 2013 article "Beguiling Eshu" discusses Afro-diasporic religions in Europe.

24. In his discussion of *La mucama*, Paul Humphrey notes that Indiana plays with "the oft-used trope in Caribbean literature of three generations of women who tell the past through their respective stories" by narrating the story from future to past, as well as complicating gender roles (111n2). I would add, however, that *La mucama* does not move linearly from past to future nor from future to past. Instead, it revels in the unobstructed flows of time, often jumping from one world to another in the span of a sentence, a characteristic driven by the copresences that populate the text.

25. A series of *patakís* about Olokun, many of which discuss betrayal and rejection, can be found in the second half of Ferrer Castro and Acosta Alegre's book *Fermina Gómez y la casa olvidada de Olókun*.

26. "During the tryst that produced Acilde, her father had told her mother he wanted to get to know Dominican beaches. Back then the island was a tourist destination with coasts full of coral, fish, and anemones" (*Tentacle* 20).

27. Denise Brennan discusses sex tourism in Sosúa, the town inhabited by Giorgio, one of Acilde's avatars. The borderlessness of *La mucama* is perpetuated by Sosúa since the majority of its inhabitants are migrants: "Dominican migrants from throughout the country; Haitian migrants; an expatriate resident community of Germans, and an assortment of other Europeans and Canadians; elderly Jewish European 'settlers' (refugees from Nazi persecution) and their descendants; and, of course, a constant stream of tourists, generally from Europe" (Brennan 13).

28. Beliso-De Jesús addresses these undercurrents in the ochascape, which "was described in neoliberal terms that offered the Internet as a site of individual freedoms from tradition" (*Electric Santería* 54).

29. Jorge Castellanos and Isabel Castellanos also describe Santería/Regla de Ocha practitioners as "servidor[es] de sus dioses" (those who serve their gods) (88).

30. Beliso-De Jesús explains, "Contractual arrangements also occur in *regla ocha* [Santería/Regla de Ocha] practices. Practitioners describe how they had to make santo, become initiated in Santería, because they 'owed the debt of their head' to the oricha. This was often the case when a parent promised to initiate a child in order to save the child's life. The child is considered *preso de santo*, a prisoner of the oricha, and must be initiated to pay the debt. Becoming a prisoner of santo can also happen

when the oricha saves someone's life, or defends the person against spiritual warfare from other copresences" (*Electric Santería* 121–122).

31. According to David Hatfield Sparks, "*Orishás* associated with lesbian/gay and/or transgendered experience include: Obatalá, Oshún, Yemayá, Olokun, Yewá, Oyá, Erinlé, Logunedé, Orúnmila" (374).

32. Other water deities are connected to the provocative triad of gender fluidity, androgyny, and healing; an example is Erinle. See Cabrera's *Yemayá y Ochún* (87) and Otero's "In the Water with Inle."

33. The purpose of divination is to provide information upon which action must be taken. Wirtz states, "Seldom do the saints directly heal or solve anything during a divination. Rather, they mostly dispense advice and suggestions upon which the client must act in order to solve the problem" (150).

34. "Nobody knows what's at the bottom of the ocean" (*Tentacle* 19).

35. "Esther had brought her a blue bead necklace from Brazil; it was consecrated to Olokun, the oldest deity in the world, the sea itself. 'Master of the unknown,' Esther explained when she put it on her. 'Wear it always because, even if you don't believe, it will protect you. One day, you're going to inherit my house. You won't understand this now but, in time, you will.' Omicunlé would get very serious and Acilde would feel very uncomfortable. She couldn't help but feel affection for the old woman who took care of her with a tenderness her own family had never shown her" (*Tentacle* 21–22).

36. "Belarminio Brito, Omidina, child of Yemayá, and he was so bad, as noxious as gas" (*Tentacle* 17). Although Indiana does not provide the translation for Omidina's name, John Mason indicates that it means "Water blocks the road" (*In Praise* 23). Notably, the children of Yemayá in the novel—Omidina, Omicunlé, and Omioloyu—have names linked to water, "omi."

37. That Esther and Eric are initiated by Omidina, a priest of Yemayá, and are identified as children of this *orisha* reinforces the role Yemayá plays in relation to Olokun throughout the text. Indeed, one of Yemayá's paths is "the doorkeeper of Olókun who inhabits the ocean" (Mason, *Olóòkun* 34).

38. The fact that Eric is initiated to Yemayá when he is nine and nine is one of Olokun's divine numbers augments the many techno-resonances between Yemayá and Olokun in the novel. "In the prophecy delivered at his initiation, it was revealed he would be the one to find Olokun's legitimate son, the one with the seven perfections, the Lord of the Deep. That's why his godfather called him Omioloyu, the Eyes of Yemayá, convinced that *one day this clever young boy would discover in the flesh* the one who knew what lies at the bottom of the sea" (*Tentacle* 50, my emphasis).

39. "A Cuban doctor with movie-star good looks, Eric didn't need to pay for sex but he was crazy about those middle-class white boys who sold themselves so they could buy the pills they were addicted to" (*Tentacle* 11).

40. "Acilde sucked him *and let him grab her head*. . . . Acilde hadn't quite finished saying 'gimme my money, faggot' when Eric launched himself on top of her, immobilizing her, face down, and stifling her screams of 'I'm a girl, shithead' with the gravel [grass] stuffed in her mouth. At this point, Eric didn't care what she was and just shoved his dry dick up her ass. When he finished and Acilde stood up to pull up her pants, he

flicked a lighter and approached her to confirm it was true that she was a woman. 'I'm gonna pay you more for the special effects,' he said. And when she saw how much more, she accepted his invitation to breakfast" (*Tentacle* 11–12, my emphasis).

41. One of the mythical stories about Olokun in Santería/Regla de Ocha recounts how the *orisha* was chained to the bottom of the ocean to prevent the destruction of the world (Cabrera, *Yemayá y Ochún* 26).

42. "Touching the *orí* [head] of a priest is regarded by many as a serious violation" (Tsang, "Beguiling Eshu" 223).

43. "Acilde had a crown of moles, dark spots that made a circle all the way around his head. Eric had noticed it when the girl . . . had knelt before him to suck him off that night at the Mirador" (*Tentacle* 51).

44. This crown is why *kari ocha* is often referred to as *coronación* (coronation).

45. "Eric stayed in the house. At first, Acilde thought the witch didn't trust her, but later she understood the anemone needed special care, which Eric would dispense in her absence. This was confirmed when she saw him spend so many dead hours holed up in the saint's room. On her return, Esther found Eric sick, with diarrhea, the shivers, and a strange discoloring on his arms. She sent him home. 'He asked for it, that bugger,' she told Acilde. 'Don't take his calls.' Despite Omicunlé's warnings, Acilde visited Eric while he was sick to bring him food and the medicine he prescribed for himself. Eric stayed in his room, where a stink of vomit and liquor reigned. There were days when he was delirious, when he sweated terrible fevers, and when he continually called out to Omicunlé: 'Oló! Kun fun me lo mo, oló kun fun.' When Acilde returned to Esther's she told her everything to try to soften her up but all she managed was to get the old lady to curse him even more, calling him a traitor, dirty, a pendejo" (*Tentacle* 20–21).

46. As Cabrera declares, "Los Santos, airados, no solamente envían enfermedades sino todo género de calamidades" (The Saints [*orishas*], when irate, not only send illness, but all sorts of calamities) (*El monte* 55).

47. This moment of techno-resonance reflects Santería/Regla de Ocha history. Fermina Gómez, the priestess of Yemayá credited with establishing Olokun worship in the Americas, was originally initiated to the *orisha* Ochún, an erroneous ritual that led her to become "'twisted' (*se trastornó*), meaning a mental or physical break" (Beliso-De Jesús, *Electric Santería* 132). Gómez was healed when another priestess, Ma Monserrate, remedied the harm "in a complicated ritual called '*virando el oro*,' reversing the initiation practice and then making her to Yemayá, the correct oricha" (Beliso-De Jesús, *Electric Santería* 132). Gómez's case is evidence of the intrinsic resonances between the waters, signaled here by the *orishas* Yemayá and Ochún, but also of the profound differences between them, differences that must be honored and respected.

48. "Eric loved the old woman like a mother and, wanting to avoid the prophecy's fatal outcome, he'd tried to improvise a way out. If he crowned himself as Omo Olokun, he could get rid of Acilde, the supposed Chosen One, but his experiments with the anemone behind Esther's back had ended up making him ill and angering her" (*Tentacle* 50–51).

49. Alison Glassie contends that the *C. gigantea* anemone represents the "anemone-like

structure" of the text, another view that supports how water is continually identified as the spiritual power center of the text.

50. In *Tentacle*, Obejas translates the name of the drug as "Rainbow Brite." In my analysis, I use the spelling from the original Spanish text.

51. "[It was] an injection making the rounds in alternative science circles that promised a complete sex change without surgery. The process had been compared to going cold turkey, although the homeless transsexuals who'd served as guinea pigs said it was much worse" (*Tentacle* 15–16).

52. Beliso-De Jesús notes that in Cuba different groups "sold Santería initiation tours to foreigners" for roughly $7,000 in the 1990s and 2000s (*Electric Santería* 17). Regarding Haitian Vodou, McCarthy Brown declares, "No one undertakes these various levels of initiation idly or out of pure curiosity. They are expensive and taxing" (351).

53. The very title of Davis's 1987 study of La 21 División, *La otra ciencia*, addresses the tradition's medicinal aspects.

54. Tejeda Ortiz also declares that *servidores* often provide medical, psychological, and psychiatric services for their communities (154).

55. In *The Price for Their Pound of Flesh*, Daina Ramey Berry documents how medical training in the United States relied on the use of Black bodies purchased through the domestic cadaver trade, a complex system that "planted, harvested, and transported" the bodies of the formerly enslaved into medical schools (154).

56. In the Dominican Republic the *cofradías* were created in the sixteenth century. Ricourt notes, "One cofradia surviving until the present day in the Dominican Republic is the Cofradia of the Congos of Villa Mella, which has been proclaimed an Intangible Cultural Heritage of Humanity by UNESCO" (*The Dominican* 109). García-Peña also discusses the Cofradía del Espíritu Santo, in San Juan de la Maguana (58–64).

57. Provocatively, in *La mucama* Indiana makes Villa Mella the birthplace of the ultraconservative evangelical terrorist movement Los Siervos del Apocalipsis (the Servants of the Apocalypse), which rises in response to President Bona's proclamation of La 21 División as the official religion of the island (59).

58. "Give herself an enema, take a bath, and shave her vulva and head" (*Tentacle* 48).

59. In preparation for *kanzo*, for example, Métraux states that initiates "'freshen' their bodies with 'baths' that is to say with water into which leaves with medical or magical properties have been infused" (195).

60. A master of ceremonies of sorts, the role of the *obá-oriaté* is "apparently without precise African antecedents," making it "both the corollary and catalyst of the condensed Lucumí pantheon within La Regla de Ocha" (D. H. Brown 150). While originally women also fulfilled this role, "very few contemporary women have attempted to or been allowed to perform the role of oriaté" (Beliso-De Jesús, *Electric Santería* 194). Some of the ritual skills associated with the *obá-oriaté* are "shaver, singer, herbalist, sacrificer, diviner" (D. H. Brown 151).

61. In his study on Santería/Regla de Ocha, Lachatañeré indicates that some individuals undergoing initiation must shave their heads and their underarms and genital areas (321).

62. In contrast, in Santería/Regla de Ocha the initiate is seated in a special *pilón* (mortar) or in a chair (Cabrera, *Yemayá y Ochún* 162).
63. "Keep the space around her body sterile" (*Tentacle* 48).
64. Davis explains, "Cada persona tiene que traer un pañuelo nuevo, siempre *blanco* 'porque el pañuelo blanco es divisional, lo puede usar cualquier misterio'" (Each person must bring a new kerchief, always *white* 'because the white kerchief is divisional; it can be used by any *misterio*') (*La otra ciencia* 285–286, emphasis in the original).
65. The role of water and the *jarro divisional* is echoed by the reception given to the *orishas* in Santería/Regla de Ocha. Cabrera offers this description: "Ofreciéndoles agua se recibe a los Orichas cuando bajan a bailar en compañía de sus hijos y devotos en las fiestas o en cualquier otra ocasión. Para 'saludarlos' se les ofrece agua; una libación precede a un ruego" (The Orichas are received with an offering of water when they come down to dance with their children and devotees at religious festivities or other occasions. To "greet them" they are offered water; a libation precedes a request) (*Yemayá y Ochún* 24).
66. "Offerings so everything will go smoothly" (*Tentacle* 48).
67. In his discussion of this spiritual technology in the worship of Olokun, Mason terms these symbols "Òṣù nílẹ̀ (ball of medicine on the ground)" (*Olóòkun* 57).
68. *Vèvè* can also be drawn with "ashes, flour, coffee grinds, brick dust, or other powders" (Rey and Stepick, "Visual Culture" 231).
69. Davis mentions that the use of *vèvè* in La 21 División is being supplanted by that of the imagery of the Catholic saints in an attempt to distance the tradition from Blackness (*La otra ciencia* 313).
70. The fact that Indiana marks Acilde's initiation as Olokun's child through direct contact with the head is a subversion of current practices in Santería/Regla de Ocha. As explained by D. H. Brown, "A number of the *orichas* in the modern pantheon, although they may be selected as the guardian angel—the initiate is their 'child'— cannot be mounted 'directly' on the head, or are rarely, or no longer, done so for various reasons. For example, Olokun (the mystery of the bottom of the sea), Oricha Oko (the earth), and Odúa (Creator of the world, time, longevity, and life and death), are grand and powerful constituent parts of the Creation; like Osain (owner of the *monte*), they are believed to be 'too big' to be contained by the head of any single individual" (136).
71. The novel presents a literary and not a traditional rendition of initiation. As described by D. H. Brown, "In the full Lucumí initiation, the Warriors [Elegguá, Ogún, Ochosi, Osun], received together in a prior initiatory step, along with the Four Pillars [Obatalá, Ochún, Yemayá, Changó] and the *cabecera* [titular *orisha*], are 'washed' with herbal *osain* liquids [*omiero*], 'presented to the head' of the initiate (with some exceptions), and 'fed' sacrifices in one day of complex ceremonies called the *asiento* or *kariocha*" (135).
72. "Esther knew what was going to happen. I'm done for [I've paid my debt]. We gave you the body you wanted and now you've given us the body we needed" (*Tentacle* 51).
73. Recorded messages are nothing new in the Afro-diasporic religious world. In *Migration and Vodou*, Karen E. Richman discusses how practitioners use cassette tapes as

letters to enable communication between distant family members as well as between the spirits and those who serve them: "Spirits possessing the bodies of ritual actors are not only aware of the recording devices, they often move to the recorder in order personally to address the absent migrant or migrants" (25).

74. "Said depends on me [you] so use the powers you have begun to discover for the good of humanity. Save the sea, Maferefún Olokun, Maferefún Yemayá" (*Tentacle* 83).

75. According to Cabrera's *Anagó*, "Maferefún Yemayá" would translate as "Gracias, bendita, o alabada seas" (Thank you, blessed be, or praised be) (205).

76. "Do I have two bodies or is my mind capable of broadcasting two different channels simultaneously?" (*Tentacle* 80).

77. When Acilde chooses the name Giorgio Menicucci for their avatar in the 1990s and 2000s they are told by the man who falsifies their documents, "You're going to do fine; in this country being white is a profession" (*Tentacle* 86). Acilde chooses the surname "Menicucci" in honor of their absent Italian father (*Tentacle* 87).

78. "After ten years in La Victoria—comfortable, calm, without any responsibilities other than to eat and breathe—he was now headed to the outside world, where the asphalt would stick to his soles like gum. He'd have to work now, that was certain. How would he deal with his stuff, his other lives, his businesses?" (*Tentacle* 123).

79. "He could sacrifice everything except this life, Giorgio Menicucci's life, his wife's company, the gallery, the lab. . . . In a little while, he'll forget about Acilde, about Roque, even about what lives in a hole down there in the reef" (*Tentacle* 132).

80. The Taíno were comprised of various ethnic groups. The term is contested, and I use it because it is the one employed in the novel. For more see Anderson-Córdova, *Surviving Spanish Conquest* 16–17.

81. Ananí's ownership of the land provides a matrilineal depiction of power that repudiates the reach of the patriarchal state.

82. "Men from the water, who came every so often to help them" (*Tentacle* 74).

83. "She was pregnant" (*Tentacle* 85).

84. "The portal to the land of the beginning" (*Tentacle* 75).

CHAPTER 3. AFRO-DIASPORIC CURRENTS IN THE GLORIA EVANGELINA ANZALDÚA PAPERS

1. A recent exception is Alicia Gaspar de Alba's poem "To Your Shadow Beast: In Memoriam," which also presents this moment as dialoguing with Afro-diasporic religions.

2. The essay where this line appears, "Let us be the healing of the wound: The Coyolxauhqui imperative—la sombra y el sueño," has been printed three times. The piece was first published in 2003 in the collection *One Wound for Another/Una herida por otra*, then it was included in the *Gloria Anzaldúa Reader*, and finally it became the first chapter of *Light in the Dark*. "Let us be the healing of the wound" begins with Anzaldúa walking by the sea in Santa Cruz, California, in an attempt to process the grief of 9/11; the chapter closes with a mention of the sounds of drumming at the

beach that Anzaldúa describes as a serenade for Yemayá (22). The second chapter, "Flights of the Imagination," also begins in the water, at the root of La Virgen's tree, which Anzaldúa explains is a special place she would often walk to along Monterrey Beach (23–24).

3. A CMAS-Benson Latin American Collection Summer Research Fellowship and the Carlos E. Castañeda Postdoctoral Research Fellowship provided me with access to the GEA Papers at the University of Texas at Austin.

4. *Conocimientos* are defined by AnaLouise Keating as "alternate ways of knowing that synthesize reflection with action to create subversive knowledge systems that challenge the status quo" ("Risking" 5).

5. In his 1998 lecture "Thinking the Diaspora," Hall speaks of the roots and routes of this Caribbean process (210). DeLoughrey expands on this construct in her book *Routes and Roots*.

6. See, for example, Arrizón's *Queering Mestizaje*.

7. This text represents what would have been Anzaldúa's PhD dissertation. She was posthumously awarded a PhD from UC Santa Cruz's Literature program, and the letters "PhD" were added to her tombstone in Hargill, Texas.

8. For a recent intervention on the changing vision of Anzaldúa within academia, see chapter 4 of Bost's *Shared Selves*.

9. For a recent exploration on embodiment see Covington-Ward's and Jouili's edited volume, *Embodying Black Religions in Africa and Its Diasporas*.

10. Anzaldúa developed the genre of the *autohistoria-teoría* in order to show "the concept that Chicanas and women of color write not only about abstract ideas but also bring in their personal history as well as the history of their community" (Anzaldúa, "Writing" 242).

11. For a discussion of Anzaldúa's birth certificates see Martínez 36–39.

12. Though these data do not appear consistently in the GEA Papers, whenever they are available I provide them in my citations.

13. "Comadres" is what Anzaldúa called those with whom she shared her writing, attesting to the communal aspect of her creative process. In Spanish, the term indicates a sense of kinship with someone who is not one's blood relation. In Catholicism, this connection is officialized through the rite of baptism in which the child's godparents become the *comadre(s)* and *compadre(s)* of the parents.

14. For more on Anzaldúa's revision process see my article "Chronic Illness and Transformation in Gloria Anzaldúa's 'Puddles.'"

15. Several of the texts I was able to locate that speak to Anzaldúa's relationship with water are barred from reproduction. All quotes from these manuscripts were taken as notes while at the Benson Library. Further information can be located on the finding aid for the GEA Papers at txarchives.org/utlac/finding_aids/00189.xml.

16. "Autoretratos de la artista as a Young Girl" and "Autohistoria de la artista as a Young Girl" contain distinct subsections that narrate Anzaldúa/Prieta's encounter with the sea, some of which share the title "En el hocico del mar." For clarity, when I cite from these longer documents I indicate the name "Autoretratos" or "Autohistoria," reserving "Hocico" only for citations from the stand-alone story.

17. Anzaldúa sometimes translates the title of this story as "In the Mouth of the Sea."
18. In a 2001 interview, Anzaldúa states that her story "En el hocico del mar" is part of a larger collection of stories centering on Prieta ("Daughter of Coatlicue" 53).
19. Bost speaks of Anzaldúa's strategies for "addressing [her] fluid self in her writing" (*Shared Selves* 104).
20. Some documents in the GEA Papers state that Anzaldúa was 11 when this happened, but 10 is the age that is most often indicated. In a 1982 interview, however, Anzaldúa says she was eight years old: "I've been dead four times: I died for a little while when I was three months old; when I was about eight I drowned for a little while at Padre Island; and then, when I fell off the hill and broke the left side of my back, I think I was dead for a minute and a half or two minutes. But during my operation the doctor said that I'd died for twenty minutes" ("Turning Points" 34). The shift in ages provides additional evidence of the problems generated by relying on chronology to address Anzaldúa's work.
21. Obatalá is the *orisha* associated with peace, purity, and wisdom. He plays a key role in the creation of human life, in particular the human body.
22. Judith Gleason observes, "The word 'orisha' literally means 'head-calabash.' Calabashes, gourds that grow on trees in tropical climates, are used as containers—of water, of food, of anything that can be put into them, magical substances as well as humdrum items" (*Oya: In Praise* 4). Gleason's book is part of Anzaldúa's personal library, which contains thousands of books. An itemized list can be requested from the Benson Library.
23. This humanization of water is replicated in an unpublished poem by Anzaldúa, "The water doesn't breath[e]," which I discuss in chapter 4.
24. Additional discussion of this vignette appears in Martínez 39–43.
25. School is often a place of trauma for Latinx children. In her memoir *When the Spirits Dance Mambo*, Afro–Puerto Rican author Marta Moreno Vega describes an eerily similar experience on her first day of school, when her teacher called out her given name, "Marta Moreno," and she did not respond to it because at home she was always called "Cotito," her nickname. This led to her teachers thinking she either did not speak English or had a learning disability (33–39).
26. For an example of this kind of critique see Alire Sáenz 85–87.
27. In her discussion of Dominican national identity, García-Peña defines "Hispanism" as the blend of "Christianity, Spanish language, and the elevated cultures of our 'mother Spain'" (31).
28. Beyond their limitations, Alicia Arrizón notes that *mestizaje* and Latinidad can generate "diasporic interventions, hybrid epistemologies, and the borderization of time and space" (48).
29. This view is also supported by Ana Castillo, who writes, "The Chicana feminist, who is of mixed European, Mexic Amerindian, and sometimes African and/or Asian origins, is making attempts at reviving the credos of her ancestors" (153–154).
30. For more on spiritual activism see Keating's "I'm a Citizen of the Universe."
31. This image is included in Aquino's 2015 zine *Gloria Anzaldúa*, from the series "The Life and Times of Butch Dykes."

32. Medina's term underscores the central role of spirituality in the development of Anzaldúa's epistemological and ontological theories. Anzaldúa's engagement with *nepantla* first appeared in *Borderlands* and continued throughout her life. The term is discussed at length in chapter 4.

33. Irene Lara explains how this recovery process can incorporate the *orisha* of sweet-waters, Ochún (31–35).

34. For Anzaldúa, *curanderismo* was a familiar system because her grandmother practiced it. Randy P. Conner notes that Anzaldúa "did not share with many people that one of her grandmothers—at least according to what she told me—had been a *curandera* and that she was destined to receive her wisdom" (190). See also Hartley, "The Curandera of Conquest."

35. As Mercedes Cros Sandoval observes, "the widespread use of herbal remedies and esoteric magical practices of *curanderismo* makes its ritual elements comparable to Santería ("Santería" 365).

36. *Borderlands* 118n7; "Turning Points" 19. This detail helps explain Yemayá's presence in the biography Anzaldúa supplied for *Bridge*.

37. Similar energies are attributed to Lasirèn, Agwe's underwater counterpart, who is often connected to profound infusions of knowledge. Additional discussion of Lasirèn appears in the prologue and chapter 1.

38. An almost verbatim rendition of this event appears in Anzaldúa's 1983 interview with Christine Weiland (112–113).

39. Delgadillo notes that Anzaldúa links spiritual *mestizaje* with the serpent (*Spiritual Mestizaje* 1).

40. This interview is also included in the 4th edition of *Borderlands/La Frontera* (267–284).

41. I was unable to secure permissions to use this image, but the series is available to view in the GEA Papers, box 146, folder 2.

42. Teish indicates that her name, "Luisah Teish," means "adventuresome spirit" (*Jambalaya* 32).

43. See p. 273 of Negrón-Muntaner's "Bridging Islands."

44. Anzaldúa recounts her advisor telling her "that Chicana literature was not a legitimate discipline, that it didn't exist, and that women's studies was not something I should do" ("Gloria" 4).

45. This course lives on at UT Austin under the title "La Chicana." It is supported by the Center for Mexican American Studies and the Department of Mexican American and Latino Studies. In spring 2018, as the Carlos E. Castañeda Postdoctoral Fellow, I taught the course, and we read *Borderlands/La Frontera*. The fact that most of my students were Chicanx was not lost on me, nor was the importance of letting them know that Anzaldúa herself had been a student at this university and had taught the very course they were taking.

46. "El Mundo Zurdo" is also the name given to the conference held annually at Trinity University by the Society for the Study of Gloria Anzaldúa.

47. For a discussion of F. Ortiz's work in relation to Afro-diasporic practices see chapter 2 of Palmié's *The Cooking of History*.

48. These metaphors of mixing, however, are far from panaceas and have been rightly criticized due to the whitening tone that can undergird them, reflective of the issues surrounding *mestizaje*.

49. For more on the connection between the *ajiaco*, Santería/Regla de Ocha, and Cuba see Beliso-De Jesús's *Electric Santería* 170–171.

50. It is possible that Anzaldúa may have been an *hija de las dos aguas*, daughter of both waters, which indicates that while her titular *orisha* was Yemayá, she might have also had a strong connection to rivers and thus to Ochún. Otero states that to be "a 'child of both waters/*hijo/a de las dos aguas*' exists as an insider category that is open, multifaceted, and not fixed" ("Yemayá y Ochún: Queering" 86).

51. For more on this debate see Beliso-De Jesús's "Contentious Diasporas."

52. Teish makes clear that Anzaldúa never underwent the initiation process into Santería/Regla de Ocha (Piña 114). Conner corroborates this assertion (187). Nonetheless, the timing of the reading Teish performed for Anzaldúa indicates that she was connected to the *orisha* in the years leading to the writing and publication of *Borderlands*.

53. Amalia is Anzaldúa's real-life mother, and Hecate and Yemayá are female representations of the divine. Hecate comes from Greek mythology, like Medusa, and is associated with witchcraft, magic, and the underworld as well as with crossroads.

54. The prose sections in *Borderlands*, which include material Anzaldúa extracted from her unpublished autobiography, are the text's most widely read sections. Though *Borderlands* was published in 1987, the poems were written before the prose sections. It was in 1985 that Anzaldúa began to work on the essays in the book (Pinkvoss 15).

55. This experience parallels what Rita Indiana expresses regarding her own interest in Santería/Regla de Ocha ("A Conversation").

56. Cabrera goes as far as to say that concrete is the worst enemy of the *orishas* (*El monte* 68–69).

57. "Yemayá" is included in *The Gloria Anzaldúa Reader* (2009), edited by Keating. Drafts of the poem are located in the GEA Papers box 88, folder 52.

58. Anzaldúa does reference drowning in her discussion of the Coatlicue state, which she described as "that deep ocean where once I dived into death. I am afraid of drowning" (*Borderlands* 70). This statement attests to the flowing connection Anzaldúa cultivated between Coatlicue and Yemayá.

59. According to Anzaldúa's records, her heart stopped for twenty minutes ("Turning Points" 34).

60. The betrayal Anzaldúa felt regarding her body began in her childhood but reached a climax when she was diagnosed with Type 1 diabetes in 1992, a condition that left its mark on every aspect of her life (Keating, "Working" 134). For more see Keating's introduction to *Light in the Dark/Luz en lo oscuro*. For a focused discussion on pain in Anzaldúa's writing see Bost, "Gloria Anzaldúa's Mestiza Pain."

61. Yemayá is viewed as the mother of all creatures, which explains why the etymology of her name alludes to motherhood. It is translated as "Mother of Fish" (Sellers 131).

62. This aspect of Anzaldúa's life resonates with Deirdre Cooper Owens's account of

how the concept of the "medical superbody" denied enslaved Black women the right to experience pain.

63. Anzaldúa's brother did not die in Vietnam, but he came back injured, both physically and psychically (Anzaldúa, "Turning Points" 44). One narration about his experiences appears in a subsection of a 1980 version of "La serpiente" titled "In Uniform with Rifle" (box 78, folder 11, pp. 103–104).

64. This is also the title of a 2014 documentary by Belén Maldonado and Álex Esteva which explores the spiritual traditions of the town of Bahía Honda, Cuba.

65. For more about the role of the *misa espiritual* in Santería/Regla de Ocha see Cabrera's *El monte* 62–63.

66. In Haitian Vodou, the living are tasked with undertaking a ceremony to "retrieve" the dead from the waters (Deren 46–53).

67. Dreams are often a conduit for spiritual messages in the Afro-diasporic religious world (Otero, *Archives* 2).

68. This description is considerably shorter than one included in an entry from an early draft from "La serpiente" dated March 15, 1980. In that description, after disclosing she has a mass in her uterus the size of a grapefruit, Teish tells Anzaldúa to perform the following ritual: "Before going to the hospital, take a bath. First rub honey on your stomach, then rub a grapefruit over the tumor until the two become one. Hide the grapefruit for 5 days, then throw it in the ocean for [*sic*] bay. . . . Only someone who is a spiritualist can throw the grapefruit into the ocean" (box 78, folder 11, p. 108). With its emphasis on honey and the number 5, this ritual is clearly aligned with the energies of Ochún, Teish's titular *orisha*.

69. In one of the first versions of "La serpiente," Anzaldúa does not mention Yemayá by name. Instead, her request for her uterus comes from her desire to perform a "ritual burial" (June–July 1984, box 68, folder 3, p. 28). Yemayá's name is added in the versions from the 2000s, attesting to the *orisha*'s constant presence in her life and how it was likely strengthened by her time on the East Coast.

70. For a discussion of a community-based *ebó* see Tsang, "Beguiling Eshu" 220–223.

71. Generally, this kind of consultation is received when the *iyalosha* (initiated priestess) or *babalosha* (initiated priest) reads the *diloggún*, a complex divinatory system involving cowrie shells, for the querent.

72. For more on Anzaldúa's poetry see Vigil, "Heterosexualization and the State."

73. The 2021 critical edition of *Borderlands*, edited by Ricardo F. Vivancos-Pérez and Norma Elia Cantú, includes an English translation of the poem (210–211). This edition also makes archival material related to *Borderlands* accessible to a broad audience.

74. In "La serpiente" Anzaldúa writes, "Where was Tlazolteotl's priest? Who would hear her confession?" (June–July 1984, box 68, folder 3, p. 15).

75. For more on anesthesiology and ether see the 2015 article "Ether in the Developing World" by Chang et al.

76. Mercedes Cros Sandoval studies the connections between Santería/Regla de Ocha and mental health. She asserts, "Santería is assisting its heterogeneous following to cope with the tensions of modernization, as well as the alienation experienced by immigrants and marginalized people who live in the shadows of a post-industrial

milieu" ("Santería" 356). Matibag's discussion of representations of Afro-Cuban religion in literature underscores that Afro-diasporic religions can "offer a kind of verbal-semiotic 'medicine' for healing" (*Afro-Cuban* 97).

77. For more on the aesthetics of "night" in Anzaldúa's writing see DeGuzmán *Buenas Noches*, 31–35.

78. "tears out my entrails, / how she tosses my womb in the trash—womb without tomb" (*Borderlands, Critical Edition* 210).

79. Anzaldúa's *facultad* provides a significant moment of spiritual and epistemic contact between Latinx and Caribbean spiritual worlds as a generative precursor to A.-M. Lara's concept of "vibe" in Afro-diasporic religions: "that intangible ripple of energy, of something that you can feel in your gut, an awakening of intuition and knowing that is beyond rational sphere. You *feel* it" (*Queer* 109–110, emphasis in the original).

CHAPTER 4. ORISHAS IN THE BORDERLANDS

1. Despite this effort Julie Avril Minich finds that "as a nationalist formation, Aztlán necessarily leaves some outside its borders, even in its most inclusive versions" (169).

2. One critical exception is Díaz-Sánchez's "Yemaya Blew That Wire Fence Down."

3. In "Borderwaters," Kyrstin Mallon Andrews observes, "Water has a place both in the politics and the experience of borderscapes." Her piece begins with an epigraph from the opening poem of Anzaldúa's *Borderlands*.

4. The same can be said of the term "boat people." The presence of Haitian migrants in Del Rio, Texas, in the summer of 2021 compounded this plight.

5. An initial development of this concept appears in my 2015 book chapter "Rippling Borders in Latina Literature."

6. For a thorough discussion of this controversy see C. J. Alvarez 143–157.

7. This is not the only instance where the shape of a poem is directly connected to its message. The poem that opens chapter 4 of *Borderlands*, "La herencia de Coatlicue/The Coatlicue State," is shaped like one of the representations of this divinity (Anzaldúa 63). In this same chapter Anzaldúa describes the experience of seeing the Coatlicue statue for the first time in the Museum of National History in New York City, reiterating the importance of taking into consideration her time on the East Coast (*Borderlands* 69). Attention to the visual rendition of the poem also takes into consideration Anzaldúa's identity as a visual artist; before she started writing she was a painter and a sculptor (Anzaldúa, "Gloria" 11).

8. In the posthumously published *Light in the Dark/Luz en lo oscuro*, Anzaldúa refers to *nepantla* as a "bridge between worlds," a place from which one's whole outlook, personal, spiritual and otherwise, is both challenged and expanded, and as a place where "ordinary and spirit realities" meet (28–29).

9. As expressed by Ana-Maurine Lara in her study of Afro-diasporic religion in the Dominican Republic, "Borders and nepantlas . . . also emerge from the sea" (*Queer Freedom* 3n6).

10. In later writings Anzaldúa would favor using *nepantla* over "borderlands" because *nepantla* underscores "a connection to the world after death and to the psychic spaces like between air and water" (Anzaldúa, "Writing Politics" 143).

11. Díaz-Sánchez addresses Eshu/Elegguá's presence in *Borderlands* (161–164).

12. Various other spellings and versions of his name exist, including "Eleda, Exu, Cxu Eleggua, Cxu Elegbara, Legba, Elegba, Elegbera, or Odara" (Falola 3).

13. In *The Signifying Monkey*, Henry Louis Gates Jr. underscores the mediator role Eshu/ Elegguá plays in Ifá divination practices and likens it to that of scholars of literature by ascertaining that this *orisha* is, in fact, "the indigenous black metaphor for the literary critic" (11).

14. Conner deepens this reading by asserting that the title of the sixth chapter of *Border-lands*, "*Tlilli, Tlapalli*/The Path of the Red and Black Ink," can also be seen as evoking Eshu/Elegguá, whose colors are red and black (192).

15. This reading of Anzaldúa's poem is inspired by Valdés's discussion of Nancy Morejón's poetry and its connection to Cuban history (99).

16. This concept aligns with Anzaldúa's Coyolxauhqui imperative and the transgressive openness of her spiritual outlook. For more see chapter 2 of Anzaldúa's *Light in the Dark*.

17. A reading of the Rio Grande/Río Bravo as an active rippling border leads readers to consider that the Chamizal dispute can be seen as the river trying to recover its territory.

18. Aside from being associated with particular numbers and having favorite foods, the *orishas* have color associations. The *orishas* also have several *caminos* (paths), so they may be associated with more than one color. For a discussion of Yemayá's *caminos* see Cabrera, *Yemaya y Ochún* 27–30.

19. Cabrera notes that Yemayá's attributes include the sun, the moon, an anchor, a life preserver, a boat, oars, a key, a star, and seven silver bangles (*Yemayá y Ochún* 268). Tellingly, silver is the color Anzaldúa gives to Yemayá's "tongues" in the posthumously published poem "Yemayá."

20. The moon and its inherent ties to the tides presents a rich point of connection between Afro-diasporic and Indigenous worlds in Anzaldúa's writing as Coyolxauhqui (the moon) abounds in scholarly engagements with Anzaldúa's work.

21. Although the *orishas* are worshipped in Mexico, their presence is marginalized in the country's dominant cultural and national narrative of Catholicism/*mestizaje* (Juárez Huet, "De 'negro brujo'" 86), an observation that elucidates how Anzaldúa's *Borderlands* aimed to use *mestizaje* differently. There is growing interest in documenting the presence of Santería/Regla de Ocha in Mexico, a practice that has been increasingly visible since the 1990s (Juárez Huet, "Religiones afroamericanas" 232). Nahayeilli Beatriz Juárez Huet finds that in Mexico "una gran parte de los adeptos a la santería hizo su primer contacto en una edad adulta" (a large part of santería practitioners had their first contact [with the religion] as an adult) (*Un pedacito* 222). This is significant in that it places Anzaldúa within the larger pattern of Santería/Regla de Ocha's diasporic movements in Mexico.

22. "I see the sea attacking / the fence at Border Field Park / with its mouth full of

water . . . I hear the sea's weeping, the wind's breath" (*Borderlands, Critical Edition* 69).

23. In footnote 26 Holslin mentions that even the mesh was likely to be short-lived, as the Border Patrol intended to "remove the mesh" and instead "place a barrier fence to keep the public 5 feet away from the wall" (153).

24. For a description of the full requirements for entry into Friendship Park see page 182 of Tocilovac's book chapter.

25. The location of Border Field Park and Friendship Park illustrates the discrepancy between national security and environmental protection. Throughout the twentieth century, this estuary's biodiversity and health were sacrificed to accommodate the need for industrial development and expansion (Holslin 142).

26. Otero asserts, "In places where Yemayá and Ochún merge, where river spills into the ocean, their subjectivities are also merged, and this enhances the kind of aché they emit into the world" (*Archives* 113). In Haitian Vodou, Gran Salin, a place where saltwaters and sweetwaters meet, is a similarly potent location (Daniels, "The Coolness").

27. Anzaldúa considered that institutionalized religion fostered an acceptance of the status quo (Anzaldúa, "Within" 73).

28. For more on Teish's relationship to La Virgen de Guadalupe see her essay "The Warrior Queen."

29. For a thought-provoking reading of this opening in the fence see Harford Vargas's article "The Undocumented Subjects of *el Hueco*."

30. Gleason notes that one of the Greek parallels to Oyá is Hecate (*Oya: In Praise* 14). This observation calls attention to Anzaldúa's claiming of Hecate as one of her divine mothers in her biography for *Bridge*.

31. Oyá is credited with helping Changó, an *orisha* strongly associated with virility and justice, defeat his enemies (Lachatañeré 373).

32. Because Yemayá's sacred number is 7 her energies are channeled into this reference since it is the seventh endnote in this chapter.

33. Anzaldúa confirms this information when she says that "Luisah Teish did a pretty detailed reading for me (she told me my mothers are Yemanja and Oya)" (Anzaldúa, "Turning Points" 19). Curiously, in Santería/Regla de Ocha it is often Yemayá who raises the children of other *orishas*, including those of Ochún (Cabrera, *Yemayá y Ochún* 83).

34. The initial poem in *Borderlands* also points to Oyá's formidable presence in the images of the broken fences and the crumbling houses as these are common sites initiates are asked to visit to pay Oyá tribute (Gleason, "Oya in the Company" 275).

35. Another common expression for this process is *asentar* (to seat or give a place to) or *hacer santo* (make saint).

36. For more on this process see chapter 7 of Lydia Cabrera's *Yemayá y Ochún*. Cabrera contends that the term "Ka ri Ocha" can be literally translated from Yoruba as "to put on top of the head," alluding again to the figure of the crown (129).

37. This entrance is also connected to wind through her blowing the fence down, once again fusing Yemayá's energies with those of Oyá.

38. Anzaldúa recalls that the image of crucifixion had always affected her: "Anyone who allowed others to nail him to a cross with nails was a puny mortal not a god. The dead man on the cross was just that, dead and a man" ("La serpiente" 1982–1983, p. 14).

39. For a thorough discussion of La Llorona see D. R. Perez, *There Was a Woman*.

40. Another important engagement with La Llorona is Anzaldúa's children's book *Prietita and the Ghost Woman/Prietita y La Llorona*.

41. Anzaldúa discusses her early poetry (from the late 1970s and early 1980s) in her interview with Linda Smuckler (Anzaldúa, "Turning Points" 52–53).

42. Keating, the editor of *The Gloria Anzaldúa Reader*, states that the last revision of this poem is from 2001 (242). The GEA Papers has an audio recording of Anzaldúa reading an early version of this poem on July 28, 1980, alongside Luisah Teish (box 158, folder 11).

43. Yemayá can be associated with the serpent, but she is also connected with Ochumare, an androgynous *orisha* associated with the rainbow. As rainbows often appear in the ocean, Ochumare is referred to as "el manto de Yemayá" (Yemayá's shawl) or "la corona de Yemayá" (Yemayá's crown) (Cabrera, *Yemayá y Ochún* 28).

44. It is difficult to know if the notes in the margin are Anzaldúa's or from one of her writing *comadres*. As with much of the materials in the archive, authorship is multiple, another way of foregrounding the need to address the recursive nature of Anzaldúa's writing and research process.

EPILOGUE. WATER AND LIGHT:
THE *BÓVEDA* AS COUNTER-ARCHIVE

1. The Massacre River's name is a reminder of the (neo)colonial violence that has been cyclically enacted upon its waters. As Michele Wucker states, "The river lost its original Taino Indian name, Guatapana, in 1728, when Spanish soldiers slaughtered thirty pirate buccaneers seized there. In honor of the slaughter, the river was christened in blood as the Río Masacre" (44).

2. Many of BOL's organizers are members of the Transnational Hispaniola collective. For more see Mayes and Jayaram, "Transnational Hispaniola."

3. Hispaniola is the name of the landmass that encompasses the islands of the Dominican Republic and Haiti.

4. For research on the 1937 Massacre, see the work of Derby, García-Peña, Paulino, and Turits, among others.

5. A detailed discussion of the initial Border of Lights event in 2012 appears in Paulino and García's essay "Bearing Witness to Genocide."

6. For this reason, Megan Jeanette Myers and Edward Paulino propose using the word "lynching" to discuss the Massacre (3–4).

7. In the late 1990s Julia Alvarez and Michele Wucker discussed the idea but were unable to put it into action (Myers and Paulino 9).

8. The mention of La Virgen de Altagracia takes place between 47:56 and 48:38.

9. La Virgen de Altagracia is the subject of J. Alvarez's children's book *A Gift of Gracias*.

Furthermore, her coffee farm in the Dominican Republic is named Alta Gracia (Myers, "A Promise" 169).

10. Jennifer Baez notes, "In an interesting twist that joins the beginnings of the story of the Altagracia cult in Hispaniola with the history of the Afrodiasporic experience in the Americas, [Nicolás de] Ovando built the first hospital of the Americas in Santo Domingo on the same spot where he found 'a pious black woman' (*negra piadosa*) tending to the sick in a hut. He named the Hospital San Nicolás de Bari and its first chapel was dedicated to the Virgin of Altagracia" (2–3).

11. Davis identifies a connection between La Virgen de la Altagracia and the *misterio* Alailá (*La otra ciencia* 94). Deive (227) and Ricourt (*The Dominican* 115) also note this correspondence, and Tejeda Ortiz includes a brief description of this *misterio* (129–130). For an image of an altar from La 21 División that includes a representation of La Virgen de la Altagracia see p. 408 of Davis's essay "A Tire Blowout."

12. Although Catholic imagery is incorporated into Santería/Regla de Ocha, it is rarely the central representation of an *orisha*.

13. For some examples see Ricourt's *The Dominican Racial Imaginary* and Thornton's *Negotiating Respect*. "Folk Catholicism" has also often been used to discuss spiritual practices in Puerto Rico, including Espiritismo (Romberg 152; Flores-Peña 88).

14. As Elizabeth Pérez points out, La Virgen de la Caridad del Cobre, though Catholic in origin, "eventually came to personify unity among Cubans of indigenous Taíno, African, European, and Asian descent" ("Crystallizing" 187).

15. According to Lauren Derby, "Creole identity was forged [in the Dominican Republic] through the two national patron saints of the country, the Virgin of Altagracia and the Virgin of las Mercedes, who protected protonationalist insurgents in the colonial period by endowing them with her miraculous charisma" (230).

16. For a discussion of the connections between Ochún and La Virgen de la Caridad del Cobre in the context of the Virgin's shrine in Miami see Tweed, pp. 48–49.

17. Alegría-Pons also notes a resonance between La Virgen de la Altagracia and Metresilí, another *misterio* of La 21 División (60). Metresilí is connected to Erzulie, a *lwa* of Haitian Vodou.

18. For more on this see Strongman, "Reading" p. 43.

19. This kind of commemoration also happens in secular spaces. A recent example is the vigil held on January 19, 2021, at the Lincoln Memorial. Here, the presidency of Joe Biden honored the 400,000 lives lost to COVID-19 in the United States in the first year of the pandemic by lighting 400 candles alongside the Lincoln Memorial's reflecting pool. For more see Kelly.

20. In his discussion of African-derived healing practices in eighteenth-century Brazil, James H. Sweet observes that practitioners "often concluded [their] healing sessions by taking a 'small piece of glass,' cutting [their] clients, and then putting black powders into the incisions" (133). Small wounds are also a part of the creation of a *pwen* (point) in Haitian Vodou. As Karen McCarthy Brown explains, *pwen* "refers to a charm or talisman. A *pwen* may consist of words, gestures, ritual objects, or herbs rubbed into a small cut in a person's skin. In all cases, the point represents the condensation and appropriation of spiritual powers" (94n1).

21. Roxane Gay's 2011 short story about the 1937 Massacre, "In the Manner of Water or Light," revolves around memory and uses the word "suffuse" to describe the omniscient presence of trauma.

22. It is common for those seeking initiation into Santería/Regla de Ocha to take part in a spiritual séance to secure the blessing of the dead for this life-changing event (E. Pérez, "Spiritist" 337, 341). Jorge Castellanos and Isabel Castellanos refer to this ritual as a "misa espiritual de coronación" (spiritual coronation mass) (91). Nonetheless, the acceptance of Espiritismo's presence in Afro-diasporic religious spaces is far from universal (E. Pérez, "Spiritist" 337).

23. Because the Massacre occurred in locations beyond the Massacre River/Dajabón River, bodies were also thrust into the sea (Ricourt, *The Dominican* 36).

24. Espírito Santo notes that in Espiritismo "metaphors of light, incandescence, ascension, evolution, and immateriality" are used to speak of "good" spirits, while "terms such as *muerto oscuro*, meaning the 'dark' dead, evoke images of beings in the underworlds" (41).

25. Myriam Moïse notes that in Edwidge Danticat's short story "Nineteen Thirty-Seven," which also recounts the legacy of this event, "water and fluidity are made central" (127).

26. See pages 17–19 of my book chapter "Transformative Currents" for a thorough discussion of this moment in Rosario's novel.

27. The original letter, available online, is in Spanish. The quote is from the translation provided by WOLA (Washington Office on Latin America): wola.org/2021/03/concern -over-initiative-to-build-a-border-wall-between-the-dominican-republic-and-haiti/.

28. For an earlier mention of the connections between "desbordar" and "overflow" see page 111 of my essay "Rippling Borders in Latina Literature."

29. For a discussion of the circulating discourses regarding Dominicans of Haitian descent in the Dominican Republic see Amezquita, "Imaginary Narratives." Candelario's "La ciguapa" also offers critical background on this law.

30. Nicole F. Scalissi notes that Báez's use of anthropophagism dialogues with Oswald de Andrade's 1928 *Manifesto Antropófago,* whose "cultural cannibalist philosophy empowered the appropriation of ideas and artistic styles of (at that time) dominant Europe as a radical aesthetic and political gesture" (101).

31. According to Miguel "Willie" Ramos, "Oshun represents the suffering of womankind, reputed to defend her daughters from the abuse of *mankind*" (69, italics in the original).

32. For Cabrera, this *pataki* indicates that the daughters of Yemayá have a predisposition for healing (*Yemayá y Ochún* 115–116).

33. For a thorough albeit metaphorical interpretation of the connections between salt, wounding, and personal history see Moraga's chapter on her relationship to Gloria Anzaldúa, "The Salt that Cures/2009," in *A Xicana Codex of Changing Consciousness* (116–130).

34. Teresa N. Washington finds that "The Africans who survived the crossing did so because Yemoja used her soothing waters to heal lacerated bodies that had been rubbed raw and anointed with feces, menstrual blood, urine, tears, and destitution. . . . She was the first God they thanked for having survived the horror that was the Middle Passage" (217).

Works Cited

Abimbọla, Wande. *Ifá Will Mend Our Broken World: Thoughts on Yoruba Religion and Culture in Africa and the Diaspora.* Aim Books, 1997.

Abiodun, Rowland. "Hidden Power: Ọ̀ṣun, the Seventeenth Odù." *Ọ̀ṣun across the Waters: A Yoruba Goddess in Africa and the Americas,* edited by Joseph M. Murphy and Mei-Mei Sanford, Indiana University Press, 2001, pp. 10–33.

———. "Who Was the First to Speak? Insights from Ifá Orature and Sculptural Repertoire." *Òrìṣà Devotion as World Religion: The Globalization of Yorùbá Religious Culture,* edited by Jacob K. Olupona and Terry Rey, University of Wisconsin Press, 2008, pp. 51–69.

Acosta, Ikam. *Boy Exile Turned Saint: Elián González as a Contested Religio-Ideological Symbol among Cuban-American Catholics.* 2016. Florida International University, master's thesis, digitalcommons.fiu.edu/etd/1103.

Alarcón, Norma. "Anzaldúa's *Frontera*: Inscribing Gynetics." *Displacement, Diaspora, and Geographies of Identity,* edited by Smadar Lavie and Ted Swedenburg, Duke University Press, 1996, pp. 41–53.

———. "Encuentros en la Encrucijada." *Borderlands/La Frontera: The New Mestiza,* by Gloria Anzaldúa, 1987, 4th ed., Aunt Lute Books, 2012, pp. 231–232.

Alcide, Evelyn. *Lasirène matennelle (Maternal Lasirèn).* 2005. Private collection. *Mami Wata: Arts for Water Spirits in Africa and Its Diasporas,* edited by Henry John Drewal, Fowler Museum at UCLA, 2008, p. 146.

Alcoff, Linda Martín. "The Unassimilated Theorist." *PMLA,* vol. 121, no. 1, 2006, pp. 255–259.

Alegría-Pons, José Francisco. *Gagá y vudú en la República Dominicana: Ensayos antropológicos.* Ediciones El Chango Prieto, 1993.

Alexander, M. Jacqui. *Pedagogies of Crossing: Meditations on Feminism, Sexual Politics, Memory, and the Sacred.* Duke University Press, 2005.

Alire Sáenz, Benjamin. "In the Borderlands of Chicano Identity, There Are Only Fragments." *Border Theory: The Limits of Cultural Politics,* edited by Scott Michaelsen and David E. Johnson, University of Minnesota Press, 1997, pp. 68–96.

Alvarado, Leticia. "Flora and Fauna Otherwise: Black and Brown Aesthetics of Relation in Firelei Báez and Wangechi Mutu." *Latin American and Latinx Visual Culture*, vol. 1, no. 3, 2019, pp. 8–24.

Alvarado, Li Yun. "Chicana in New York City: Gloria Anzaldúa on Spirituality and the City." *MELUS*, vol. 44, no. 2, Summer 2019, pp. 71–92.

Alvarez, C. J. *Border Land, Border Water: A History of Construction on the US-Mexico Divide*. University of Texas Press, 2019.

Alvarez, Julia. *A Gift of Gracias*. Illustrated by Beatriz Vidal. Random House, 2005.

Alvarez, Julia, and Vanessa Pérez-Rosario. "Off the Page: Julia Alvarez and Vanessa Pérez-Rosario in Conversation." Kupferberg Center for the Arts, YouTube, 20 Apr. 2021, youtube.com/watch?v=Fv1YKt5_c0g.

Amezquita, Gloria. "Imaginary Narratives about *Dominicanos* of Haitian Descent: Media Debates Concerning Sonia Pierre and Juliana Dequis." *Pan-Caribbean Integration: Beyond CARICOM*, edited by Patsy Lewis et al., Routledge, 2017, pp. 138–150.

Anaya, Rudolfo, et al., editors. *Aztlán: Essays on the Chicano Homeland*. Revised and expanded ed., University of New Mexico Press, 2017.

Anderson-Córdova, Karen F. *Surviving Spanish Conquest: Indian Fight, Flight, and Cultural Transformation in Hispaniola and Puerto Rico*. University of Alabama Press, 2017.

Andrews, Kyrstin Mallon. "Borderwaters: Conversing with Fluidity at the Dominican Border." *Cultural Anthropology*, 29 Oct. 2019, culanth.org/fieldsights/borderwaters.

Anzaldúa, Gloria. "Autohistoria de la artista as a Young Girl." Box 57, folder 10, Gloria Evangelina Anzaldúa Papers, Nettie Lee Benson Latin American Collection, University of Texas Libraries, University of Texas at Austin.

———. "Autoretratos de la artista as a Young Girl." May 1991, box 57, folder 12, Gloria Evangelina Anzaldúa Papers, Nettie Lee Benson Latin American Collection, University of Texas Libraries, University of Texas at Austin.

———. "Border Arte: Nepantla, el Lugar de la Frontera." *The Gloria Anzaldúa Reader*, edited by AnaLouise Keating, Duke University Press, 2009, pp. 176–186.

———. *Borderlands/La Frontera: The New Mestiza*. 1987, 4th ed., Aunt Lute Books, 2012.

———. *Borderlands/La Frontera: The New Mestiza, Critical Edition*, edited by Ricardo F. Vivancos-Pérez and Norma Elia Cantú, Aunt Lute Books, 2021.

———. "Canción de cascabel." 2001, box 68, folder 6, Gloria Evangelina Anzaldúa Papers, Nettie Lee Benson Latin American Collection, University of Texas Libraries, University of Texas at Austin.

———. "Canción de cascabel." Box 68, folder 7, Gloria Evangelina Anzaldúa Papers, Nettie Lee Benson Latin American Collection, University of Texas Libraries, University of Texas at Austin.

———. "Canciones de la Luna Reading at Bound Together." Gloria Anzaldúa and Luisah Teish, 28 July 1980, box 158, folder 11, MP3 no. 186, Gloria Evangelina Anzaldúa Papers, Nettie Lee Benson Latin American Collection, University of Texas Libraries, University of Texas at Austin.

———. Correspondence with Aunt Lute Books. 1987–2004, box 7, folder 4, Gloria Evangelina Anzaldúa Papers, Nettie Lee Benson Latin American Collection, University of Texas Libraries, University of Texas at Austin.

———. Correspondence with Rudolfo Anaya. 1989–1990, box 6, folder 11, Gloria Evangelina Anzaldúa Papers, Nettie Lee Benson Latin American Collection, University of Texas Libraries, University of Texas at Austin.

———. "Counsels from the Firing . . . past, present, future: Foreword to the Third Edition, 2001." *This Bridge Called My Back: Writings by Radical Women of Color*, edited by Cherríe Moraga and Gloria Anzaldúa, 1981, 4th ed., SUNY Press, 2015, pp. 261–266.

———. "Daughter of Coatlicue: An Interview with Gloria Anzaldúa." Interview by Irene Lara. *EntreMundos/AmongWorlds: New Perspectives on Gloria E. Anzaldúa*, edited by AnaLouise Keating, Palgrave Macmillan, 2005, pp. 41–55.

———. "Doing Gigs—Speaking, Writing, and Change: An Interview with Debbie Blake and Carmen Abrego (1994)." *Interviews/Entrevistas*, edited by AnaLouise Keating, Routledge, 2000, pp. 211–233.

———. "En el hocico del mar." June 1997, box 70, folder 3, Gloria Evangelina Anzaldúa Papers, Nettie Lee Benson Latin American Collection, University of Texas Libraries, The University of Texas at Austin.

———. "En el hocico del mar." 1989, box 70, folder 3, Gloria Evangelina Anzaldúa Papers, Nettie Lee Benson Latin American Collection, University of Texas Libraries, University of Texas at Austin.

———. "Esperando la serpiente con plumas/Waiting for the Feathered Serpent." July 1981–September 1982, box 78, folder 9, Gloria Evangelina Anzaldúa Papers, Nettie Lee Benson Latin American Collection, University of Texas Libraries, University of Texas at Austin.

———. Foreword. *Cassell's Encyclopedia of Queer Myth, Symbol and Spirit: Gay, Lesbian, Bisexual, and Transgender Lore*. Reprint, *The Gloria Anzaldúa Reader*, edited by AnaLouise Keating, Duke University Press, 2009, pp. 229–231.

———. Gloria Evangelina Anzaldúa Papers, Nettie Lee Benson Latin American Collection, University of Texas Libraries, University of Texas at Austin.

———. "Gloria Anzaldúa: Writer, Editor, Critic, and Third-World Lesbian Women-of-Color Feminist." Interview by Karin Ikas, *Chicana Ways: Conversations with Ten Chicana Writers*, University of Nevada Press, 2001, pp. 1–24.

———. "Haciendo caras, una entrada: An Introduction by Gloria Anzaldúa." *Making Face, Making Soul, Haciendo Caras: Creative and Critical Perspectives by Feminists of Color*, edited by Gloria Anzaldúa, Aunt Lute Books, 1990, pp. xv–xxviii.

———. "Lesbian Wit: Conversation with Jeffner Allen (late 1980s)." Interview by Jeffner Allen, *Interviews/Entrevistas*, edited by AnaLouise Keating, Routledge, 2000, pp. 129–150.

———. "Let us be the healing of the wound: The Coyolxauhqui imperative—la sombra y el sueño." *One Wound for Another/Una herida por otra: testimonios de Latin@s in the U.S. through Cyberspace (11 de septiembre 2001–11 de marzo 2002)*, edited by Claire Joysmith and Clara Lomas, Centro de Investigaciones Sobre América del Norte, Universidad Autónoma de México, Colorado College, Whittier College, 2003, pp. 92-103.

———. "Let us be the healing of the wound: The Coyolxauhqui imperative—la sombra y el sueño." Reprint, *The Gloria Anzaldúa Reader*, edited by AnaLouise Keating, Duke University Press, 2009, pp. 303-317.

———. *Light in the Dark/Luz en lo oscuro: Rewriting Identity, Spirituality, Reality*, edited by AnaLouise Keating, Duke University Press, 2015.

———. "Matriz sin tumba o 'el baño de la basura ajena.'" *Borderlands/La Frontera: The New Mestiza*. 1987, 4th ed., Aunt Lute Books, 2012, pp. 158–160.

———. "The New Mestiza Nation: A Multicultural Movement." *The Gloria Anzaldúa Reader*, edited by AnaLouise Keating, Duke University Press, 2009, pp. 203–216.

———. "On the Process of Writing *Borderlands/La Frontera*." *The Gloria Anzaldúa Reader*, edited by AnaLouise Keating, Duke University Press, 2009, pp. 187–197.

———. "La Prieta." *This Bridge Called My Back: Writings by Radical Women of Color*, edited by Cherríe Moraga and Gloria Anzaldúa, 1981, 4th ed., SUNY Press, 2015, pp. 198–209.

———. *Prietita and the Ghost Woman/Prietita y La Llorona*. Illustrated by Maya C. González. Children's Books Press, 1995.

———. "Reading and Discussion of *Borderlands*, Mama Bear's." 16 Sep. 1987, box 155, folder 1, MP3 no. 101, Gloria Evangelina Anzaldúa Papers, Nettie Lee Benson Latin American Collection, University of Texas Libraries, University of Texas at Austin.

———. "La serpiente que se come su cola." 1980, box 78, folder 11, Gloria Evangelina Anzaldúa Papers, Nettie Lee Benson Latin American Collection, University of Texas Libraries, University of Texas at Austin.

———. "La serpiente que se come su cola." 1982–1983, box 78, folder 10, Gloria Evangelina Anzaldúa Papers, Nettie Lee Benson Latin American Collection, University of Texas Libraries, University of Texas at Austin.

———. "La serpiente que se come su cola." June–July 1984, box 68, folder 3, Gloria Evangelina Anzaldúa Papers, Nettie Lee Benson Latin American Collection, University of Texas Libraries, University of Texas at Austin.

———. "Spiritual Activism: Making Altares, Making Connections." 4 Nov. 1996, box 64, folder 19, Gloria Evangelina Anzaldúa Papers, Nettie Lee Benson Latin American Collection, University of Texas Libraries, University of Texas at Austin.

———. "Turning Points: An Interview with Linda Smuckler (1982)." Interview by Linda Smuckler, *Interviews/Entrevistas*, edited by AnaLouise Keating, Routledge, 2000, pp. 17–70.

———. "The water doesn't breath [*sic*]." 1980, box 88, folder 40, Gloria Evangelina Anzaldúa Papers, Nettie Lee Benson Latin American Collection, University of Texas Libraries, University of Texas at Austin.

———. "Within the Crossroads—Lesbian/Feminist/Spiritual Development: An Interview with Christine Weiland (1983)." *Interviews/Entrevistas*, edited by AnaLouise Keating, Routledge, 2000, pp. 71–127.

———. "Writing: A Way of Life: An Interview with María Henríquez Betancor (1995)." *Interviews/Entrevistas*, edited by AnaLouise Keating, Routledge, 2000, pp. 235–249.

———. "Writing, Politics, and *las Lesberadas*: Platicando con Gloria Anzaldúa." Interview by AnnLouise [*sic*] Keating. *Chicana Leadership: The Frontiers Reader*, edited by Yolanda Flores Niemann et al., University of Nebraska Press, 2002, pp. 120–143.

———. "Yemaya." 1980, box 88, folder 52, Gloria Evangelina Anzaldúa Papers, Nettie

Lee Benson Latin American Collection, University of Texas Libraries, University of Texas at Austin.

———. "Yemayá." *The Gloria Anzaldúa Reader*, edited by AnaLouise Keating, Duke University Press, 2009, p. 242.

Aparicio, Frances R. "Latinx Studies: Notes from an Emerita." *The Latinx Project*, New York University, 5 Feb. 2021, latinxproject.nyu.edu/intervenxions/latinx-studies -notes-from-an-emerita.

Apátrida (Stateless). Directed by Michèle Stephenson, Hispaniola Productions and National Film Board of Canada, 2020.

Apter, Andrew. *Oduduwa's Chain: Locations of Culture in the Yoruba-Atlantic*. University of Chicago Press, 2017.

Aquino, Eloisa. *Gloria Anzaldúa*. Vol. 7, no. 1, B and D Press, 2015.

Arrizón, Alicia. *Queering Mestizaje: Transculturation and Performance*. University of Michigan Press, 2006.

"At Full Steam, Haiti Opens Channel to Take Water from the Massacre River." *Dominican Today*, 7 May 2021, dominicantoday.com/dr/local/2021/05/07/at-full-steam -haiti-opens-channel-to-take-water-from-the-massacre-river.

Bachelard, Gaston. *Water and Dreams: An Essay on the Imagination of Matter*. Translated by Edith R. Farrell, 1983. Pegasus Foundation, 2006.

Báez, Firelei. *Becoming New (a tignon for Mami Wata)*. 2016. Courtesy of the artist and James Cohan, New York.

———. "Firelei Báez: An Open Horizon (or) the Stillness of a Wound." Art21, *New York Close Up*, YouTube, 10 Feb. 2021, youtube.com/watch?v=-RjY0hiJ5Sw.

———. "Firelei Báez on Generosity and Freedom in Art." Interview by Angie Cruz, *Asterix Journal*, 6 Jul. 2017, asterixjournal.com/firelei-baez.

———. *For Améthyste and Athénaire (Exiled Muses Beyond Jean-Luc Nancy's Canon), Anacaonas*. 2018, Museum of Modern Art, New York.

———. *Ode to la Sirène (and to muses beyond Jean-Luc Nancy's Canon)*. 2014. Courtesy of the artist and James Cohan, New York.

———. "Studio Visit: Firelei Báez." Interview by Isabel Custodio, *MoMA Magazine*, 14 Nov. 2018, moma.org/magazine/articles/16.

———. *TC/0168.13 (Anthropophagist wading in the Artibonite River)*. 2014. Photo © by Scott McCrossen/FIVE65 Desi. Courtesy of the artist and James Cohan, New York.

Báez, Firelei, and Franklin Sirmans. "Artwork: Firelei Báez Introduced by Franklin Sirmans." *Art Journal*, vol. 76, nos. 3–4, 2017, pp. 78–79.

Baez, Jennifer. "Modeling Black Piety and Community Membership in the Virgin of Altagracia Medallions." *Arts*, vol. 10, no. 37, 2021, pp. 1–23.

Banet-Weiser, Sarah. "Elián González and the 'Purpose of America': Nation, Family, and the Child-Citizen." *American Quarterly*, vol. 55, no. 2, 2003, pp. 149–178.

Barnet, Miguel. "La Regla de Ocha: The Religious System of Santería." *Sacred Possessions: Vodou, Santería, Obeah, and the Caribbean*, edited by Margarite Fernández Olmos and Lizabeth Paravisini-Gebert, Rutgers University Press, 2000, pp. 79–100.

Beliso-De Jesús, Aisha M. "Brujx: An Afro-Latinx Queer Gesture." *Critical Dialogues in*

Latinx Studies: A Reader, edited by Ana Y. Ramos-Zayas and Mérida M. Rúa, New York University Press, 2021, pp. 528–538.

———. "Contentious Diasporas: Gender, Sexuality, and Heteronationalisms in the Cuban Iyanifa Debate." *Signs*, vol. 40, no. 4, Summer 2015, pp. 817–840.

———. *Electric Santería: Racial and Sexual Assemblages of Transnational Religion*. Columbia University Press, 2015.

Bellegarde-Smith, Patrick. *Haiti: The Breached Citadel*. Revised and updated ed., Canadian Scholar's Press, 2004.

Benítez-Rojo, Antonio. *The Repeating Island: The Caribbean and the Postmodern Perspective*. Translated by James E. Maraniss, Duke University Press, 1996.

Berry, Daina Ramey. *The Price for Their Pound of Flesh: The Value of the Enslaved, from Womb to Grave, in the Building of a Nation*. Beacon Press, 2017.

Blum, Hester. "The Prospect of Oceanic Studies." *PMLA*, vol. 125, no. 3, 2010, pp. 670–677.

Bost, Suzanne. "Gloria Anzaldúa's Mestiza Pain: Mexican Sacrifice, Chicana Embodiment, and Feminist Politics." *Aztlán: A Journal of Chicano Studies*, vol. 30, no. 2, Fall 2005, pp. 5–31.

———. "Messy Archives and Materials that Matter: Making Knowledge with the Gloria Evangelina Anzaldúa Papers." *PMLA*, vol. 130, no. 3, 2015, pp. 615–630.

———. *Shared Selves: Latinx Memoir and Ethical Alternatives to Humanism*. University of Illinois Press, 2019.

Brady, Mary Pat. "The Fungibility of Borders." *Nepantla: Views from South*, vol. 1, no. 1, 2000, pp. 171–190.

Brandon, George Edward. "From Oral to Digital: Rethinking the Transmission of Tradition in Yorùbá Religion." *Òrìṣà Devotion as World Religion: The Globalization of Yorùbá Religious Culture*, edited by Jacob K. Olupona and Terry Rey, University of Wisconsin Press, 2008, pp. 448–469.

Brathwaite, Edward Kamau. "Caribbean Man in Space and Time: A Bibliographical and Conceptual Approach." *Savacou*, no. 11–12, Sep. 1975, pp. 1–11.

Braziel, Jana Evans. *Riding with Death: Vodou Art and Urban Ecology in the Streets of Port-au-Prince*. University Press of Mississippi, 2017.

Brennan, Denise. *What's Love Got to Do with It?: Transnational Desires and Sex Tourism in the Dominican Republic*. Duke University Press, 2004.

Brown, David H. *Santería Enthroned: Art, Ritual, and Innovation in an Afro-Cuban Religion*. University of Chicago Press, 2003.

Brown, Kimberly Juanita. *The Repeating Body: Slavery's Visual Resonance in the Contemporary*. Duke University Press, 2015.

Broyles-González, Yolanda. "Indianizing Catholicism: Chicana/India/Mexicana Indigenous Spiritual Practices in Our Image." *Chicana Traditions: Continuity and Change*, edited by Norma E. Cantú and Olga Nájera-Ramírez, University of Illinois Press, 2002, pp. 117–132.

Brüske, Anne, and Wiebke Beushausen. "Writing from Lòt Bò Dlo: The Aesthetics and Poetics of Vodou in Edwidge Danticat and Myriam Chancy." *Vodou in Haitian Memory: The Idea and Representation of Vodou in Haitian Imagination*, edited by Celucien L. Joseph and Nixon S. Cleophat, Lexington Books, 2016, pp. 145–178.

Butler, Kim D. "Defining Diaspora, Refining a Discourse." *Diaspora: A Journal of Transnational Studies*, vol. 10, no. 2, 2001, pp. 189–219.

Cabrera, Lydia. *Anagó: Vocabulario lucumí (El yoruba que se habla en Cuba)*. 1957. Ediciones Universal, Miami, 2007.

———. *El monte: Igbo, finda, ewe orisha, vititi nfinda (Notas sobre las religiones, la magia, las supersticiones y el folklore de los negros criollos y el pueblo de Cuba)*. 1954, 8th ed., Ediciones Universal, 2000.

———. *Yemayá y Ochún: Kariocha, Iyalorichas y Olorichas*. 1974. Ediciones Universal, 1996.

Candelario, Ginetta E. B. *Black behind the Ears: Dominican Racial Identity from Museums to Beauty Shops*. Duke University Press, 2007.

———. "*La ciguapa y el ciguapeo*: Dominican Myth, Metaphor, and Method." *Small Axe*, vol. 20, no. 3 (51), 2016, pp. 100–112.

Cañete Ochoa, Jesús. *Cartas de Yemayá a Changó: Epistolario inédito de Lydia Cabrera y Pierre Verger*. Archivo de la Frontera, 2011.

Cantú, Norma Elia, and Aída Hurtado. "Breaking Borders/Constructing Bridges: Twenty-Five Years of *Borderlands/La Frontera*." *Borderlands/La Frontera: The New Mestiza*, by Gloria Anzaldúa, 1987, 4th ed., Aunt Lute Books, 2012, pp. 3–13.

Capó Crucet, Jennine. *Make Your Home among Strangers*. St. Martin's Press, 2015.

Carr, C. Lynn. *A Year in White: Cultural Newcomers to Lukumi and Santería in the United States*. Rutgers University Press, 2015.

Castellanos, Isabel. "A River of Many Turns: The Polysemy of Ochún in Afro-Cuban Tradition." *Ọ̀ṣun across the Waters: A Yoruba Goddess in Africa and the Americas*, edited by Joseph M. Murphy and Mei-Mei Sanford, Indiana University Press, 2001, pp. 34–45.

Castellanos, Jorge, and Isabel Castellanos. *Cultura Afrocubana 3: Las religiones y las lenguas*. Ediciones Universal, 1992.

Castillo, Ana. "Brujas and Curanderas: A Lived Spirituality." *Massacre of the Dreamers: Essays on Xicanisma. Twentieth Anniversary Updated Edition*, University of New Mexico Press, 2014, pp. 153–172.

Castillo, Debra A. "Anzaldúa and Transnational American Studies." *PMLA*, vol. 121, no. 1, 2006, pp. 260–265.

Chancy, Myriam J. A. *From Sugar to Revolution: Women's Visions of Haiti, Cuba, and the Dominican Republic*. Wilfrid Laurier University Press, 2012.

———. "'A Solidarity of Dreams': Searching for Unity in the Works of Edwidge Danticat, Ana Lydia Vega, Julia Alvarez and Cristina García." *Journal of Caribbean Literatures*, vol. 3, no. 1, Summer 2001, pp. 27–34.

Chang, Connie Y., et al. "Ether in the Developing World: Rethinking an Abandoned Agent." *BMC Anesthesiology*, vol. 15, no. 149, 2015.

Chaves Daza, Maria Paula. "Horizontal Contact Zones: Undocumented Latina's Coalitional Practices During Hurricane Katrina." *Chicana/Latina Studies*, vol. 19, no. 2, Spring 2020, pp. 82–203.

Cisneros, Sandra. "A Note to Gloria from the Bottom of the Sea." *Borderlands/La*

Frontera: The New Mestiza, by Gloria Anzaldúa, 1987, 4th ed., Aunt Lute Books, 2012, pp. 241–242.

Clitandre, Nadège T. *Edwidge Danticat: The Haitian Diasporic Imaginary*. University of Virginia Press, 2018.

"Concern over Initiative to Build a Border Wall between the Dominican Republic and Haiti." *WOLA: Advocacy for Human Rights in the Americas*, 18 Mar. 2021, wola.org/2021/03/concern-over-initiative-to-build-a-border-wall-between-the -dominican-republic-and-haiti.

Concha-Holmes, Amanda D. "Decolonizing the Imaging of African-Derived Religions." *Afro-Descendants, Identity, and the Struggle for Development in the Americas*, edited by Bernd Reiter and Kimberly Eison Simmons, Michigan State University Press, 2012, pp. 243–267.

Conner, Randy P. "Santa Nepantla: A Borderlands Sutra" (Plenary Speech). *El Mundo Zurdo: Selected Works from the Meetings of the Society for the Study of Gloria Anzaldúa 2007 and 2009*, edited by Norma E. Cantú et al., Aunt Lute Books, 2010, pp. 177–202.

Covington-Ward, Yolanda. *Gesture and Power: Religion, Nationalism, and Everyday Performance in Congo*. Duke University Press, 2016.

Covington-Ward, Yolanda, and Jeanette S. Jouili, editors. *Embodying Black Religions in Africa and Its Diasporas*. Duke University Press, 2021.

Cruz, Angie. *Let It Rain Coffee*. Simon and Schuster, 2006.

Daniels, Kyrah Malika. "The Coolness of Cleansing: Sacred Waters, Medicinal Plants and Ritual Baths of Haiti and Peru." *ReVista: Harvard Review of Latin America*, vol. 16, no. 1, Fall 2016, pp. 21–24.

———. "Sea, Stone, Sky, and Cemetery: Vodou's Divine Nature and Religious Archetypes in Edwidge Danticat's *Krik? Krak!* and *After the Dance*." *The Bloomsbury Handbook to Edwidge Danticat*, edited by Jana Evans Braziel and Nadège T. Clitandre, Bloomsbury Publishing, 2021, pp. 305–345.

Danticat, Edwidge. "All Geography Is Within Me: Writing Beginnings, Life, Death, Freedom, and Salt." *World Literature Today*, vol. 93, no. 1, Winter 2019, pp. 59–65.

———. "Children of the Sea." *Krik? Krak!*, Vintage Books, 1996, pp. 1–29.

———. Introduction. *The Butterfly's Way: Voices from the Haitian Dyaspora in the United States*, edited by Edwidge Danticat, Soho Press, 2001, pp. ix–xvii.

———. "Nineteen Thirty-Seven." *Krik? Krak!*, Vintage Books, 1996, pp. 31–49.

———. "We Are Ugly but We Are Here." *Women Writing Resistance: Essays on Latin America and the Caribbean*, edited by Jennifer Browdy, Beacon Press, 2017, pp. 21–26.

Daut, Marlene L. "Beyond Trouillot: Unsettling Genealogies of Historical Thought." *Small Axe*, vol. 25, no. 1 (64), 2021, pp. 132–154.

Dávila, Arlene. *Latinx Art: Artists, Markets, and Politics*. Duke University Press, 2020.

Davis, Martha Ellen. *La otra ciencia: El vodú dominicano como religión y medicina populares*. Editora Universitaria de la Universidad Autónoma de Santo Domingo, 1987.

———. "A Tire Blowout Gives Entry into the World of Spiritism." *The Dominican Republic Reader: History, Culture, Politics*, edited by Eric Paul Roorda et al., Duke University Press, 2014, pp. 406–410.

Dayan, Colin (Joan). "Vodoun, or the Voice of the Gods." *Sacred Possessions: Vodou,*

Santería, Obeah, and the Caribbean, edited by Margarite Fernández Olmos and Lizabeth Paravisini-Gebert, Rutgers University Press, 2000, pp. 13–36.

De Ferrari, Guillermina. "Science Fiction and the Rules of Uncertainty." *Small Axe,* vol. 24, no. 1 (61), 2020, pp. 1–10.

DeGuzmán, María. *Buenas Noches, American Culture: Latina/o Aesthetics of Night.* Indiana University Press, 2012.

———. "Latinx: ¡Estamos aquí!, or being 'Latinx' at UNC–Chapel Hill." *Cultural Dynamics,* vol. 29, no. 3, 2017, pp. 214–230.

Deive, Carlos Esteban. *Vodú y magia en Santo Domingo.* 1975. Fundación Cultural Dominicana, 1996.

De La Torre, Miguel A. *La lucha for Cuba: Religion and Politics on the Streets of Miami.* University of California Press, 2003.

Delgadillo, Theresa. "African, Latina, Feminist, and Decolonial: Marta Moreno Vega's Remembrance of Life in El Barrio in the 1950s." *Theories of the Flesh: Latinx and Latin American Feminisms, Transformation, and Resistance,* edited by Andrea J. Pitts et al., Oxford University Press, 2020, pp. 157–170.

———. *Spiritual Mestizaje: Religion, Gender, Race, and Nation in Contemporary Chicana Narrative.* Duke University Press, 2011.

DeLoughrey, Elizabeth M. *Routes and Roots: Navigating Caribbean and Pacific Island Literatures.* University of Hawai'i Press, 2007.

De Maeseneer, Rita, and Jordi De Beule. "Cinco zambullidas en *boat people.*" *Confluencia,* vol. 25, no. 2, Spring 2010, pp. 94–105.

Derby, Lauren. *The Dictator's Seduction: Politics and the Popular Imagination in the Era of Trujillo.* Duke University Press, 2009.

Deren, Maya. *Divine Horsemen: The Living Gods of Haiti.* 1953. McPherson and Company, 2004.

Desmangles, Leslie G. *The Faces of the Gods: Vodou and Roman Catholicism in Haiti.* University of North Carolina Press, 1992.

Díaz-Sánchez, Micaela. "'Yemaya Blew That Wire Fence Down': Invoking African Spiritualities in Gloria Anzaldúa's *Borderlands/La Frontera: The New Mestiza* and the Mural Art of Juana Alicia." *Yemoja: Gender, Sexuality, and Creativity in the Latina/o and Afro-Atlantic Diasporas,* edited by Solimar Otero and Toyin Falola, SUNY Press, 2013, pp 153–186.

"Dominican Republic Announces Plans for Haiti Border Fence." *BBC News,* 28 Feb. 2021, bbc.com/news/world-latin-america-56227999.

Drewal, Henry John. "Charting the Voyage." *Sacred Waters: Arts for Mami Wata and Other Divinities in Africa and the Diaspora,* edited by Henry John Drewal, Indiana University Press, 2008, pp. 1–18.

———, editor. *Mami Wata: Arts for Water Spirits in Africa and Its Diasporas.* Fowler Museum at UCLA, 2008.

———. "Sources and Currents." *Mami Wata: Arts for Water Spirits in Africa and Its Diasporas.* Fowler Museum at UCLA, 2008, pp. 23-69.

Duany, Jorge. *The Puerto Rican Nation on the Move: Identities on the Island and in the United States.* University of North Carolina Press, 2002.

Dubois, Laurent. *Haiti: The Aftershocks of History.* Metropolitan Books, 2012.

Duchesne-Winter, Juan. "Rita Indiana y sus nuevos misterios." *80 Grados*, 15 May 2015, 80grados.net/rita-indiana-y-sus-nuevos-misterios.

Dunning, Nicholas P. "Life and Death from the Watery Underworld: Ancient Maya Interaction with Caves and Cenotes." *Sacred Waters: A Cross-Cultural Compendium of Hallowed Springs and Holy Wells*, edited by Celeste Ray, Routledge, 2020, pp. 50–58.

Espírito Santo, Diana. *Developing the Dead: Mediumship and Selfhood in Cuban Espiritismo.* University Press of Florida, 2015.

Falola, Toyin. "Èṣù: The God without Boundaries." *Èṣù: Yoruba God, Power, and the Imaginative Frontiers*, edited by Toyin Falola, Carolina Academic Press, 2013, pp. 3–37.

"Families Resuming Tradition of Gathering at Friendship Park." *EFE World News Service*, 27 Oct. 2014.

Feliciano-Santos, Sherina. *A Contested Indigeneity: Language, Social Practice, and Identity within Puerto Rican Taíno Activism.* Rutgers University Press, 2021.

Fernández, Alexander. *Odú in Motion: Afro-Cuban Orisha Hermeneutics and Embodied Scholarship, Life Reflections of a Lukumí Priest.* 2014. Florida International University, master's thesis, digitalcommons.fiu.edu/etd/1142.

Fernández Olmos, Margarite. "Spirited Identities: Creole Religions, Creole/U.S. Latina Literature, and the Initiated Reader." *Contemporary U.S. Latino/a Literary Criticism*, edited by Lyn Di Iorio Sandín and Richard Perez, Palgrave Macmillan, 2007, pp. 63–92.

Fernández Olmos, Margarite, and Lizabeth Paravisini-Gebert. *Creole Religions of the Caribbean: An Introduction from Vodou and Santería to Obeah and Espiritismo.* New York University Press, 2011.

Fernández Retamar, Roberto. *Calibán: Apuntes sobre la cultura en nuestra América.* Editorial Diógenes, 1971.

Ferrer Castro, Armando, and Mayda Acosta Alegre. *Fermina Gómez y la casa olvidada de Olókun.* Editorial José Martí, 2007.

Figueroa-Vásquez, Yomaira C. *Decolonizing Diasporas: Radical Mappings of Afro-Atlantic Literature.* Northwestern University Press, 2020.

Flores-Peña, Ysamur. "Candles, Flowers, and Perfume: Puerto Rican Spiritism on the Move." *Botánica Los Angeles: Latino Popular Religious Art in the City of Angels*, UCLA Fowler Museum of Cultural History, 2004, pp. 88–98 and 131–133.

Fortilus, Nadine. *Santa Marta Ora.* 2007. Private Collection. *Mami Wata: Arts for Water Spirits in Africa and Its Diasporas*, edited by Henry John Drewal, Fowler Museum at UCLA, 2008, p. 150.

Frerichs, Ralph R. *Deadly River: Cholera and Cover-Up in Post-Earthquake Haiti.* ILR Press/Cornell University Press, 2016.

Garcia Lopez, Christina. *Calling the Soul Back: Embodied Spirituality in Chicanx Narrative.* University of Arizona Press, 2019.

García-Peña, Lorgia. *The Borders of Dominicanidad: Race, Nation, and Archives of Contradiction.* Duke University Press, 2016.

Gaspar de Alba, Alicia. "To Your Shadow Beast: In Memoriam." *Entre Guadalupe y Malinche: Tejanas in Literature and Art*, edited by Inés Hernández-Ávila and Norma Elia Cantú, University of Texas Press, 2016, pp. 33–35.

Gates, Henry Louis, Jr. *The Signifying Monkey: A Theory of African-American Literary Criticism*. 1988. Oxford University Press, 2014.

Gay, Roxane. "In the Manner of Water or Light." *Firelei Báez: Bloodlines*, edited by María Elena Ortiz, Pérez Art Museum, 2015, pp. 28–33.

Gilroy, Paul. *The Black Atlantic: Modernity and Double Consciousness*. Harvard University Press, 1993.

Glassie, Alison. "Into the Anemone: Ocean, Form, and the Anthropocene in *Tentacle*." *SX Salon*, vol. 34, June 2020, smallaxe.net/sxsalon/discussions/anemone.

Gleason, Judith. *Oya: In Praise of an African Goddess*. 1987. HarperCollins, 1992.

———. "Oya in the Company of Saints." *Journal of the American Academy of Religion*, vol. 68, no. 2, 2000, pp. 265–292.

Glissant, Édouard. *Caribbean Discourse: Selected Essays*. 1989. University Press of Virginia, 1999.

———. *Poetics of Relation*. Translated by Betsy Wing, University of Michigan Press, 1997.

Goldman, Francisco. "The Magical Realism of the Elian Chronicle." *Los Angeles Times*, 30 Apr. 2000, latimes.com/archives/la-xpm-2000-apr-30-op-24956-story.html.

González, José Luis. "En el fondo del caño hay un negrito." *Revista Asomante*, no. 3, July-Sep. 1950, pp. 88–91.

González-Wippler, Migene. *The Santería Experience*. Prentice Hall, 1982.

Graziano, Frank. *Undocumented Dominican Migration*. University of Texas Press, 2013.

Guidotti-Hernández, Nicole M. "Affective Communities and Millennial Desires: Latinx, or Why My Computer Won't Recognize Latina/o." *Cultural Dynamics*, vol. 29, no. 3, 2017, pp. 141–159.

———. *Archiving Mexican Masculinities in Diaspora*. Duke University Press, 2021.

"Haiti Warning: Dominican Nationalists March in Demand Detention Canal Rio Massacre." Dímelo TV Official, YouTube, 4 Jun. 2021, youtube.com/watch?v=bX1ZLOZGmBk.

Hall, Stuart. "Subjects in History: Making Diasporic Identities." 1998. *Selected Writings on Race and Difference*, edited by Paul Gilroy and Ruth Wilson Gilmore, Duke University Press, 2021, pp. 329–338.

———. "Thinking the Diaspora: Home-Thoughts from Abroad." *Essential Essays Vol. 2: Identity and Diaspora*, edited by David Morley. Duke University Press, 2018, pp. 206–226.

Hamilton, Njelle W. "'Another Shape to Time': Tentacle's Spiral Now." *SX Salon*, vol. 34, June 2020, smallaxe.net/sxsalon/discussions/another-shape-time-tentacles-spiral-now.

Harford Vargas, Jennifer. "The Undocumented Subjects of *el Hueco*: Theorizing a Colombian Metaphor for Migration." *Symbolism: An International Annual of Critical Aesthetics*, vol. 17, *Latina/o Literature: The Trans-Atlantic and the Trans-American in Dialogue*, edited by Rüdiger Ahrens et al., Walter De Gruyter, 2017, pp. 31–53.

Hartley, George. "The Curandera of Conquest: Gloria Anzaldúa's Decolonial Remedy." *Aztlán: A Journal of Chicano Studies*, vol. 35, no. 1, Spring 2010, pp. 135–161.

———. "'Matriz sin tumba': The Trash Goddess and the Healing Matrix of Gloria Anzaldúa's Reclaimed Womb." *MELUS*, vol. 35, no. 3, Fall 2010, pp. 41–61.

Hebblethwaite, Benjamin. *A Transatlantic History of Haitian Vodou: Rasin Figuier, Rasin Bwa Kayiman, and the Rada and Gede Rites*. University Press of Mississippi, 2021.

———. *Vodou Songs in Haitian Creole and English*. Temple University Press, 2011.

Hernandez, Jasmin. *We Are Here: Visionaries of Color Transforming the Art World*. Abrams, 2021.

Herrera, Cristina. "'Undesirable Women?' Afro–Puerto Rican Mother-Daughter Relationships and Puerto Rican Heritage in Dahlma Llanos-Figueroa's *Daughters of the Stone*." *Chicana/Latina Studies*, vol. 12, no. 1, Fall 2012, pp. 32–78.

Herrero-Martín, Rosana. "Olokun or the Caribbean Quantum Mind: An Analysis of Transculturated Metaphysical Elements within Rita Indiana's Novel *Tentacle*." *Journal of West Indian Literature*, vol. 27, no. 2, 2019, pp. 52–67 and 81.

Hey-Colón, Rebeca L. "Chronic Illness and Transformation in Gloria Anzaldúa's 'Puddles.'" *Aztlán: A Journal of Chicano Studies*, vol. 47, no. 1, Spring 2022, pp. 15-42.

———. "'Por el mar que nos une': *boat people's* Living Waters." *Chicana/Latina Studies*, vol. 20, no. 2, Spring 2021, pp. 28–59.

———. "Rippling Borders in Latina Literature." *The Image of the River in Latin/o American Literature: Written in the Water*, edited by Jeanie Murphy and Elizabeth G. Rivero, Lexington Books, 2018, pp. 95–115.

———. "Toward a Genealogy of Water: Reading Julia de Burgos in the Twenty-First Century." *Small Axe*, vol. 21, no. 3 (54), 2017, pp. 179–187.

———. "Transformative Currents: An Exploration of the Sea and Identity in the Works of Angie Cruz and Nelly Rosario." *Negotiating Latinidades, Understanding Identities within Space*, edited by Kathryn Quinn-Sánchez, Cambridge Scholars Publishers, 2015, pp. 9–29.

Hoffnung-Garskof, Jesse. *A Tale of Two Cities: Santo Domingo and New York After 1950*. Princeton University Press, 2008.

Holslin, Jill M. "Friendship Park: Environmental Placemaking at the US-Mexico Border." *The Nature of Hope: Grassroots Organizing, Environmental Justice, and Political Change*, edited by Char Miller and Jeffrey Crane, University Press of Colorado, 2019, pp. 139–154.

Hu-DeHart, Evelyn, and Kathleen López. "Asian Diasporas in Latin America and the Caribbean: An Historical Overview." *Afro-Hispanic Review*, vol. 27, no. 1, Spring 2008, pp. 9–21.

Humphrey, Paul. "'El manto que cubre el mar': Religion, Identity, and the Sea in Rita Indiana's *La mucama de Omicunlé*." *Sargasso*, nos. 1–2, 2016–2017, pp. 109–125.

Hurston, Zora Neale. *Tell My Horse: Voodoo and Life in Haiti and Jamaica*. 1938. HarperCollins, 2009.

Hurtado, Aída. "Theory in the Flesh: Toward an Endarkened Epistemology." *International Journal of Qualitative Studies in Education*, vol. 16, no. 2, 2003, pp. 215–225.

Hyppolite, Joanne. "Dyaspora." *The Butterfly's Way: Voices from the Haitian Dyaspora in the United States*, edited by Edwidge Danticat, Soho Press, 2001, pp. 7–11.

Idowu, E. Bọlaji. *Olódùmarè: God in Yoruba Belief.* Longmans, 1962.

Ikú lobi Ocha: El muerto hace el Santo. Directed by Belén Maldonado and Álex Esteva. Universidad de Cadiz, 2014.

Indiana, Rita. *La mucama de Omicunlé.* Editorial Periférica, 2015.

———. *Tentacle.* Translated by Achy Obejas, And Other Stories, 2018.

Indiana, Rita, et al., panelists. "A Conversation with Rita Indiana." 24 Mar. 2021, online event, Fordham University, New York.

Ingersoll, Karin Amimoto. *Waves of Knowing: A Seascape Epistemology.* Duke University Press, 2016.

Irizarry, Ylce. *Chicana/o and Latina/o Fiction: The New Memory of Latinidad.* University of Illinois Press, 2016.

Jean-Charles, Régine Michelle. "'A Border between Geographies of Grief': River Crossings and Crossroads between Haiti and the Dominican Republic." *Transnational Hispaniola: New Directions in Haitian and Dominican Studies,* edited by April J. Mayes and Kiran C. Jayaram, University of Florida Press, 2018, pp. 81–103.

Jiménez Román, Miriam, and Juan Flores. Introduction. *The Afro-Latin@ Reader: History and Culture in the United States,* edited by Miriam Jiménez Román and Juan Flores, Duke University Press, 2010, pp. 1–15.

Johnson, Paul Christopher, and Stephan Palmié. "Afro-Latin American Religions." *Afro-Latin American Studies: An Introduction,* edited by Alejandro de la Fuente and George Reid Andrews, Cambridge University Press, 2018, pp. 438–485.

Jones, Jennifer A. "Afro-Latinos: Speaking through Silences and Rethinking the Geographies of Blackness." *Afro-Latin American Studies: An Introduction,* edited by Alejandro de la Fuente and George Reid Andrews, Cambridge University Press, 2018, pp. 569–614.

———. "Blackness, Latinidad, and Minority Linked Fate." *Critical Dialogues in Latinx Studies: A Reader,* edited by Ana Y. Ramos-Zayas and Mérida M. Rúa, New York University Press, 2021, pp. 425–437.

Juárez Huet, Nahayeilli Beatriz. "De 'negro brujo' a patrimonio cultural: Circulación transnacional de la 'tradición orisha.'" *Desacatos,* vol. 53, 2017, pp. 74–89.

———. *Un pedacito de Dios en casa. Circulación transnacional, relocalización y praxis de la santería en la ciudad de México.* Publicaciones de la Casa Chata, 2014.

———. "Religiones afroamericanas en México: Hallazgos de una empresa etnográfica en construcción." *Revista Cultura y Religión,* vol. 8, no. 1, 2014, pp. 219–241.

Keating, AnaLouise. "Archival Alchemy and Allure: The Gloria Evangelina Anzaldúa Papers as Case Study." *Aztlán: A Journal of Chicano Studies,* vol. 35, no. 2, Fall 2010, pp. 159–171.

———. "Editor's Introduction: Re-envisioning Coyolxauhqui, Decolonizing Reality: Anzaldúa's Twenty-First-Century Imperative." *Light in the Dark/Luz en lo oscuro: Rewriting Identity, Spirituality, Reality,* edited by AnaLouise Keating, Duke University Press, 2015, pp. ix–xxxvii.

———. "'I'm a Citizen of the Universe': Gloria Anzaldúa's Spiritual Activism as Catalyst for Social Change." *Feminist Studies,* vol. 34, nos. 1–2, Spring/Summer 2008, pp. 53–69.

———. Introduction to "Yemayá." *The Gloria Anzaldúa Reader*, edited by AnaLouise Keating, Duke University Press, 2009, p. 242.

———. "Risking the Personal: An Introduction." *Interviews/Entrevistas by Gloria Anzaldúa*, edited by AnaLouise Keating, Routledge, 2000, pp. 1–15.

———. "'Working toward Wholeness': Gloria Anzaldúa's Struggles to Live with Diabetes and Chronic Illness." *Speaking from the Body: Latinas on Health and Culture*, edited by Angie Chabram-Dernersesian and Adela de la Torre, University of Arizona Press, 2008, pp. 133–143.

Keating, AnaLouise, and Gloria González-López, editors. *Bridging: How Gloria Anzaldúa's Life and Work Transformed Our Own*. University of Texas Press, 2011.

Kelly, Mary Louise. "400 Lights, for 400,000 Dead, Illuminate Lincoln Memorial Reflecting Pool." NPR, 19 Jan. 2021, npr.org/sections/coronavirus-live-updates /2021/01/19/958449203/400-lights-for-400-000-dead-to-illuminate-lincoln -memorial-reflecting-pool.

King, Tiffany Lethabo. *The Black Shoals: Offshore Formations of Black and Native Studies*. Duke University Press, 2019.

Lachatañeré, Rómulo. *El sistema religioso de los afrocubanos*. 1992. Editorial de Ciencias Sociales, 2007.

Laó-Montes, Agustín. "Afro-Latinidades and the Diasporic Imaginary." *Iberoamericana*, vol. 5, no. 17, 2005, pp. 117–130.

Laó-Montes, Agustín, and Mirangela Buggs. "Translocal Space of Afro-Latinidad: Critical Feminist Visions for Diasporic Bridge-Building." *Translocalities/Translocalidades: Feminist Politics of Translation in the Latin/a Américas*, edited by Sonia E. Alvarez et al., Duke University Press, 2014, pp. 381–400.

Lara, Ana-Maurine. *Erzulie's Skirt*. Redbone Press, 2006.

———. "I Wanted to Be More of a Person: Conjuring [Afro] [Latinx] [Queer] Futures." *Bilingual Review/Revista Bilingüe*, vol. 33, no. 4, 2017.

———. *Queer Freedom: Black Sovereignty*. SUNY Press, 2020.

Lara, Irene. "Bruja Positionalities: Toward a Chicana/Latina Spiritual Activism." *Chicana/Latina Studies*, vol. 4, no. 2, Spring 2005, pp. 10–45.

Martínez, Diana Isabel. *Rhetorics of Nepantla, Memory, and the Gloria Evangelina Anzaldúa Papers: Archival Impulses*. Lexington Books, 2022.

Martínez-San Miguel, Yolanda. "Rethinking the Colonial Latinx Literary Imaginary: A Comparative and Decolonial Research Agenda." *The Cambridge History of Latina/o American Literature*, edited by John Morán González and Laura Lomas, Cambridge University Press, 2018, pp. 93–118.

Mason, John. *In Praise of Our Mothers*. Yorùbá Theological Archministry, 2016.

———. *Olóòkun: Owner of Rivers and Seas*. Yorùbá Theological Archministry, 1996.

Matibag, Eugenio. *Afro-Cuban Religious Experience: Cultural Reflections in Narrative*. 1996. University Press of Florida, 2017.

———. "Ifá and Interpretation: An Afro-Caribbean Literary Practice." *Sacred Possessions: Vodou, Santería, Obeah, and the Caribbean*, edited by Margarite Fernández Olmos and Lizabeth Paravisini-Gebert, Rutgers University Press, 2000, pp. 151–170.

Matory, J. Lorand. *Black Atlantic Religion: Tradition, Transnationalism, and Matriarchy in the Afro-Brazilian Candomblé*. Princeton University Press, 2005.

———. "Free to Be a Slave: Slavery as Metaphor in the Afro-Atlantic Religions." *Journal of Religion in Africa*, vol. 37, 2007, pp. 398–425.

———. "The Many Who Dance in Me: Afro-Atlantic Ontology and the Problem with 'Transnationalism.'" *Transnational Transcendence: Essays on Religion and Globalization*, edited by Thomas J. Csordas, University of California Press, 2009, pp. 231–262.

Mayes, April J. "To Be Haitian Means to Leave: Refusal and Survivance from Brazil to Mexico." 5 Nov. 2020, online event, University of Colorado Boulder.

Mayes, April J., and Kiran C. Jayaram. Introduction. *Transnational Hispaniola: New Directions in Haitian and Dominican Studies*, edited by April J. Mayes and Kiran C. Jayaram, University of Florida Press, 2018, pp. 1–19.

McAlister, Elizabeth. *Rara!: Vodou, Power, and Performance in Haiti and Its Diaspora*. University of California Press, 2002.

———. "Sacred Waters of Haitian Vodou: The Pilgrimage of Sodo." *Sacred Waters: A Cross-Cultural Compendium of Hallowed Springs and Holy Wells*, edited by Celeste Ray, Routledge, 2020, pp. 259–265.

———. "Soundscapes of Disaster and Humanitarianism: Survival Singing, Relief Telethons, and the Haiti Earthquake." *Small Axe*, vol. 16, no. 3 (39), 2012, pp. 22–38.

McCarthy Brown, Karen. *Mama Lola: A Vodou Priestess in Brooklyn*. 1991. University of California Press, 2010.

Medina, Lara. "*Nepantla* Spirituality: Negotiating Fluid Identities, Faiths, and Practices." *El Mundo Zurdo: Selected Works from the Meetings of the Society for the Study of Gloria Anzaldúa 2007 and 2009*, edited by Norma E. Cantú et al., Aunt Lute Books, 2010, pp. 205–214.

Méndez, Susan C. "'Like a Dialect Freaked by Thunder': Spiritual Articulations of Survival and Identity in Cristina García's *Dreaming in Cuban* and *Monkey Hunting*." *Chicana/Latina Studies*, vol. 11, no. 1, Fall 2011, pp. 124–157.

Métraux, Alfred. *Voodoo in Haiti*. 1959. Translated by Hugo Charteris, Schocken Books, 1972.

Milian, Claudia. "Extremely Latin, XOXO: Notes on LatinX." *Cultural Dynamics*, vol. 29, no. 3, 2017, pp. 121–140.

———. *LatinX*. University of Minnesota Press, 2019.

Minich, Julie Avril. "Aztlán Unprotected: Reading Gil Cuadros in the Aftermath of HIV/AIDS." *GLQ: A Journal of Lesbian and Gay Studies*, vol. 23, no. 2, 2017, pp. 167–193.

Misterios. Directed by Giovanni Savino, Magnetic Arts Productions, 2005.

Moïse, Myriam. "Vodou Symbolism and 'Poto Mitan' Women in Edwidge Danticat's Work." *Vodou in Haitian Memory: The Idea and Representation of Vodou in Haitian Imagination*, edited by Celucien L. Joseph and Nixon S. Cleophat, Lexington Books, 2016, pp. 125–143.

Molina Guzmán, Isabel. "Disorderly Bodies and Discourses of Latinidad in the Elián González Story." *From Bananas to Buttocks: The Latina Body in Popular Film and Culture*, edited by Myra Mendible, University of Texas Press, 2007, pp. 219–241.

Moraga, Cherríe L. *A Xicana Codex of Changing Consciousness: Writings, 2000–2010.* Duke University Press, 2011.

Moraga, Cherríe, and Gloria Anzaldúa, editors. "Entering the Lives of Others: Theory in the Flesh." *This Bridge Called My Back: Writings by Radical Women of Color.* 1981, 4th ed., SUNY Press, 2015, p. 19.

———. "El Mundo Zurdo: The Vision." *This Bridge Called My Back: Writings by Radical Women of Color.* 1981, 4th ed., SUNY Press, 2015, pp. 195–196.

———. *This Bridge Called My Back: Writings by Radical Women of Color.* 1981, 4th ed., SUNY Press, 2015.

Mordecai, Pamela, and Betty Wilson, editors. *Her True-True Name: An Anthology of Women's Writing from the Caribbean.* Heinemann, 1990.

Moreno, Marisel. "Bordes líquidos, fronteras y espejismos: El dominicano y la migración intra-caribeña en *boat people* de Mayra Santos-Febres." *Revista de Estudios Hispánicos,* vol. 34, no. 2, 2007, pp. 17–32.

Moreno Vega, Marta. "Afro-Boricua: Nuyorican de Pura Cepa." *Women Warriors of the Afro-Latina Diaspora,* edited by Marta Moreno Vega et al., Arte Público Press, 2012, pp. 77–95.

———. *The Altar of My Soul: The Living Traditions of Santería.* Random House, 2000.

———. "The Ancestral Sacred Creative Impulse of Africa and the African Diaspora: Àse, the Nexus of the Black Global Aesthetic." *Lenox Avenue: A Journal of Interarts Inquiry,* vol. 5, 1999, pp. 45–57.

———. "The Candomblé and Eshu-Eleggua in Brazilian and Cuban Yoruba-Based Ritual." *Black Theatre: Ritual Performance in the African Diaspora,* edited by Paul Carter Harrison et al., Temple University Press, 2002, pp. 153–166.

———. "*Espiritismo* in the Puerto Rican Community: A New World Recreation with the Elements of Kongo Ancestor Worship." *Journal of Black Studies,* vol. 29, no. 3, 1999, pp. 325–353.

———. *When the Spirits Dance Mambo: Growing Up Nuyorican in El Barrio.* Three Rivers Press, 2004.

Morrison, Toni. "The Site of Memory." *Inventing the Truth: The Art and Craft of Memoir,* 2nd ed., edited by William Zinsser, Houghton Mifflin, 1995, pp. 83–102.

Murphy, Joseph M. *Botánicas: Sacred Spaces of Healing and Devotion in Urban America.* University Press of Mississippi, 2015.

———. "'Chango 'Ta Veni'/Chango Has Come': Spiritual Embodiment in the Afro-Cuban Ceremony, Bembé." *Black Music Research Journal,* vol. 32, no. 1, Spring 2012, pp. 69–94.

———. "Òrìṣà Traditions and the Internet Diaspora." *Òrìṣà Devotion as World Religion: The Globalization of Yorùbá Religious Culture,* edited by Jacob K. Olupona and Terry Rey, University of Wisconsin Press, 2008, pp. 470–484.

———. *Santería: African Spirits in America.* 1988. Beacon Press, 1993.

Myers, Megan Jeanette. "*Dos rayanos-americanos* Rewrite Hispaniola: Julia Alvarez and Junot Díaz." *Confluencia,* vol. 32, no. 1, Fall 2016, pp. 161–181.

———. "A Promise Kept: A Conversation with Julia Álvarez." *Afro-Hispanic Review,* vol. 31, no. 1, Spring 2012, pp. 169–176.

Myers, Megan Jeanette, and Edward Paulino. "Bearing Witness on and Beyond the Border." *The Border of Lights Reader: Bearing Witness to Genocide in the Dominican Republic*, edited by Megan Jeanette Myers and Edward Paulino, Amherst College Press, 2021, pp. 1–40.

Nancy, Jean-Luc. *The Muses*. Translated by Peggy Kamuf, Stanford University Press, 1996.

Negrón-Muntaner, Frances. "Bridging Islands: Gloria Anzaldúa and the Caribbean." *PMLA*, vol. 121, no. 1, 2006, pp. 272–278.

Oliver, José R. *Caciques and Cemi Idols: The Web Spun by Taíno Rulers Between Hispaniola and Puerto Rico*. University of Alabama Press, 2009.

Olupona, Jacob K., and Terry Rey. Introduction. *Òrìṣà Devotion as World Religion: The Globalization of Yorùbá Religious Culture*, edited by Jacob K. Olupona and Terry Rey, University of Wisconsin Press, 2008, pp. 3–28.

O'Neil, Deborah, and Terry Rey. "The Saint and Siren: Liberation Hagiography in a Haitian Village." *Studies in Religion/Sciences Religieuses*, vol. 41, no. 2, 2012, pp. 166–186.

Ortíz, Fernando. "Los factores humanos de la cubanidad." *Revista Bimestre Cubana*, vol. 45, 1940, pp. 161–186.

Ortiz, María Elena, editor. *Firelei Báez: Bloodlines*, Pérez Art Museum, 2015.

———. "A Future Yet to Be Unfolded." *Firelei Báez: Bloodlines*, edited by María Elena Ortiz, Pérez Art Museum, 2015, pp. 11–19.

Ortiz, Ricardo. "Edwidge Danticat's *Latinidad*: *The Farming of Bones* and the Cultivation (of Fields) of Knowledge." *Aftermaths: Exile, Migration, and Diaspora Reconsidered*, edited by Marcus Bullock and Peter Y. Paik, Rutgers University Press, 2008, pp. 150–172.

Otero, Solimar. *Archives of Conjure: Stories of the Dead in Afrolatinx Cultures*. Columbia University Press, 2020.

———. "Èṣù at the Transatlantic Crossroads: Locations of Crossing Over." *Èṣù: Yoruba God, Power, and the Imaginative Frontiers*, edited by Toyin Falola, Carolina Academic Press, 2013, pp. 191–213.

———. "In the Water with Inle: Santería's Siren Songs in the CircumCaribbean." *The Southern Quarterly*, vol. 55, no. 4, Summer 2018, pp. 143–161.

———. "Yemayá y Ochún: Queering the Vernacular Logics of the Waters." *Yemoja: Gender, Sexuality, and the Creativity in the Latina/o and Afro-Atlantic Diasporas*, edited by Solimar Otero and Toyin Falola, SUNY Press, 2013, pp. 85–111.

Overmyer-Velázquez, Mark. "Global Latin(X) AmericanXs: Charting New Ontological and Epistemological Cartographies beyond US LatinX Studies." *Cultural Dynamics*, vol. 31, nos. 1–2, 2019, pp. 35–49.

Owens, Deirdre Cooper. *Medical Bondage: Race, Gender, and the Origins of American Gynecology*. University of Georgia Press, 2017.

Palmié, Stephan. *The Cooking of History: How Not to Study Afro-Cuban Religion*. University of Chicago Press, 2013.

———. *Wizards and Scientists: Explorations in Afro-Cuban Modernity and Tradition*. Duke University Press, 2002.

Past, Mariana. "'But the Captain Is Haitian': Issues of Recognition within Ana Lydia

Vega's 'Encancaranublado.'" *Racialized Visions: Haiti and the Hispanic Caribbean*, edited by Vanessa K. Valdés, SUNY Press, 2020, pp. 159–176.

Patterson, Tiffany Ruby, and Robin D. G. Kelley. "Unfinished Migrations: Reflections on the African Diaspora and the Making of the Modern World." *African Studies Review*, vol. 43, no. 1, 2000, pp. 11–45.

Paulino, Edward. *Dividing Hispaniola: The Dominican Republic's Border Campaign against Haiti, 1930–1961*. University of Pittsburgh Press, 2016.

Paulino, Edward, and Scherezade García. "Bearing Witness to Genocide: The 1937 Haitian Massacre and the Border of Lights." *Afro-Hispanic Review*, vol. 32, no. 2, Fall 2013, pp. 111–118.

Pedraza, Silvia. *Political Disaffection in Cuba's Revolution and Exodus*. Cambridge University Press, 2007.

Perez, Domino Renee. *There Was a Woman: La Llorona from Folklore to Popular Culture*. University of Texas Press, 2008.

Pérez, Elizabeth. "Crystallizing Subjectivities in the African Diaspora: Sugar, Honey, and the Gods of Afro-Cuban Lucumí." *Religion, Food, and Eating in North America*, edited by Benjamin E. Zeller et al., Columbia University Press, 2014, pp. 175–194.

———. "Nobody's Mammy: Yemayá as Fierce Foremother in Afro-Cuban Religions." *Yemoja: Gender, Sexuality, and Creativity in the Latina/o and Afro-Atlantic Diasporas*, edited by Solimar Otero and Toyin Falola, SUNY Press, 2013, pp. 9–41.

———. "Portable Portals: Transnational Rituals for the Head across Globalizing Orisha Traditions." *Nova Religio: The Journal of Alternative and Emergent Religions*, vol. 16, no. 4, 2013, pp. 35–62.

———. "Spiritist Mediumship as Historical Mediation: African-American Pasts, Black Ancestral Presence, and Afro-Cuban Religions." *Journal of Religion in Africa*, vol. 41, no. 4, 2011, pp. 330–365.

———. "Willful Spirits and Weakened Flesh: Historicizing the Initiation Narrative in Afro-Cuban Religions." *Journal of Africana Religions*, vol. 1, no. 2, 2013, pp. 151–193.

Pérez-Rosario, Vanessa. "Translator's Note." *Boat People*, by Mayra Santos-Febres. Cardboard House Press, 2021, pp. 75–80.

Pérez-Torres, Rafael. "The Embodied Epistemology of Chicana/o Mestizaje." *Routledge Handbook of Chicana/o Studies*, edited by Francisco A. Lomelí et al., 2018, pp. 229–241.

Perkins, Alexandra Gonzenbach. "Queer Materiality, Contestatory Histories, and Disperse Bodies in *La mucama de Omiculé*." *Journal of Latin American Cultural Studies*, vol. 30, no. 1, 2021, pp. 47–60.

Piña, Sarah Elisabeth. *The Atlantis Effect: Aquatic Invocations and the (Re)Claiming of Women's Space through the Works and Archives of Lydia Cabrera, Gloria Anzaldúa, and Tatiana de la Tierra*. 2017. University of Houston, PhD dissertation, uh-ir.tdl.org /handle/10657/2037.

Pinkvoss, Joan. Editor's Note. *Borderlands/La Frontera: The New Mestiza*, by Gloria Anzaldúa, 1987, 4th ed., Aunt Lute Books, 2012, pp. 15-16.

Pressley-Sanon, Toni. *Istwa across the Water: Haitian History, Memory, and the Cultural Imagination*. University Press of Florida, 2017.

Quinn, Rachel Afi. *Being La Dominicana: Race and Identity in the Visual Culture of Santo Domingo*. University of Illinois Press, 2021.

Ramos, Miguel "Willie." "Afro-Cuban Orisha Worship." *Santería Aesthetics in Contemporary Latin American Art*, edited by Arturo Lindsay, Smithsonian Institution Press, 1996, pp. 51–76.

Ramsey, Kate. *The Spirits and the Law: Vodou and Power in Haiti*. University of Chicago Press, 2011.

Reti, Irene. "Living in the House of Nepantla." *EntreMundos/AmongWorlds: New Perspectives on Gloria E. Anzaldúa*, edited by AnaLouise Keating, Palgrave Macmillan, 2005, pp. 57–59.

Rey, Terry. "The Life of the Dead in African and African Diasporic Religion." *Death and Dying in World Religions: An Anthology*, edited by Lucy Bregman, Kendall Hunt Publishing, 2009, pp. 153–167.

———. *Our Lady of Class Struggle: The Cult of the Virgin Mary in Haiti*. Africa World Press, 1999.

———. "Vodou, Water, and Exile: Symbolizing Spirit and Pain in Port-au-Prince." *Religion, Violence, Memory, and Place*, edited by Oren Baruch Stier and J. Shawn Landres, Indiana University Press, 2006, pp. 198–213.

Rey, Terry, and Alex Stepick. *Crossing the Water and Keeping the Faith: Haitian Religion in Miami*. New York University Press, 2013.

———. "Visual Culture and Visual Piety in Little Haiti: The Sea, the Tree, and the Refugee." *Art in the Lives of Immigrant Communities in the United States*, edited by Paul DiMaggio and Patricia Fernández-Kelly, Rutgers University Press, 2010, pp. 229–248.

Ribó, John D. "'Neither Strangers nor Friends': Transnational Hispaniola and the Uneven Intimacies of *The Farming of Bones*." *The Bloomsbury Handbook to Edwidge Danticat*, edited by Jana Evans Braziel and Nadège T. Clitandre, Bloomsbury Publishing, 2021, pp. 470–488.

Richman, Karen E. *Migration and Vodou*. University Press of Florida, 2005.

Ricourt, Milagros. *The Dominican Racial Imaginary: Surveying the Landscape of Race and Nation in Hispaniola*. Rutgers University Press, 2016.

———. "Reaching the Promised Land: Undocumented Dominican Migration to Puerto Rico." *CENTRO Journal*, vol. 19, no. 2, Fall 2007, pp. 225–243.

Rivera, Fredo. "Precarity + Excess in the *latinopolis*: Miami as Erzulie." *Cultural Dynamics*, vol. 31, nos. 1–2, 2019, pp. 62–80.

Rivera, Juan Pablo. "Lírica, sabor y saber: *Anamú y manigua* y *Boat People*." *Lección errante: Mayra Santos Febres y el Caribe contemporáneo*, edited by Nadia V. Celis and Juan Pablo Rivera, Editorial Isla Negra, 2011, pp. 171–186.

Rivera-Rideau, Petra R., et al., editors. *Afro-Latin@s in Movement: Critical Approaches to Blackness and Transnationalism in the Americas*. Palgrave Macmillan, 2016.

Roberts, Brian Russell. *Borderwaters: Amid the Archipelagic States of America*. Duke University Press, 2021.

Rodríguez, Juana María. *Sexual Futures, Queer Gestures, and Other Latina Longings*. New York University Press, 2014.

Rodríguez Vélez, Wendalina. *El turbante blanco: Muertos, santos y vivos en la lucha política.* Museo del Hombre Dominicano, 1982.

Rogers, Charlotte. "Rita Indiana's Queer Interspecies Caribbean and the Hispanic Literary Tradition." *SX Salon,* vol. 34, June 2020. smallaxe.net/sxsalon/discussions/rita-indianas-queer-interspecies-caribbean-and-hispanic-literary-tradition.

Romberg, Raquel. "From Charlatans to Saviors: *Espiritistas, Curanderos,* and *Brujos* Inscribed in Discourses of Progress and Heritage." *CENTRO Journal,* vol. 15, no. 2, Fall 2003, pp. 147–172.

Rosario, Nelly. *Song of the Water Saints.* Vintage Books, 2002.

Rosen, Norma. "Chalk Iconography in Olokun Worship." *African Arts,* vol. 22, no. 3, 1989, pp. 44–53 and 88.

Sabau, Ana. *Riot and Rebellion in Mexico: The Making of a Race War Paradigm.* University of Texas Press, 2022.

Saldívar-Hull, Sonia. Introduction to the Second Edition. *Borderlands/La Frontera: The New Mestiza.* 1987, 4th ed., Aunt Lute Books, 2012, pp. 251–263.

Sánchez-Carretero, Cristina. "*Santos y Misterios* as Channels of Communication in the Diaspora: Afro-Dominican Religious Practices Abroad." *Journal of American Folklore,* vol. 118, no. 469, Summer 2005, pp. 308–326.

Sandoval, Mercedes Cros. "Santería in the Twenty-First Century." *Òrìṣà Devotion as World Religion: The Globalization of Yorùbá Religious Culture,* edited by Jacob K. Olupona and Terry Rey, University of Wisconsin Press, 2008, pp. 355–371.

———. *Worldview, the Orichas, and Santería: Africa to Cuba and Beyond.* University Press of Florida, 2006.

Santos-Febres, Mayra. *boat people.* Ediciones Callejón, 2005.

———. *Boat People.* Translated by Vanessa Pérez-Rosario, Cardboard House Press, 2021.

Scalissi, Nicole F. "*Firelei Báez: Bloodlines*: The Andy Warhol Museum, February 17–May 21, 2017." *Contemporaneity: Historical Presence in Visual Culture,* vol. 6, no. 1, Fall 2017, pp. 97–102.

Sellers, Allison P. "Yemoja: An Introduction to the Divine Mother and Water Goddess." *Yemoja: Gender, Sexuality, and the Creativity in the Latina/o and Afro-Atlantic Diasporas,* edited by Solimar Otero and Toyin Falola, SUNY Press, 2013, pp. 131–149.

Sharpe, Christina. *In the Wake: On Blackness and Being.* Duke University Press, 2016.

Sharpe, Jenny. *Immaterial Archives: An African Diaspora Poetics of Loss.* Northwestern University Press, 2020.

Shufro, Cathy. "Professor of Mambo: Robert Farris Thompson—Master T—Teaches 'the Black Aesthetics of the Cool.'" *Yale Alumni Magazine,* vol. 73, no. 6, Jul./Aug. 2010, yalealumnimagazine.com/articles/2919-professor-of-mambo?page=1.

Sirmans, Franklin. "Preface and Acknowledgements/Prólogo y agradecimientos." *Firelei Báez: Bloodlines,* edited by María Elena Ortiz, Pérez Art Museum, 2015, pp. 7–9.

Smartt Bell, Madison. Preface. *Nan Dòmi: An Initiate's Journey into Haitian Vodou* by Mimerose P. Beaubrun, translated by D. J. Walker, City Light Books, 2013, pp. 11–30.

Sparks, David Hatfield. "Dancing the River: Fluidity of Eros and Gender in Music and

Dance of African Diasporic Spiritual Traditions." *Postscripts: The Journal of Sacred Texts, Cultural Histories, and Contemporary Contexts*, vol. 4, no. 3, 2008, pp. 367–388.

Strongman, Roberto. *Queering Black Atlantic Religions: Transcorporeality in Candomblé, Santería, and Vodou*. Duke University Press, 2019.

———. "Reading through the Bloody Borderlands of Hispaniola: Fictionalizing the 1937 Massacre of Haitian Sugarcane Workers in the Dominican Republic." *Journal of Haitian Studies*, vol. 12, no. 2, Fall 2006, pp. 22–46.

Sweet, James H. *Domingos Álvares, African Healing, and the Intellectual History of the Atlantic World*. University of North Carolina Press, 2011.

Tejeda Ortiz, Dagoberto. *El Vudú en Dominicana y en Haití*. Ediciones Indefolk, 2013.

Teish, Luisah. *Jambalaya: The Natural Woman's Book of Personal Charms and Practical Rituals*. 1985. HarperCollins, 1988.

———. "O.K. Momma, Who the Hell Am I? An Interview with Luisah Teish." Interview by Gloria Anzaldúa, *This Bridge Called My Back: Writings by Radical Women of Color*. 1981, 4th ed., edited by Cherríe Moraga and Gloria Anzaldúa, SUNY Press, 2015, pp. 221–231.

———. "The Warrior Queen: Encounters with a Latin Lady." *Goddess of the Americas: Writings on the Virgin of Guadalupe*, edited by Ana Castillo, Riverhead Books, 1996, pp. 137–146.

Thompson, Robert Farris. *Flash of the Spirit: African and Afro-American Art and Philosophy*. 1983. Vintage Books, 2010.

Thornton, Brendan Jamal. *Negotiating Respect: Pentecostalism, Masculinity, and the Politics of Spiritual Authority in the Dominican Republic*. University Press of Florida, 2016.

Tinsley, Omise'eke Natasha. "Black Atlantic, Queer Atlantic: Queer Imaginings of the Middle Passage." *GLQ: A Journal of Lesbian and Gay Studies*, vol. 14, nos. 2–3, 2008, pp. 191–215.

Tocilovac, Marko. "(Dis)Continuities of the Border Spectacle: An Analysis of a Binational Park in a San Diego, California." *Permeable Borders: History, Theory, Policy, and Practice in the United States*, edited by Paul Otto and Susanne Berthier-Foglar, Berghahn Brooks, 2020, pp. 177–193.

Torres, Lourdes. "Latinx?." *Latino Studies*, vol. 16, 2018, pp. 283–285.

Torres-Saillant, Silvio. "Afro-Latinidad: Phoenix Rising from a Hemisphere's Racist Flames." *The Cambridge History of Latina/o American Literature*, edited by John Morán González and Laura Lomas, Cambridge University Press, 2018, pp. 276–305.

Trouillot, Michel-Rolph. *Silencing the Past: Power and the Production of History*. Beacon Press, 1995.

———. *Stirring the Pot of Haitian History*. 1977. Translated and edited by Mariana Past and Benjamin Hebblethwaite, Liverpool University Press, 2021.

Tsang, Martin A. "Beguiling Eshu: Motion and Commotion in London." *Èṣù: Yoruba God, Power, and the Imaginative Frontiers*, edited by Toyin Falola, Carolina Academic Press, 2013, pp. 215–229.

———. "A Different Kind of Sweetness: Yemayá in Afro-Cuban Religion." *Yemoja: Gender, Sexuality, and the Creativity in the Latina/o and Afro-Atlantic Diasporas*, edited by Solimar Otero and Toyin Falola, SUNY Press, 2013, pp. 113–130.

―――. "On Becoming the Archive." *Lydia Cabrera: Between the Sum and the Parts*, edited by Karen Marta and Gabriela Rangel, Koenig Books, 2019, pp. 61–66.

―――. "The Power of Containing and the Containing of Power: Creating, Collecting, and Documenting an Afro-Cuban Lukumí Beaded Vessel." *Journal of Museum Ethnography*, no. 30, Mar. 2017, pp. 125–147.

―――. "¿Tienes memoria? Have you got Memory? Religious Knowledge Transfers via el Paquete." *Cuba Counterpoints*, 2016, cubacounterpoints.com/archives/712.html.

―――. "Write into Being: The Production of the Self and Circulation of Ritual Knowledge in Afro-Cuban Religious Libretas." *Material Religion*, vol. 17, no. 2, 2021, pp. 228–261.

Turits, Richard Lee. *Foundations of Despotism: Peasants, the Trujillo Regime, and Modernity in Dominican History*. Stanford University Press, 2003.

―――. "A World Destroyed, a Nation Imposed: The 1937 Haitian Massacre in the Dominican Republic." *Hispanic American Historical Review*, vol. 82, no. 3, 2002, pp. 589–635.

Tweed, Thomas A. *Our Lady of the Exile: Diasporic Religion at a Cuban Catholic Shrine in Miami*. Oxford University Press, 1997.

Valdés, Vanessa K. *Oshun's Daughters: The Search for Womanhood in the Americas*. SUNY Press, 2014.

―――, editor. *Racialized Visions: Haiti and the Hispanic Caribbean*. SUNY Press, 2020.

Vázquez-Fernández, Carmen. *Balseros cubanos*. Editorial Betania, 1999.

Vega, Ana Lydia. *Encancaranublado y otros cuentos de naufragio*. 1982, 7th ed., Editorial Cultural, 2001.

Victoriano-Martínez, Ramón Antonio. *Rayanos y Dominicanyorks: La dominicanidad del siglo XXI*. Instituto Internacional de Literatura Iberoamericana, 2014.

Vigil, Ariana. "Heterosexualization and the State: The Poetry of Gloria Anzaldúa." *Chicana/Latina Studies Journal*, vol. 16, no. 1, Fall 2016, pp. 86–109.

Washington, Teresa N. "'The Sea Never Dies': Yemoja: The Infinitely Flowing Mother Force of Africana Literature and Cinema." *Yemoja: Gender, Sexuality, and Creativity in the Latina/o and Afro-Atlantic Diasporas*, edited by Solimar Otero and Toyin Falola, SUNY Press, 2013, pp. 215–266.

Winters, Lisa Ze. *The Mulatta Concubine: Terror, Intimacy, Freedom, and Desire in the Black Transatlantic*. University of Georgia Press, 2016.

Wirtz, Kristina. *Ritual, Discourse, and Community in Cuban Santería: Speaking a Sacred World*. University Press of Florida, 2007.

Wucker, Michele. *Why the Cocks Fight: Dominicans, Haitians, and the Struggle for Hispaniola*. Hill and Wang, 1999.

Zamora, Omaris Z. "(Trance)forming AfroLatina Embodied Knowledges in Nelly Rosario's *Song of the Water Saints*." *Label Me Latina/o*, vol. 7, Summer 2017, pp. 1–16.

Zaytoun, Kelli D. "'Now Let Us Shift' the Subject: Tracing the Path and Posthumanist Implications of La Naguala/The Shapeshifter in the Works of Gloria Anzaldúa." *MELUS*, vol. 40, no. 4, Fall 2015, pp. 69–88.

Index

Page locators in *italics* indicate figures.

Anaya, Rudolfo, 118
ancestor worship: dead/*egun* as linked
    to *orishas*, 89, 107–109, 120–127;
    foundational role of, 31, 64; water in,
    18, 39, 140–144
Andrade, Oswald de, 178n30
Andrews, Kyrstin Mallon, 173n3
androgyny, 24, 58–59, 64, 67, 131, 176n43
Antero (La 21 División healer), 158n29
anthropophagism, 146–147
Anzaldúa, Gloria Evangelina: Afro-
    diasporic traditions and, 86, 94–95,
    97, 100–102, 104–105, 122, 130,
    134–135; Afro-Latinidad and, 13–14;
    autohistoria-teoría, 87–88, 101;
    Blackness and, 114, 119; "bridging" as
    life's work, 24, 84, 102, 173n8; career/
    personal migrations of, 100–105,
    168n7; Catholicism and, 123–126,
    129–130; *cenotes* and, 133–134;
    childhood/family of, 88, 90–91, 100,
    107, 125, 170n34; coalitional Latina
    practices and, 50; Coatlicue and, 105,
    109, 111, 114, 128–129, 131, 171n58;
    Coyolxauhqui and, 86, 94, 99, 105,
    114, 131, 174n16, 174n20; dominant
    academic view of, 85–86, 91, 100,
    113–114, 122, 128–129; East Coast as
    influence on, 103–105, 172n69, 173n7;
    female divinity and, 102, 105, 114, 125,
    129, 175n30; hysterectomy/health of,
    100, 106–112; Indigeneity and, 86,
    93, 101–102, 119, 134–135; lifelong
    relationship with water, 24, 83–84,
    86, 88–90, 134–136, 148; memorials
    for, 127–128; on *mestizaje*, 91–92, 94,
    111, 170n39; near-drowning of, 83,
    87–88, 94–96, 98–99, 104–106, 124,
    135; *nepantla* and, 92–93, 117–120,
    123, 129; ocean's energy felt by, 88–91,
    94–96, 98–99; personal library of, 95,
    104, 127, 169n22; Prieta (literary alter
    ego), 88, 91, 106, 108, 110; queerness
    and, 85, 92, 131; scholarship of as

spiritual, 133–134, 152n8; on shape-
    shifting/*la naguala*, 91, 96–97, 113;
    shifting chronologies and, 169n20;
    spiritual activism of, 91–92, 130–131;
    on spirituality, 86, 91, 103–104, 108,
    125–126; writing *comadres* of, 87, 98,
    176n44; Yemayá as spiritual mother
    to, 83–84, 88, 92, 93, 98, 102, 128;
    Yemayá's energies felt by, 94–99,
    104–105, 107–109, 111–112; Yemayá's
    initial introduction to, 100–104
—GEA Papers: Afro-diasporic research
    evidenced in, 104–105; on Anzaldúa's
    health/body, 106–112; Anzaldúa's
    multifaceted personhood and, 85–87;
    Anzaldúa's relationship to water
    made clear, 24, 94–95, 99, 135–136;
    Anzaldúa's revision process evidenced
    in, 87–88, 105, 133–136; contents of/
    access to, 84, 87–88, 176n42, 176n44;
    value of for scholarship, 91, 135–136
—Works (archival and published):
    "Autohistoria de la artista as a
    Young Girl," 87, 90–91, 94–95, 133;
    "Autoretratos de la artista as a Young
    Girl," 87–88; "Canción de cascabel,"
    95, 108, 111; "En el hocico del mar,"
    87–88, 95–96; "Esperando la serpiente
    con plumas," 104–105; "Let us be the
    healing of the wound," 94; *Light in the
    Dark/Luz en lo oscuro*, 86, 132, 134,
    173n8; "Matriz sin tumba," 109–111;
    "La Prieta," 88, 101, 110; *Prietita and the
    Ghost Woman*, 176n40; "La serpiente
    que se come su cola," 103, 106–107,
    110, 112, 125, 172nn68–69, 172n74,
    176n38; "Spiritual Activism," 91; "The
    water doesn't breath[e]," 133, 169n23;
    "Yemayá," 105, 134–135, 174n19. See
    also *Borderlands/La Frontera*; *This
    Bridge Called My Back*
Aparicio, Frances R., 4
Apter, Andrew, 97
Aquino, Eloisa, 92, 93

bordering, 6, 85

borderlands: vs. borderwaters, 114–115; *nepantla* and, 92–93, 117–120, 123, 129; *rayano* consciousness and, 9; rippling borders and, 116–117, 174n17

Borderlands/La Frontera (Anzaldúa), 113–133; on Anzaldúa's living death experiences, 106; Aztlán in, 113, 118; Border Field Park in, 113, 123–124, 126; borders torn down in, 129–133; borderwaters of, 114–121; Cisneros on, 99; critical edition of, 172n73; Eshu/Elegguá addressed in, 119–121, 128–130; on *la facultad*, 112; genre/ linguistic crossing of, 116–117, 120; initiation in, 2, 18; La Llorona in, 131–132; literary *ebó* in, 109–111; on *mestizaje*, 92; *nepantla* in, 117–120, 123, 129, 170n32; new *mestiza* in, 113, 117–121, 132; opening poem of, 96, 113, 116–119, 121–127, 129–130, 132; Oyá/wind in, 122–123, 126–130, 133, 135, 175n37; rippling borders in, 116–117, 174n17; tension between land and water in, 113, 132; transnational reflections in, 100; visual shape of poems in, 117, 121–123; water's role and destructive force in, 24–25, 83, 115–117, 121–123; writing of, 103, 171n52; Yemayá and fluidity in, 96, 113–116, 118, 121–123; Yemayá's motherly rage in, 129–132; Yemayá's personal connection to Anzaldúa in, 95, 122, 125, 128–129, 133, 135

borderlessness, 28–31, 47, 96, 114–115, 162n27

Border of Lights (BOL): candlelight vigil as *bóveda*, 25, 137–138, *138*, 140–144, 148; diasporic origins, 138–140; opposition to border wall, 145

Bost, Suzanne, 87, 119, 168n8, 169n19, 171n60

botpipèl (Kreyòl term), 28–29, 36, 39, 43, 173n4

bóveda (Espiritismo altar), 25, 138, 142–144

braceros, 155n55

Brady, Mary Pat, 115

Brathwaite, Edward Kamau, 157n15, 158n32

Braziel, Jana Evans, 43

Brazil, 5, 14, 16–17, 42, 66, 177n20

Brennan, Denise, 162n27

bridges/bridging, 24, 84, 86, 93, 102, 173n8

Brotons, Elisabet, 36

Brown, David H., 17–18, 166n70, 166n71

Brown, Kimberly Juanita, 35

Buggs, Mirangela, 9

Cabrera, Lydia: ethnography of, 151n6, 155n61, 161n14, 172n65, 175n36; and F. Ortiz, 158n26; on illnesses, 164n46; on nature, 104, 171n56; on *omiero*/water, 21–22, 34–35, 60–61, 155n58, 163n32, 166n65; *patakís* recounted by, 157n12, 161n16, 178n32; on religious names, 45; Tsang on, 21, 152n9, 159n42; on Yemayá, 34, 157n14, 161n14, 167n75, 174nn18–19, 178n32

Candelario, Ginetta E. B., 63, 137, 178n29

Candomblé, 14, 66

Cantú, Norma Elia, 100, 111, 156n9, 172n73

Capó Crucet, Jennine, 157n17

Carfour/Legba (*lwa/misterio*), 40, 70, 76, 119

Caribbean Sea, 14–15, 27–28, 36, 40, 62. See also *boat people*; *La mucama de Omicunlé*

Carr, C. Lynn, 18, 78, 155n56

Castellanos, Isabel, 147, 162n29, 178n22

Castellanos, Jorge, 162n29, 178n22

Castillo, Ana, 169n29

Castillo, Debra A., 91

Castro, Fidel, 35

program in, 155n55; *cofradías* (mutual-aid societies), 72; Haitian-descended citizens in, 145–147, 158n37, 162n27; Hispanism in, 169n27; non-Caribbean migrants to, 156n4, 162n27; "La Sentencia," 146–148; state treatment of Afro-diasporic religions in, 61, 72–73, 153n24; Trujillo regime, 47, 51, 137, 144, 153n24; US invasions of, 60; La Virgen de la Altagracia and, 139–140; *yoleros*/migrants, 28–30, 32, 36, 43, 47–48, 63. *See also* La 21 División

dreams, 20, 39, 78, 89, 106, 108, 127

Drewal, Henry John, 47, 159nn47–48, 160n57

Dubois, Laurent, 42

Dunning, Nicholas P., 134

Duvalier, François "Papa Doc," 42–43, 47, 51

Duvalier, Jean-Claude "Baby Doc," 43, 47, 51

Elegguá (*orisha*). *See* Eshu/Elegguá

elekes (sacred necklaces), 1, 65–66, 68

El Paso (TX), 13–14, 116

Erinle (*orisha*), 163nn31–32

Erzulie Freda (*lwa*), 8, 147–148, 177n17

Eshu/Elegguá (*orisha*), 25, 38, 69–70, 111, 114, 119–121, 128–130, 157n19

Espiritismo: *bóveda* (altar), 25, 138, 142–144; *darle luz al muerto* (to give light to the dead), 141; feminisms and, 152n12; as "folk Catholicism," 177n13; Santería and, 17, 74, 78, 142, 153n25, 160n4; spiritual mediumship and, 56

Espírito Santo, Diana, 141, 178n24

Esteva, Álex, 172n64

Falola, Toyin, 120

Feliciano-Santos, Sherina, 50, 158n39

feminisms. *See* Afro-Latinx feminisms; Chicana feminisms

Fernández, Alexander, 44, 159n41

Fernández Olmos, Margarite, 2–3, 61

Fernández Retamar, Roberto, 36

Figueroa-Vásquez, Yomaira C., 4

Flores, Juan, 5–6, 152n17

Flores-Peña, Ysamur, 142

Fortilus, Nadine, 47, 48

Frerichs, Ralph R., 145

Friendship Park (CA), 123–124, 126

García, Scherezade, 140–141

Garcia Lopez, Christina, 7, 94

García-Peña, Lorgia, 6–7, 9, 72, 85, 155n55, 158n34, 169n27, 176n4

Gaspar de Alba, Alicia, 167n1

Gates, Henry Louis, Jr., 174n13

Gay, Roxane, 178n21

Gede (*lwa*), 42–43

Gilroy, Paul, 13, 30

Ginen/Guinée (spiritual realm), 39, 41–42, 51, 97

Glassie, Alison, 164n49

Gleason, Judith, 126–127, 169n22, 175n30

Glissant, Édouard, 14, 156n5, 157n15

Gloria Evangelina Anzaldúa Papers (GEA Papers). *See* Anzaldúa, Gloria Evangelina

Goldman, Francisco, 35

Gómez, Fermina (priestess of Santería/Regla de Ocha), 59–60, 164n47

González, Elián, 35–36

González, José Luis, 159n45

González, Juan Miguel, 35

González López, Gloria, 99

González-Wippler, Migene, 104

Grande, Reyna, 156n9

Graziano, Frank, 36

Greek mythology, 12–13, 102, 129, 175n30

Guidotti-Hernández, Nicole M., 4

Guinée/Ginen (spiritual realm), 39, 41–42, 51, 97

medical/pharmaceutical industry, 69–74,
77, 106–111
"medical superbody," 71–72, 171n62
Medina, Lara, 92–93
Medusa, 129, 171n53
Méndez, Susan C., 35
mestizaje: Anzaldúa on, 91–92, 94, 111,
170n39; issues surrounding, 91–92,
171n48, 174n21; Latinidad and, 91–92,
152n13. *See also* new *mestiza*
Métraux, Alfred, 2, 19, 22, 74–75, 165n59
Metresilí (*misterio*), 148, 177n17
Mexica, 113, 128, 135. *See also* Coatlicue;
Coyolxauhqui
Mexico: *bracero* program, 155n55; Haitians
in, 157n10; religion/spirituality in, 94,
174n21; territorial struggles of, 116,
122. *See also* US/Mexico border
Miami (FL), 1, 8, 35–36
Michael, Saint (archangel), 71
Middle Passage, 12, 17–18, 21, 28, 35, 40,
47, 52, 148
migration: Anzaldúa's, 100–105;
borderlessness and, 162n27; *braceros*,
155n55; constant motion and,
116–117; Cuban *balseros*, 29–30,
35–36, 43; dictatorships and, 42–43,
47; Dominican *yoleros*, 28–30, 32, 36,
43; falsified documentation and, 43–45,
167n77; forced, 18, 28, 115–116;
gendering of, 35–36; Haitian *botpipèl*,
28–29, 36, 39, 43, 173n4; "illegal,"
41–42, 145; *mojado* (wetback),
115; "La Sentencia" and, 146–148;
undocumented, 27–31, 40, 52. *See also*
boat people
Milian, Claudia, 4, 152n10
Minich, Julie Avril, 173n1
misterios (La 21 División deities): Alailá,
177n11; Belié Belcán, 71; coexistence
with Catholic saints, 71, 97, 139; colors
and, 74, 166n64; communal groupings
of, 153n26; dwelling places of, 16;
ethnic origins of, 154n45; in initiation,

19, 22–23; Legba, 40, 70, 76, 119;
Metresilí, 148, 177n17; possession and,
77, 142; Santa Marta la Dominadora,
47–50, 48; *servidores* (devotees) of, 20,
22–23, 64, 71, 148; Yoruba and, 17–18
Moïse, Myriam, 178n25
Mona Passage, 28
moon, 94. *See also* Coyolxauhqui
Moraga, Cherríe, 100, 126. See also *This
Bridge Called My Back*
Morejón, Nancy, 174n15
Moreno Vega, Marta, 31, 89–90, 152n12,
169n25
Morrison, Toni, 145
Movimiento de Mujeres Dominico-
Haitianas (MUDHA), 138–139, 145
La mucama de Omicunlé (Indiana), 55–82;
Acilde as Omo Olokun (child of
Olokun) in, 69, 75–80; Afro-diasporic/
Indigenous convergences in, 80–82;
divination in, 62, 64–65; initiation in, 2,
18, 60, 66–70, 72–77; ocean as techno-
resonant being in, 58, 87; Olokun in,
24, 58–61, 64–69, 72, 75, 77; opening
scene of, 55, 57–58; productive techno-
resonances in, 60–66, 148; queerness
in, 55, 60, 64, 67, 70–72, 74; Rainbow
Bright drug in, 70–75, 77; sea anemone
(*C. gigantea*) in, 63, 68–70, 72, 75–76,
81; techno-resonances conceptualized,
24, 56–58; temporalities of, 57, 77–78,
162n24; transnational transactions in,
63–66, 167n77; La 21 División in, 7,
61, 73; violent techno-resonances in,
66–69; water as source of knowledge in,
60–63, 65–66, 81–82
Murphy, Joseph M., 74, 153n25, 154n40
Museum of Modern Art (MoMA), 154n36
Myers, Megan Jeanette, 176n6

Nancy, Jean Luc, 12
nation, 16–17
nepantla, 92–93, 117–120, 123, 129

new *mestiza*, 113, 117–121, 132. See also
    mestizaje
New Orleans Vodou, 101–102, 151n4
New York City, 1, 100, 103–105, 173n7
9/11 attack, 83, 94, 123
1937 Massacre, 25, 137, 139–141, 143–144
Nixon, Richard, 123

Obatalá (*orisha*), 38, 89, 134, 155n61,
    163n31
Obejas, Achy, 160n2
ochascape, 56, 162n28
Ochumare (*orisha*), 176n43
Ochún (*orisha*): Anzaldúa/Teish and, 93,
    97, 100, 102; attributes/associations
    of, 1, 12, 38, 107, 139, 147, 163n31,
    172n68, 175n33; in *kari ocha*, 21–22,
    34; sacredness of water and, 35, 61, 124,
    148–149, 159n48, 164n47
ofeicitá (in Santería/Regla de Ocha), 44,
    159nn40–41
Ogún (*orisha*), 38
Oliver, José R., 81, 160n53
Olokun (*orisha*): attributes of, 62–64,
    67, 131; cult of, 59–60, 74, 164n47,
    166n67; in *La mucama de Omicunlé*, 24,
    58–61, 64–69, 72, 75, 77; Omo Olokun
    (child of Olokun) and, 69, 75–80; Taíno
    cosmology and, 81; water and, 27,
    52–53, 67, 135–136, 159n48; Yemayá
    and, 52–53, 58–60, 64, 66, 69, 77, 80,
    131, 164n47
Olupona, Jacob K., 17
O'Neil, Deborah, 51
orishas (Santería/Regla de Ocha deities):
    caminos (paths) of, 59, 97, 120–121,
    131, 174n18; Changó, 38, 175n31;
    coexistence with Catholic saints, 97,
    125, 177n12; color associations of,
    74, 174n18; dwelling places of, 16,
    40, 52–53, 58, 60, 90, 104–105, 124,
    127–128, 135; *egun* (dead/ancestors)
    and, 89, 107–109, 120, 127; Erinle,

163nn31–32; feeling of *corriente* and,
    89–90; gender fluidity of, 64, 131;
    inheritance of, 155n53; in initiation, 19,
    44–45; invocation of, 33; Obatalá, 38,
    89, 134, 155n61, 163n31; ochascape
    and, 56, 162n28; Ochumare, 176n43;
    Ogún, 38; as one and multiple, 58–59;
    Orula, 38, 161n16; *osun*/markings and,
    68, 75; possession and, 77, 142; ritual
    greeting of, 166n65; shape-shifting by,
    97, 127; Siete Potencias Africanas, 38,
    62, 74, 95; spiritual transactions and,
    64–65, 76; wrath of, 68–69; Yoruba
    and, 17–18. See also Eshu/Elegguá;
    Ochún; Olokun; Oyá; Yemayá
Ortiz, Fernando, 102, 158n26
Ortiz, María Elena, 8, 10, 153n30
Ortiz, Ricardo, 6
Orula (*orisha*), 38, 161n16
Otero, Solimar: on archive, 3, 84; on
    cultural convergences, 139; on Eshu/
    Elegguá, 120; on queer strategies,
    151n7; on *vèvè* (ritual symbols), 75; on
    water, 18, 38, 163n32, 171n50, 175n26
ounsi (Haitian Vodou initiate). See *kanzo*
Ovando, Nicolás de, 177n10
Owens, Deirdre Cooper, 71–72, 171n62
Oyá (*orisha*), 25, 114, 122–123, 126–131,
    133, 135, 163n31, 175n37

pain, 39–40, 52, 71–72, 88, 106–110, 138,
    140–141, 147–149
Palmié, Stephan: on biases against Afro-
    diasporic religions, 49, 153n23,
    158n33, 161n10; on digital circulation
    of religions, 56, 161n5, 162n20; on
    F. Ortiz, 170n47; on head's role in
    initiations, 73, 76
Paravisini-Gebert, Lizabeth, 61
Past, Mariana, 156n8
patakís (mythical stories), 34, 64, 148–149,
    161n16, 162n25, 164n41
Patterson, Tiffany Ruby, 154n37

Paulino, Edward, 138, 140–141, 176nn4–6
Pedraza, Silvia, 36
Pérez, Elizabeth, 19, 125, 143, 155n61, 160n4, 177n14
Pérez, Emmy, 156n9
Pérez Art Museum Miami (PAMM), 8
Pérez-Rosario, Vanessa, 156n2
Pérez-Torres, Rafael, 92
Perkins, Alexandra Gonzenbach, 65
pharmaceutical/medical industry, 69–74, 77, 106–111
Pierre, Sonia, 138
Pratt, Mary Louise, 50
Puerto Rico: as crossroads, 40; "folk Catholicism" in, 177n13; Indigeneity and, 51, 160n54; internal/external migration, 28, 32, 63, 159n45; maroon communities in, 42

queerness: Anzaldúa and, 85, 92, 131; in "Latinx" and, 4, 50; *La mucama de Omiculné*, 55, 60, 64, 67, 70–72, 74; *orisha* gender fluidity, 64, 131; pathologizing of, 85; secrecy as strategy, 151n7
Quinn, Rachel Afi, 56

Ramos, Miguel "Willie," 178n31
Ramsey, Kate, 7, 42, 153n27
religion (term), 7–8, 175n27
residence time, 46
Rey, Terry: on Afro-diasporic traditions, 17, 138, 155n50; on Haitian migrants, 39, 158n27; on Little Haiti, 8, 153n28; on water in Haitian Vodou, 39, 51, 61, 154n38
Ribó, John D., 9, 152n16
Richman, Karen E., 21, 32, 155n55, 166n73
Ricourt, Milagros: on *cofradías*, 165n56; on Dominican migration, 32, 36; on La 21 División, 71, 81, 153n26, 154n46, 177n11, 177n13

Rio Grande/Río Bravo, 14–15, 30, 116, 132, 135, 174n17
rituals/rites: artifacts of, 1, 12–13, 42, 65–66, 68, 74, 143, 170n35, 177n20; *bautizo* (baptism), 20, 22–23, 62, 73, 89, 134; death/burial, 40, 50, 127–128, 140–144, 172n69; Easter, 123–125, 129–130, 140; *ebó* (sacrifical offerings), 15, 64, 101, 108–111, 119–120, 134, 140–141; healing, 108–111, 130, 140–141; *misa espiritual* (spiritual mass), 107, 178n22; purification, 73–74, 110–111, 133–134; reversed initiation, 164n47; sacrifice, 119–121; secrecy of, 151n7; *vèvè* (ritual symbols), 13, 74–75, 148. *See also* divination; initiations; sacred colors; sacred numbers
Rivera, Fredo, 8
Rivera-Rideau, Petra R., 5
Rodríguez, Juana María, 85
Rodríguez Vélez, Wendalina, 158n29
Rosario, Nelly, 144
Rosen, Norma, 79

Sabau, Ana, 152n18
sacred colors: blue, 10–11, 122, 135–136, 147; rainbow, 74, 176n43; red and black, 174n14; silver, 122; white, 73, 110–111, 133–134, 155n61; yellow, 1, 147
sacred numbers: five, 172n68; nine, 62, 163n38; seven, 38, 62, 94–95, 128, 143, 158n25, 163n38, 175n32; three, 69. *See also* rituals/rites
Saldívar-Hull, Sonia, 131–132
Sánchez-Carretero, Cristina, 139, 162n23
San Diego (CA), 123–124
Sandoval, Mercedes Cros, 17, 170n35, 172n76
Santa Marta la Dominadora (*misterio*), 47–50, *48*
Santería/Regla de Ocha: Black Atlantic and, 13–14; *boat people* and, 33–35;

Chicana spirituality and, 93–94; copresences in, 57, 59, 73, 78–80, 114, 162n30; cult of Olokun, 59–60, 74, 164n47, 166n67; death and regeneration in, 40, 52–53, 111–112; *diloggún/itá*/divination, 33–34, 44–45, 65, 76, 158n25, 161n16, 172n71; *ebó/ servicios* (ritual offerings), 15, 64, 101, 108–111, 119–120, 134; *egun* (dead/ ancestors), 57, 89, 107–109, 120, 127, 178n22; *elekes* (necklaces), 1, 65–66, 68; Espiritismo and, 17, 74, 78, 142, 160n4; estuaries as spiritual sites in, 14, 124, 132–133; female *santeras* in, 58–60, 100–102, 108, 125–128, 161n16; guarded nature of, 103–104, 126; head as sacred in, 67–68, 73, 75–76, 89–90, 95, 155n61; *iyaworaje* period in, 78–79, 134; Latina feminisms and, 101–102, 104, 130–132, 152n12; legal/societal recognition of, 7, 174n21; male *babalawos* in, 59, 102, 161n16; mental health and, 172n76; *misa espiritual* (spiritual mass), 107, 178n22; names for, 7, 153n27; nature as divine in, 90, 104–105; Olodumare (supreme deity), 17; origins/survival of, 104, 115–116, 119, 151n4, 174n21; *osogbo* and *iré* (opposing energies), 57, 109, 111, 134; *patakís* (mythical stories), 34, 64, 148–149, 161n16, 162n25, 164n41; ritual sacrifice in, 119–121; sacred and secular in, 30–31; symbiosis with other Afro-diasporic religions, 16–17, 61, 66, 81–82; water as intrinsic to cosmology of, 34–35, 53, 61, 64, 107. See also *aché*; *iyawo*; *kari ocha*; *orishas*

Santos-Febres, Mayra, 27. See also *boat people*

Scalissi, Nicole F., 178n30

scholarship. *See* archive(s); writing/ scholarship

September 11 attack, 83, 94, 123

servidores (La 21 División initiates/ devotees), 20, 22–23, 64, 71, 148

Shakespeare, William, 36

shape-shifting, 91, 96–97, 113, 127

Sharpe, Christina, 46

Sharpe, Jenny, 31, 158n32

Siete Potencias Africanas, 38, 62, 74, 95

Simbi Dlo (*lwa*), 12

Sims, Marion, 72

Sirmans, Franklin, 8

Smartt Bell, Madison, 97

snakes/serpents: Lasirèn and, *11*, 12; Mami Wata and, 47, *48–49*; Rio Grande/Río Bravo as, 131–132, 135; Yemayá/*orishas* and, 92, *93*, 97, 129, 176n43

South Padre Island (TX), 83, 87–88, 94, 96, 98–99, 104–106, 124, 135

Sparks, David Hatfield, 104, 163n31

Spiritism. *See* Espiritismo

spiritual activism, 91–92, 131–132

spirituality: *mestizaje* and, 91–92, 94, 111, 170n39; *nepantla* and, 92–93, 117–120, 129; vs. religion, 7–8, 175n27; as survival, 86, 126, 178n34

spiritual mediumship, 39, 56–57, 89, 108, 127, 166n73

spiritual possession, 22, 61, 77–78, 108, 142

Stepick, Alex, 8, 138, 153n28, 154n38

Strongman, Roberto, 77, 177n18

Sweet, James H., 177n20

Taíno, 50, 81–82, 158n39, 176n1, 177n14

techno-resonance: Afro-diasporic/ Indigenous, 80–82; conceptualized, 24, 56–58; copresences and, 57, 59, 73, 78–80, 162n24; medical/spiritual node of, 70–75, 77, 110–111, 177n10; possession and, 77–78; "redes" (webs) and, 62; "transacción" and, 63–65, 76; *vèvè* (ritual symbols) and, 74–75; violent forms of, 66–69; virtual messages and, 76–77. See also *La mucama de Omicunlé*

Teish, Luisah: on Alarcón's dream of Anzaldúa, 127–128; Anzaldúa's spiritual reading by, 128, 171n52, 175n33; healing ritual for Anzaldúa by, 108–109, 172n68; *Jambalaya*, 101–102; name of, 170n42; poetry reading by, 176n42; woman-centered spirituality of, 100–102, 125–126, 175n28

Tejeda Ortiz, Dagoberto, 20, 165n54, 177n11

"theory in the flesh," 30, 86–87, 112

This Bridge Called My Back (Moraga and Anzaldúa): bridge metaphor in, 156n62; "El Mundo Zurdo" in, 101–102, 126; "theory in the flesh" in, 30, 86–87, 112; writing/publication of, 100–102; Yemayá in, 83, 102, 126, 170n36, 175n30

Thompson, Robert Farris, 13–14, 154n39

Tijuana (Mexico), 123–124, 157n10

Tinsley, Omise'eke Natasha, 86

Tlazolteotl. *See* Coatlicue

Tocilovac, Marko, 123

Torres-Saillant, Silvio, 5, 152n15

Torres Sanchez, Jenny, 156n9

Tower of Babel, 120

transculturation, 38

trauma: ancestral, 63, 108; collective, 83, 94, 123; generational, 32, 35, 107; historical, 25, 143, 178n21; school-based, 90–91; woman's, 87–88, 107, 178n31

"trigueña," 62–63

Trouillot, Michel-Rolph, 18, 153n21

Trujillo, Rafael, 47, 51, 137, 144, 153n24

Tsang, Martin A.: on Cabrera, 21, 152n9, 159n42; on *ebó*, 172n70; on European connections, 154n41, 162n23; on head and feet, 89, 120; on *libreta*, 44; on *ofeicitá*, 159n40; on *la religión*, 153n25

Turits, Richard, 176n4

Tweed, Thomas A., 139, 177n16

La 21 División: Black Atlantic and, 13–14; in *boat people*, 47–50; Catholicism and, 97, 139; *claves* (ritual symbols) in, 74–75; divination in, 158n29; Gran Dios (supreme deity), 17; healing and, 71; Indigeneity and Blackness in, 50, 81–82, 160n56, 166n69; in *La mucama de Omicunlé*, 7, 61, 73; name of, 7–8, 48, 151n4; *el nombre prestado* (borrowed name), 159n44; political invisibility of, 61, 72–73; purification/hair removal in, 73–74, 134; scholarship on, 48, 154n43; *servidores* (devotees), 20, 22–23, 64, 71, 148; symbiosis with other Afro-diasporic religions, 16–17, 22, 48, 61, 81–82, 161n6; water in, 50, 74, 142, 153n31. See also *bautizo; misterios*

University of Texas at Austin, 84, 100

Urrea, Luis Alberto, 156n9

US/Mexico border: Anzaldúa's hometown and, 90–91, 132; Border Field/Friendship Park (CA), 113, 123–124, 126; *botánicas* and, 13; Chamizal dispute and, 116, 174n17; as cutting through Anzaldúa's body, 85, 130; discourse of, 30, 123–124; visibility of, 115–117

US Supreme Court, 7

Valdés, Vanessa K., 30–31, 121, 152n18, 174n15

Valva, Annie F., 99

Vázquez-Fernández, Carmen, 157n21

Vega, Ana Lydia, 30

Verger, Pierre, 157n14

Victoriano-Martínez, Ramón Antonio, 9

Villa Mella (Dominican Republic), 72–73

La Virgen de Guadalupe, 92, *93*, 101, 114, 125–127

La Virgen de la Altagracia, 139–140

La Virgen de la Caridad del Cobre, 139

La Virgen de Regla, 125

Vivancos-Pérez, Ricardo, 111, 172n73
Vodou. *See* Haitian Vodou
Voodoo (New Orleans Vodou), 101–102, 151n4

Washington, Teresa N., 178n34
water: Anzaldúa's near-drowning, 83, 87–88, 94–96, 98–99, 104–106, 124, 135; as archive, 16, 31, 35, 38, 87–88; blood and, 10–11, 46, 105, 144–145; borderlessness/vastness of, 28–31, 47, 96, 114–115; as bridge, 86, 93; capacity to overflow/*desbordar*/resist, 14–15, 92, 116, 145, 178n28; *cenotes* (subterranean pools), 133–134; destructive force of, 121–123; drowning, 31–34, 37–38, 41, 46, 51–53, 88; in Haitian Vodou, 39–42; as horizontal contact zone, 50–51; in initiations, 18, 21–23, 41, 53; light and, 140–144; as living energy, 88–91, 94–96, 98–99; Mami Wata and, 27, 47–48; memory of, 38, 40, 145, 148–149; mystery of, 53, 60, 64, 135–136; *nepantla* and, 117–119; omnipresence of in Afro-diasporic religions, 1–3, 10, 13, 15–18, 21–23, 25, 34–35, 39, 61; sea as womb, 32, 106–108; seascape epistemology and, 122; as shape-shifter, 96–97; as source of knowledge, 60–63, 65–66, 81–82, 88, 98, 112, 134; sweet/salty confluences, 14, 35, 101, 124, 132–133, 135, 145, 147–148; transformative power of, 31–34, 101, 105; waves, 41, 58, 61, 77, 90, 94–95, 121–122, 126, 128, 133; wind and, 122–123, 126, 128–129; wounds inflicted on, 124, 144–145; as wound with healing powers, 140–141. *See also named bodies of water*
wind, 122–123, 126–129, 135, 175n37
Winters, Lisa Ze, 52
Wirtz, Kristina, 19, 56, 155n51, 158n38, 163n33

womb: in initiation, 33–34, 44, 73, 82, 155n56; Middle Passage as, 17; mouth and, 33–34, 44; sea as, 32, 106–108; as source of trauma, 107–111
writing/scholarship: citation practices, 159n42; confining/sanitizing, 14–15, 85–86, 91–92; vs. *conocimientos*, 168n4; spiritually inflected, 3, 44, 99, 108–111, 119–120, 133–134; violence of documentation and, 44, 48–50, 137–138
Wucker, Michele, 176n1, 176n7

Yemayá (*orisha*): Anzaldúa as daughter of, 83–84, 88, 92, 93, 98, 102, 128; Anzaldúa on energies of, 24–25, 94–99, 104–105, 107–109, 111–112; Anzaldúa's initial introduction to, 100–104; Anzaldúa's poem in honor of, 105, 134–135, 174n19; in *boat people*, 38, 52–53; as border crosser, 115–116; in *Borderlands/La Frontera*, 24–25, 95–96, 113–116, 118, 121–123, 125, 128–133, 135; daughters of, 34, 65, 83, 98, 102, 128, 159n41, 171n50, 178n32; divine feminine and, 102, 105, 114, 125, 129, 175n30; healing/salvation by, 35, 52–53, 113, 148–149; as maternal/mother, 34–35, 106–107, 127, 130–132, 171n61, 175n33; in *La mucama de Omicunlé*, 58, 60–62, 65–66, 69, 77, 80; offerings to, 108–109, 111, 134; Olokun and, 52–53, 58–60, 64, 66, 69, 77, 80, 131, 164n47; sacred number seven, 38, 62, 94–95, 128, 143, 158n25, 163n38; La Virgen and, 125–127; water/waves and, 27, 34–35, 40, 58, 61, 77, 122–124, 126, 128–129, 135, 147, 159n48
Yoruba, 17–18, 75, 119, 125, 127, 153n23, 159n48, 175n36. *See also* Lukumí

Zamora, Omaris Z., 31
Zaytoun, Kelli D., 97